WORK WON'T LOVE YOU BACK

The Dual Career Couple's Survival Guide

WORK WON'T LOVE YOU BACK

Stevan E. Hobfoll, Ph.D.
and Ivonne H. Hobfoll, Ph.D.

W. H. Freeman and Company
New York

Library of Congress Cataloging-in-Publication Data

Hobfoll, Stevan E., 1951–
    Work won't love you back : the dual career couple's survival guide
    Stevan E. Hobfoll and Ivonne H. Hobfoll.
       p.   cm.
    Includes bibliographical references (p.   ).
    ISBN 0-7167-2598-3. — ISBN 0-7167-2593-2 (pbk.)
    1. Dual-career families—United States.   2. Work and family—
  United States.   3. Marriage—United States.   I. Hobfoll, Ivonne H.
  II. Title.
HQ536.H62   1994
306.872—dc20   94-11992
                                                      CIP

Printed in the United States of America

1 2 3 4 5 6 7 8 9 0 VB 9 9 8 7 6 5 4

*We dedicate this book to
the loving memory of Ivonne's parents,
Elena and Genaro Heras.*

We also offer our thanks and love to Estela and Tony Lopez and to Jerry and Raul Heras, Ivonne's sister and brother-in-law and her two brothers. They sheltered and loved her and made sure Ivonne had the means to receive her education. For them, Ivonne's education was of paramount importance, whether it meant books, quiet to study, a car to get to school, or a dress to sew for the prom.

CONTENTS

ABOUT THE AUTHORS

IVONNE Heras Hobfoll was born in Juarez, Mexico, and was raised in Juarez and El Paso, Texas. She received her Ph.D. in psychology at Stanford University and worked on her dissertation with Dr. Alberta Siegel and T. Berry Brazelton of Harvard University. She received pre- and postdoctoral training at the Stanford Institute of Psychiatry and as a captain in the U.S. Air Force, respectively. Dr. Hobfoll has worked as a clinical psychologist for eighteen years, specializing in work with children and women, in Texas, Alaska, Illinois, and Ohio and in Israel. She was a faculty member at the Advanced Institute of Psychotherapy, Tel Aviv University, and she was one of the first Hispanic women in the United States to receive a Ph.D. in psychology. A popular lecturer and leader of workshops, Dr. Hobfoll is currently in private practice in Hudson, Ohio, and is an adjunct associate professor of psychology at Kent State University.

Stevan E. Hobfoll was born and raised in Chicago and received his Ph.D. in psychology at the University of South Florida. He has served on the faculties of Ben Gurion University and Tel Aviv University in Israel and is currently a professor of psychology and director of the Applied Psychology Center at Kent State University. He also has a private consulting practice in psychology. Concentrating in the area of stress, Dr. Hobfoll is the author of more than 100 publications, the recipient of numerous research grants, and the editor of *Anxiety, Stress, and Coping: An International Journal.* He was co-chair of the American Psychological Association's Commission on Stress and War during Operation Desert Storm. Dr. Hobfoll has received numerous awards for his research and work concerning women and ethnic minorities. His 1988 book, *The Ecology of Stress,* was selected by *Encyclopaedia Britannica* as an exceptional contribution to human knowledge.

The Hobfolls live in Hudson, Ohio, and have three children, Ari, Sheera, and Jonathan.

PREFACE

WE cannot remember precisely when we decided to write this book, but a number of influences pressed us in that direction. First of all, we are ourselves in a dual career marriage and have experienced dual career challenges from the beginning. Immediately after being married, we shipped off to Alaska so that Ivonne could complete her military commitment as a psychologist. Stevan didn't know if he would be able to work as a psychologist or would instead be trapping grizzlies, but followed his true love into the North Country. In 1979 we moved to Israel and brought our dual career life (now with child) with us. After seven exciting, challenging, wonderful years, we returned to the United States, and with two more children.

Over the years we became impressed with how common and troubling was the stress experienced by dual career couples and families. We saw this in our clinical work, in the stress workshops we conducted, and among our friends. Often people remarked that we seemed to know some special secrets about dual career life; we even heard this from friends who shared our professional expertise. What they didn't realize is that we also were flying by the seat of our pants and had to invent new ways of coping at each step of the way. We felt that we were flying without a flight manual in a learn-as-you-go program.

So this book is a kind of flight manual for successful dual career life. It is not that we have been free of bumps and bruises in our marriage and in raising our children, but we seem to have been successful in handling problems when they arise. We have certainly made mistakes, since others might not have had such problems in the first place, but our position is that success is a matter of working together, caring, and loving.

We also felt it was important to base our book on a combination of research findings, clinical experience, and common sense. Don't be fooled by the "sacredness" of any of these three domains. Research is always open to interpretation and selection, clinical experience is biased by how therapists see the world, and common sense is sometimes all too common. Rather, read what we have to say, consider it, and try it on for size. Use the book as a basis for discussion in your own dual career relationship, not as an endpoint.

Finally, we wish to acknowledge some of our own biases. We tend to have a liberal, rather than a traditional, relationship, and we firmly believe that men and women are equal and should have equal say, equal responsibility, and an equal work load. We are very traditional, however, in believing in the primary importance of family and faithfulness to that family. We have been shaped by the fact that we come from working-class families and now work and live in a middle-class environment. It is not always clear how our pasts have shaped our beliefs, but we feel that knowing these things about us will help you to appreciate our viewpoints. We have not been shy in asserting our opinions in this book. After all, how could you benefit from a flight manual that said, "In such an emergency, maybe you should pull up abruptly on the throttle and bank left, but then again, maybe not"?

ACKNOWLEDGMENTS

WE wish to thank a number of individuals for their help. Our editor, Susan Finnemore Brennan, and the staff at W. H. Freeman and Company were consistently helpful. Susan was always supportive, believed in us and our project, and was able to guide us in many ways. She even turned problems into opportunities. What a great editor! And speaking of great editors, Mary Louise Byrd, our project editor, directed the production of the book with professional aplomb. A number of good friends and colleagues read the manuscript and provided insightful feedback. For sharing their wisdom we wish to thank William and Marlene Brazz, Victoria and Todd Burdette, Don and Wendy Katchman, Linda Kahn-Seton, and Barbara and Dr. Harvey Altman. We also received superb secretarial support from Judy Jerkich and Lori West. Judy also had excellent insights about the content of the book; she's a gem. Dr. John Harvey and Dr. Barbara Sarason, two prominent scholars in the field of interpersonal relationships, offered excellent, critical feedback. We also received much help from two expert reviewers who chose to remain anonymous.

We wish to acknowledge the assistance, support, and love provided by our three children, Ari, Sheera, and Jonathan. They were interested in the project from the start, offered truly valuable advice, and kept a sense of humor through it all. Sections of the book became dinner discussions, and they always let us know the "real" ways our own dual career family was operating. These discussions increased our appreciation of how much children know and can express about their families.

AUTHORS' NOTE

THE case histories in this book are drawn from the experiences of clients in treatment with us, from workshops, and from personal contacts. However, each story is a compilation of individuals' and couples' stories, and we have changed important details to protect their privacy.

The book is intended especially for couples who want to prevent problems in their dual career family but who are not currently experiencing problems of a serious nature. We urge the reader to remember that this book should not be a substitute for professional psychological, psychiatric, medical, religious, or legal assistance. If any aspect of your career, family, or personal life is troubling you, speak to a professional. We urge you to err on the side of caution and consult with a professional if you are in any doubt; this book may serve as an adjunct to therapy in such cases. Indications of a more serious problem include ongoing depression or anxiety, frequent or heavy use of alcohol or drugs, signs of physical illness, frequent serious arguments with family members, thoughts of suicide, planning or acting on a plan for suicide, signs of family violence, or withdrawal (that is, avoiding contact with others) by one or more family members. If any of these signs or symptoms occur in your life or in the life of a family member, immediately consult a mental health professional or your family physician.

Chapter 1

*Must Two Careers
Create Twice the
Stress?*

Dual career life is like stunt flying loop-de-loops in an old biplane while trying to regain contact with the copilot, whom you haven't heard from in awhile. If you have children, you are off to pick up one of them while the other is belted in so she doesn't fall out. You have never had a proper flying lesson, but you have clocked up thousands of hours, under all kinds of conditions. You never saw the manual that should have come with the plane, and at times some instructions would be quite valuable. This book is that flight manual, and we offer it realizing fully that you may already be a decorated dual career pilot.

We know you are eager to find solutions to the problems you face and that you might be reading this on the train to work, standing at the kitchen counter, or in the few minutes you have before you fall into an exhausted sleep after a long dual career kind of day. Time is precious. First, however, let us briefly examine our own view of recent history and how dual career families have arrived at where they are today. Whether or not you have children, whether you are a dual career couple or are only considering it, and whatever your stance may be on the ways society has changed in the past twenty years or so, this discussion will be relevant to you.

THEN . . .

Many of us grew up in a different world, a world where mom stayed home (or maybe wished she could) and dad went off to work. Indeed, before 1960, most women were either homemakers or cooked, cleaned, and scrubbed for someone else.[1,2] Meanwhile, we kids trotted off to school and were mostly taught by working women who seemed quite a bit different from mom. We saw a few other women who worked outside the home—nurses, cleaning women, waitresses—but, on the whole, that was not what women did. Women were home preparing meals and cleaning house, always available to kiss our cuts and tend to our bruised bodies and little developing egos. They were probably in the kitchen when we brought legions of friends over and shut the door to our room. Mom was busy, but what she did didn't seem much like what we were told was work.

Ivonne comes from a traditional Hispanic family. Even though her mom raised her as a single parent, Ivonne's older siblings contributed to the household so that mom did not have to work outside. She raised chickens in the backyard for eggs (until they were stolen), she fed a parade of family members and local folks, but she was never employed outside her home. Stevan's mom went to work outside the home when he was six. She was one of the few mothers on their working-class street to work, and her part-time employment was a big source of local discussion, not to mention family upheaval.

From our perspective as adults, we can see that our mothers were working a lot harder than it seemed. They did much of what needed to be done while we were away. Mom took us to doctor appointments

WORK WON'T LOVE YOU BACK

and scout meetings, and was in charge of representing the family at parent nights at school, although dad sometimes went along, too. If your mom was employed outside the home, she probably stayed up late at night packing lunches and getting ahead on chores for the next day, or trying to straighten up the house that lay at her feet in disarray.

Although dad worked, it wasn't always clear what he was doing. Even when we understood the job's name, it felt like he just went off and then came back tired. Our fathers were laborers: Ivonne's dad drove a taxi and Stevan's dad was, and still is, a butcher. They left the house before we were even awake and came home for dinner. Mom served dinner to all of us, a big hearty meal, as this was long before the days of Weight Watchers, cholesterol, and aerobic bouncing were popularized. Men worked hard, that was clear to us, and somehow it was also clear that mom should be there to serve dinner when dad got home. On the weekends, dad rested up and did the lawn (neither family had a very big lawn, if the truth be told). Sometimes he was more industrious and got under the sink or the car. It was even a little harder to tell what was going on there.

We could have known more about what our parents were doing, but television did a lot to disguise any semblance of reality. After all, so many families appeared on popular TV shows—"Leave It to Beaver," "Ozzie and Harriet," "Bewitched," and "Dick van Dyke." These shows could have let us in on how hard mom was working and just what dad did. They didn't, not at all. Instead, the moms on TV wore high heels, never had a hair out of place, and had big kitchens that were never messy. They were never depressed, and always stood behind their man. They were loving to their children, but a little distant, too (our mothers hugged and kissed a lot more than Beaver's mom, Mrs. Cleaver). Can you recall The Beaver ever getting really smooched by Mrs. Cleaver? Dad was only pictured when he came home from work. He usually got a newspaper with the deal and sometimes smoked a pipe. He was wise and understanding, and his hair, like mom's, was always in place.

What we were shown was a picture of what mom and dad *appeared* to do. And it looked like dad worked (somewhere) and mom had easy things to do, like preparing the ever-increasing wonder foods designed to save her labor. Dad earned money and did important stuff; mom was cherished for cooking delicious Thanksgiving Day dinners.

Another way to look at all this is to consider what dad and mom didn't do. These messages were subtle but more realistic. Dad did not change diapers, make dinner, clean the house, bathe the kids, sew, wash, iron, make beds, play dolls with his daughters, or deal with minor infractions of household law. Dad did not cook, set the table, serve the food, or wash the dishes from Thanksgiving or Christmas dinner. Mom didn't mow the lawn, fix the car, repair the washer, light the furnace, leave the house to work, or earn a lot of money. Can you remember the first time you seriously thought about the dollar value of mom's enormous efforts at home or the multitude of tasks she was capable of handling? Do you think your mother felt as if she earned the money she spent?

That was a different world, and maybe what you hear us saying is that the world we saw as children was only a shadow of the real world. A couple of generations earlier, children were more likely to understand how hard their parents labored and to see what their labor was; on the farm or in the village, children mostly stayed at home and watched their parents work. Men worked nearer the home where they could be seen, and it was very clear that if mom did not make the clothes, cook, can, and teach her children, then the children would not eat, have clothing, or be educated. We might have grown up in a world that was not quite as hard on folks, but a lot more work went on than we were led to believe. If you have children and you do your own wash, you know just what we mean. Until someone invents an automatic clothes sorter, folder, and put-away-er, a lot of work will remain to be done.

Let us begin to adopt the resource perspective that is the theme of this book. When mom stayed home, most of her resources were poured directly into the family. These resources included her time, energy, and labor. They also included her emotional resources, such as her sense of self and her ability to instill a sense of worth into her children. With each meal came the message: What I do as mom is important and since I do it for you, you are important. This lesson was harder to accept on liver and onions night, but we learned it nonetheless.

Dad's resources were devoted to the family, too, but only indirectly. Instead, most of his resources were directly devoted to work, where he invested his time, energy, and sense of self. This produced money for the family. Thus, the division of labor produced a division of resource

WORK WON'T LOVE YOU BACK

investment that was almost entirely determined by gender; dad gave at work, mom gave at home. Because wherever we directly invest our resources becomes the major focus of our attention, dad's attention was dominated by work and mom's by the home.

. . . AND NOW

If you've read this far or bought this book, you are probably a member of a dual career family. There are some interesting recent trends of which you might wish to take note. Until about 1950, single women (that is, those who never married) were likely to work outside the home, but married women were unlikely to be in the paid labor force. By 1960, however, more than half of married women had entered the work force. Since World War II, there has been a slow but steady growth in the number of single women working outside the home. Meanwhile, the percentage of employed, married women has *tripled* during this same period. In other words, not only are more and more women working outside the home, but married women have been taking jobs outside the home in droves.[3, 4]

Let's look a little further. The fastest-growing segment of women working outside the home from 1940 to 1960 was the group between the ages of forty-five and sixty-four. These were women whose children had mostly left home for college, marriage, and their own families. During the mid-1960s, women with children at home began entering the work force in greater numbers. By 1984, almost two-thirds of women with school-aged children and over half of those with children under age six were participating in the labor force. And statistics for the 1990s show that over half of women with infants are now working outside the home! The housewife seems to be a vanishing species, whether you mourn or celebrate her disappearance.[3, 4]

What these statistics represent, then, is the growth of the dual career family. No longer are women working only until they marry or only if they are divorced or widowed. No longer are the majority of women staying home to mend socks and chauffeur kids to piano lessons until the children are grown and independent. Now the norm is the woman who works outside the home when her children are young, when they are growing up, and after they've gone off on their own. True, many women with young children still take some time off to be with their children, but this is increasingly rare. Today, the dual career family is the norm. Dad's resources are still being directed into work, but now so are mom's. The question arises, Are resources being invested in the family—in love, in romance, in children?

WE CHANGED; THE WORLD STAYED THE SAME

What we are describing is a change in resource investment and distribution in the labor force and in the family more vast, rapid, and significant than the one that occurred during the Industrial Revolution. Our history books teach us about the enormity of the evolution in society that was brought about by the machine factory. Yet that change actually took place over a much longer period than the change we are now experiencing as men and women work together on the job and share that burden as partners.

Our institutions, meanwhile, have remained static and unyielding to the changing demands of our families. Day care in North America is still in a primitive state. Licensing of day care is sporadic, and most licensing procedures merely attempt to establish minimal health standards and reasonable teacher-to-child ratios. Few day-care workers are professionally trained or supervised. There is no national day-care plan, no clear set of goals and expectations, and rarely any coordination between care and the different stages of young children's development.

Our day-care system is actually an amalgamation of independent and church-sponsored organizations, many of which are no more formal than a woman taking a few children into her home. One recent survey showed that the average family uses up to ten different kinds of care (including grandparents, babysitters, older siblings, and formal day care) for their children in a given year. Families usually work out a plan (few children are lost in the shuffle), but only at great expense and often by settling for less than they really want for their children.

Even when children are old enough to attend school, the situation remains far from a dual career parent's ideal. If your needs as a dual career family are not being met by the schools, you are in good company. Most other dual career parents would probably tell you that they feel the same. Kindergarten in most schools is still half-day. Educators often argue that this is as long as the young child can handle, yet the dual career child has usually been in full-time day care from two to

WORK WON'T LOVE YOU BACK

five years before entering the hallowed halls of kindergarten. It may be that kindergarten teachers would find it hard to keep five-year-olds interested in a daylong academic curriculum. However, it is our contention that if schools were seen as being part of a dual career society, innovative ideas would be implemented.

Following kindergarten, children are in school from about 8:30 or 9:00 in the morning until 3:00 or 3:30 in the afternoon. Many single career families become dual career families at this point, one parent (usually mom) having chosen to stay at home until now. With the children in school, either mom or dad must now jump the hurdles involved in straddling the pick-up and drop-off periods. Alternatively, mom or dad can take a part-time job, leaving one of them available to drive the daylong transportation route. Of course, this is usually mom. Precare and aftercare programs have begun to appear, but their availability and quality are spotty at best.

Take a look at your child's school calendar for the coming year. How many teacher conference days, teacher meeting days, holidays, and other no-school days do you count? Now take out your real calendar, the one from work. How many of those days do you have free? How open is your boss, your business, or your job to your taking days off? If you're like us, you bump and squeeze and get very creative in coming up with ways to cover child care. If you're lucky, your children are now old enough to stay home alone. If you're unlucky, you either have to lose workdays or perhaps leave your young children unattended.

And then there is summer vacation. No doubt children need a break from school and deserve sunshine and play. But this is also the time when society tells the dual career family that what happens to their children is up to them because society is off duty. Day care is poorly coordinated and offers spotty care, but summer camp is worse. Schedules, start-up dates, break periods, and transportation are designed to frustrate the most logistically adept dual career parent. Most of the camps advertised in our area begin later in the day than school, end earlier or at the same time school ends, and have funny between-session breaks. Summers are when we most wish we could have a three-parent family or live-in help (we always wish for this, but especially during the summer). Our other fantasy is to be so wealthy that we could take the entire family away for the summer. (Of course, we would also have a nanny with us so that we could have the evenings to ourselves after spending lovely, relaxed days with the children.) However, like you, we can only sigh and cope with the reality instead.

How have those who control the workplace responded to the dual career family? For the most part, they have pretended it doesn't exist. Indeed, recent economic trends have caused many employers to adopt what has been termed the "leaner and meaner" approach. Lean and mean translates to fewer workers working more hours more aggressively. In a recent visit to a car manufacturer for stress consulting, we found a new openness to working women that was refreshing. However, workers were expected to put in a forty-five- to fifty-hour workweek. Moreover, executives were expected to take work home and laborers were required to perform substantial overtime as well. This kind of schedule is overtaxing for any dual career parent. It is especially burdensome for women, because they are typically expected to put in another full day of work when they get home. Some recent research indicates that it is also becoming increasingly problematic for men in dual career families.[5, 6]

The attitude of American business toward the family is clearly reflected in the following anecdote:

———

Ted came to Chicago to manage the regional office of a large service industry. A young rising star, he not only did well, he was credited with a multi-million-dollar increase in sales while still decreasing costs. Along with a substantial raise, however, he received a phone call one Friday. He had until Monday to decide whether to accept a new, more senior position with the firm—in another city. He was also told quite directly that his refusal would probably spell the beginning of the end of his tenure with the company. But what about his wife's career, what about his children's school and social adjustment, and what about his own friendships and organizational affiliations?

Business in America too often continues to operate according to the "Leave it to Beaver" model, in which dad is the breadwinner and where and when he goes, the family follows. American corporations hope to emulate the success of Japanese businesses without showing any of the loyalty that businesses in Japan guarantee their workers. Perhaps what they really wish is for our society to emulate the continued trend in Japan for women to stay at home so that men can work ten-hour days and then have dinner with other men from the office. This division of labor is already causing strains in Japan, and it is totally inconsistent with social trends in North America, where dual career families are the norm.

Now that the Family and Medical Leave Act has been enacted into U.S. law, we expect to see greater change in the workplace. However, this law mandating unpaid leave in the event of a family crisis is only one small, albeit significant, part of the larger picture. We will know that business has changed when it sees the family as a resource, rather than as an adversary that is vying for the worker's time, attention, and energy. These changes will certainly come, because dual career families make up the vast majority of the labor pool. As the last older generation of managers who come from single career families retires, change will follow because their places will be filled by women and men from dual career families.

The two of us often go to the movies when we are able to take a night out without the children. This allows us to have family time in the early evening and our own time as a couple later on. Upon our return to the United States after living abroad for many years, we were shocked to be invited to dinner at 6:30 or 7:00 in the evening or to cocktails at 5:00 on Sunday afternoon. People were surprised (some were angry) when we declined dinner invitations for Friday evenings because that was a time we reserved to be at home with our children. Friday night was a haven for Monopoly, for watching G-rated videos (they're not easy to find), and for reading books with the kids on our laps. Families are seldom invited for dinner with their children (understandable, even if regrettable), so going out meant leaving our children with the babysitter after a week of school, day care, homework, dance classes, soccer practice, and often late-returning parents.

Clearly, whether we look at day care, school, business, or recreation, society has not kept pace with the change from single to dual career families. Society has stayed still, as if families of the 1990s were living like the families of decades earlier. Only fast-food chains seem to have taken the dual career family's needs into account. Not always the best food, but think of the time you've saved! Dual career families want and deserve better than this. We do not want the educational or business equivalents of fast-food chains, but we do want and require adjustments to be made that ensure our quality of life, the well-being of our families, and the healthy, productive development of our children. Whether we work because we want to, need to, or like to, this is the way we have contrived to best live our lives. Society needs our labor and our contribution, yet it has lagged behind in supporting our life-style. We need communities and workplaces that take into account our families' demands on our resources and that support our families.

OF HUSBANDS AND WIVES AND THEIR WELL-BEING

Given the increased stress placed on the dual career family's resources and the poor societal support for them, it would seem that the members of such families must be in great difficulty. Research indicates, however, that the reverse is often the case. Dual careerism carries both costs and dividends.

First of all, on the financial plane, dual career families obviously have an income advantage over single career families. In many dual career families, both spouses would work outside the home even if it were not economically advantageous, but for most the economic aspect is important. For some, a second income allows the family to purchase extra luxuries. For many others, it is needed to pay the monthly bills, to cover the cost of children's clothing or education, and perhaps to live in a better neighborhood or afford an automobile that is not constantly on the verge of breakdown. Without this income, many dual career families would be in serious financial straits, or at least would need to live much more frugally than they do now. Nor should one feel guilty about wanting money to eat out occasionally at a nice restaurant or even buy tickets for the ballet or a sporting event. We live in a society in which we need to let off steam, enjoy life, and defuse from the pressures of work, home, and the evening news.

The experience of the dual career family is a little different for men and women. Men have historically worked outside the home and been the principal income producer. Percentage-wise this is still the case. For women, the dual career family has meant a change. Now they, too, leave the home and dedicate their resources to the family indirectly, by producing income.

You would think that when women work outside the home, husbands and other family members would pitch in so that the family work load is shared more equitably. However, what women are finding is that after working part- or full-time jobs, they are still expected to perform the vast majority of household labor. They must cook, clean, shop, and care for children significantly more than men. In fact, women in dual career families in the United States today work from eleven to thirty more hours per week than their spouses, depending on the survey and the region of the country examined.

There are indications that men's participation in household labor is increasing and women's decreasing. This trend is heartening, but it may not be occurring fast enough. Indeed, even those who emphasize the change acknowledge that men are doing only about one-third of the housework, which is still far from equal.[7]

The situation for dual career women may look dire. However, studies also show that women who work outside the home are physically and psychologically healthier than women who do not enter the labor market. This difference is especially striking among mothers of young children. Those who stay at home are much more likely to experience clinical depression, a severe psychological disorder that often leads to hospitalization and certainly causes much pain and anxiety. A recent survey by Dr. Helen Cleminshaw and her colleagues showed that despite work and home pressures, working women in academia were more satisfied than nonworking women with their marriages, their children, and their life-style in general.[8] Academic women are a rather specialized sample, as not every working woman teaches at a university, but studies of women across various job categories also indicate that in many ways it is healthier to work.

For men, the challenge of the dual career life-style is less clear. There are numerous books about the plight of working women, but little has been written about men. We think the answer for men is simple and straightforward, at least regarding their contribution to the household. If your wife wants to work outside the home, or if your finances dictate that the family would be in significantly better shape if she did, then you need to make significant changes as well. Some of these are changes at work. Extra hours may have to be curtailed at the office, career moves may have to be reconsidered, and you may have to organize your day around dropping little Suzy off at school. Outside of work, Sunday golf may have to be limited to nine holes (or less), Monday bowling may just have to be cancelled, and you must pitch in as a full partner at home. Just as work outside the home is no longer a man's world, household labor can no longer be women's work. If you can't take the heat, you may have to get out of the kitchen, but don't forget to do the laundry, help your daughter with her homework, and bathe a kid while you're at it.

Most men are resisting this readjustment. If the man in your house is making a major contribution to housework and child rearing, we applaud you both. However, take note that this is the exception. National figures indicate that men are doing more household labor than their fathers did but still far less than their partners do.[7, 9] They continue to invest most of their resources at work. We firmly believe that this situation will have to change. Much of this book addresses just how this can be done. For now, however, we'll just say that our own lives and the lives of many couples and families that we know from counseling, as well as our research, suggest that the adjustments bring ample rewards.

When men contribute their share of resources directly to the total family labor load, it creates a cycle of family satisfaction. For example, as a father you will gain a closer relationship with your children. They will run to you when they fall and cut their knees, not just to mom. Your wife may begin to feel sexy again (add eleven hours to your weekly work load and see how romantic *you* feel!). Toilet cleaning has little romantic appeal to men or women, but doing only half makes the job bearable. Putting together simple, nutritious meals does not require a degree in rocket science; you can do it. And remember, many of the great chefs are men. Nor does that entitle you to work your cooking magic and leave the kitchen looking like Hurricane Andrew just passed through. No one can sabotage your adjustment to a new life-style as well as you can by doing a horrible job of it. And no one but you can ensure success.

Look at your own work. You not only work for money, but probably also for a sense of satisfaction and accomplishment. You feel good bringing home a paycheck as well, because in this way you have contributed to your family. When you do a job particularly well, you have

WORK WON'T LOVE YOU BACK

a special feeling of pride that can help see you through many weeks of day-to-day drudgery. Women are working for the same reasons. Your partner is not that different from you. She, too, works to gain a sense of accomplishment and contribution. These are not selfish reasons; in no way do they deny her feelings for you or your children, nor do they minimize the importance she places on the household. Indeed, research repeatedly shows that women who work outside the home remain significantly concerned about domestic problems.

Psychologically speaking, the situation for men is not so straightforward. Just as men will need to support their partners' careers and participate in the household labor, women will have to support their partners through the psychological transition to a new world. Men are showing a budding willingness to take on multiple roles in the dual career family and to pull some of their attention away from work in order to develop a sense of self that includes both work and home. They are exploring worlds that are threatening to them and to all they were taught about what it means to be men. You will need to help them through this, for in a sense you did it first and know more about how to cope with being pulled from both work and home. There's no other way around it. Men and women will have to nurture and support each other through the strains of work, home, and the interactions between them.

Keep in mind that even if both of you make the changes that we recommend, your life will not be stress-free. However, if stress is kept at a reasonable level and the rewards are sufficient, life will not only be tolerable, it will be enriched. We would choose a dual career life-style no matter what our finances were. You might or might not do the same. Each of us, however, must cope with the special difficulties and resource demands that are part and parcel of the dual career family experience.

MAKING CHANGES

This book is about ways to influence or directly change your situation at home and in the workplace. However, we have no illusions about how difficult some of these changes are to bring about. Many aspects of home and work are relatively resistant to change or are outside our direct sphere of influence. Businesses are going to change as a result of special pressures already being exerted by dual career families. Still, even if some changes in the workplace are only a year off (most, unfortunately, are likely to take longer), you cannot be expected to wait around passively for the new social order to arrive.

We will, therefore, present ideas for change that can be implemented now because they are under your control. Indeed, we hope that you will often put down this book in excitement to speak to your partner or to a friend about some great idea that you just came across. But no change, however convinced you are of its merit, will come about easily. Your family, like ours, has routines that are deeply entrenched. Some of these have been carefully planned (even if they don't work well); others just sort of developed over time. Change almost always meets with some resistance. It is easier to swim with the current, but change means swimming upstream for a bit until the current adjusts to the new situation. We will work together with you through the chapters of this book, developing suggestions, ideas, plans, and alternatives. Our goal is to enrich your life and the lives of your children by providing blueprints for change that are suited to the needs of dual career parents and their families.

We refer to dual career couples and families throughout this book, but we recognize that this is a richly diverse category. Families and couples come in so many packages that it would be naive to base our thinking on the traditional nuclear family alone. Many families, for example, are "blended families" that include children from prior marriages. Similarly, we have directed this book toward heterosexual partners, but much of what we have to say should be helpful for same-gender relationships as well. Ivonne's heritage is Mexican-American and Stevan comes from a line of Polish kosher butchers; in some ways these differences are reflected in our families of origin as well as in who we are today. We not only acknowledge all these differences, we are excited by them. They make our life and work more interesting, and we have tried to be sensitive to issues of gender, ethnicity, culture, and family type. The couples and families whose stories we present represent a rainbow of racial and ethnic diversity.

Let us now look at how we can frame the stresses common to almost every dual career family in such a way that you can better react to them and prevent them from building up to unmanageable or damaging levels.

Chapter 2

A Proven Strategy for Coping

We now introduce an overall strategy to help you organize and implement the various ideas we will present for dealing with, surviving, and thriving in dual career families. This strategy or game plan should serve as a backdrop for raising children, interacting with your partner, making changes, and deciding whether a particular change is a good one for you and your loved ones. We call this strategy the *theory of conservation of resources.* Understanding what we mean by "resource conservation" will help you make the right decisions for you and your family and will give you a yardstick with which to measure how well you are doing.

We developed the theory of conservation of resources in our research and clinical work, and it has led to a book, numerous book chapters, and many research articles.[1-7] It has also helped guide our work with families. But *conservation of resources* (or *COR*) is not a stuffy, intellectual theory. Though complex, it can be easily understood and applied by everyday thinking people. We have found its principles to be readily appreciated and adopted by the many people with whom we work, despite their different educational backgrounds and viewpoints.

Before presenting COR theory, it is important to emphasize that it addresses the very sources of stress. Other stress theories address the symptoms and perceptions of stress, suggesting your stress is all in your head. Not COR theory! There are real underlying causes of dual career stress. It is *not* merely a product of your perceptions. Nor can you alleviate stress by simple solutions such as better time management or a three times weekly aerobics class. Sure, those may be useful, but you have probably tried many such things. Have the results been overwhelming? Probably not. We must approach stress with much greater respect. It's as big as the green monster in Japanese B-movies and as resistant to attack. We cannot merely close our eyes and await the next scene, because when we open them again the oversized reptile will still be menacing.

The sources of stress include your career and job, the company you work for, what you do in your free time, how you divide household labor, how much you give to your partner, and what you do at home with your children. How far do you commute? Are family members together or apart during leisure time? What percentage of your income goes to luxury items or rooms in the house that you could do without?

Because our resources are finite, we must use them judiciously and be sure that we get all we can out of them. Some of the circumstances that determine how our resources are used are virtually unchangeable, but many can be changed or reshaped, and it is on them that we must concentrate our attention. But these are still sources of stress and strain, where the horrible beast lies in wait. Moreover, changing the way we use our resources is never as easy as attending to mere symptoms. However, we guarantee that the product of such changes will be a hundred times more satisfying.

CONSERVATION OF RESOURCES: THE BASIC PREMISE

COR begins with a simple premise: *People strive to obtain and retain those things that they value.* Indeed, this is a basic characteristic of all species. We are genetically programmed and socialized to work toward increasing those things that we value, preventing the loss of what we value, and creating a life-style that enhances the possibility of achieving those goals.

There are hundreds of examples of this in your life. You work to increase many things that you value, such as the financial stability that allows you to pay for your home, car, clothes, and kids' music lessons. You also work to increase your self-esteem and your sense of mastery over your environment. You work to increase the likelihood of finding the kind of people you like and to accomplish the kinds of things you value in this world. Clearly, people balance these various goals differently. Some of you are social workers, devoting more hours for less pay than, say, an attorney. You probably do so because you have certain social values that supersede some of your financial needs. Others work in a job they dislike, but do so because the financial remuneration is necessary. People have different values and live their lives and make decisions accordingly.

You do the same in your love life. You strive to improve the quality of your marriage, to enhance your close relationships, and to ensure that you receive what you need from your partner. Many of you give less than you should to your partner, but you probably try to keep the balance of benefits in the relationship above some minimum. When this minimum is not met, relationships begin to undergo serious problems. Again, we seek to obtain and retain what we value, and we react negatively when circumstances cause us to experience their loss.

WHEN DOES STRESS OCCUR?

Every psychological and biological system has a threshold point where an alarm goes off that says, Pay attention to me or you're in trouble. How can we know in advance when we are likely to run into this situation, which we call stress?

COR theory states that psychological stress occurs in any one of three situations:

1. When individuals are *threatened* with the possibility of loss of valued resources.
2. When individuals experience the *actual* loss of valued resources.
3. When individuals *fail to gain* resources following significant resource investment.

To clarify this definition and help you understand the nature of stress, we must explain what we mean by *resources*. Resources are *those things that we value or that serve as a means of obtaining what we value.* We speak about four kinds of resources:

1. *Objects,* such as a car, house, diamond ring, or furniture.
2. *Personal characteristics and skills,* such as self-confidence, a professional skill, social skills, or leadership ability.
3. *Conditions,* such as a good marriage, seniority on the job, home ownership, or good health.
4. *Energies,* such as money, credit, time, or stamina.

There are literally hundreds of individual resources that people have and that you have yourself. Basically, COR theory says that we all do what we can to increase our resources (those things we value) and that stress follows when we experience a significant loss of those resources.

Your resources can be likened to a mountain-climbing expedition. Object resources include the ropes, tackle, special boots, oxygen tanks, and other equipment you need for the ascent. The personal characteristics and skills you need include mountain-climbing experience, bravado, and self-confidence. Being a member of an experienced team could be an important resource condition, increasing the likelihood that others will be available should you need help. Finally, energy resources include your personal stamina and physical conditioning. No one resource group is sufficient for success; it is the combination of resources that is key. Hence, the loss of any part of this resource web can be devastating. Similarly, dual career lives depend on complex combinations of resources necessary to ensure the well-being of each individual and the family as a whole. (For the dual career family, many days also feel like a climb up Mount Everest!)

Let us now look at some examples of each of the three situations that cause stress (the threat of loss, actual loss, and the failure to gain), taken from the real lives of dual career families. We have changed important details in order to protect the anonymity of the individuals described, while preserving the essential elements of their stories.

Threat to Resources

Tom and Sandra were doing well, beginning to stabilize their dual career marriage and the myriad arrangements necessary for their children in their new community. Tom was a mechanic and Sandra had for a long period remained at home to care for their children and the household. Before that, she had been a sales clerk at a department store, and when the opportunity arose to rent a small shop in the corridor of a nearby mall—basically, three glass counters and a register—Sandra seized it. What began almost as a whim had, after about two years of hard work, become a reasonably successful enterprise. Now, however, two larger stores that had leased space in the mall were threatening Sandra's business. Both Tom and Sandra were quite distressed over this state of affairs.

Sandra, in particular, was both angry and depressed and was very short with the kids and Tom. The origin of her stress was not financial, as Tom's salary and their savings were sufficient to see the family through any short-term financial problems that might ensue. Nor had any real loss yet been experienced; the new stores had not even cut their opening-day ribbons. Rather, both Tom and Sandra realized that the store's success had become a great source of pride, enhancing self-confidence for Sandra, who had had many doubts about her ability to enter the work-a-day world after ten years at home raising the children. The stress they experienced arose from the threat that the changed conditions posed to their newfound resources, so important to the family's feeling of well-being. Tom was sensitive enough to understand that just as he worked not for the money alone, so too did his wife need to contribute to the family's financial resources and develop her own sense of purpose. Indeed, Tom's understanding and support and the fact that he didn't minimize the problem were key resources that helped them weather the crisis and engage in successful problem solving to combat their stress.

Sandra has since moved to a new mall and obtained an expanded commercial loan for a larger store. She is currently considering a second venture back at the original location that would provide merchandise more up-scale than what her competitors there sell. The family kids her, nicknaming her "the tycoon," but her sizable financial success is no laughing matter. She also has joined a group of women entrepreneurs who advise other women considering commercial ventures. Tom and Sandra's two daughters operate a lunch wagon outside local factories during the summer, and this has paid for the extras they want. They beat the competition by offering gourmet sandwiches the size of breadboxes. They will probably never have doubts about their ability to succeed in the business world!

Actual Loss of Resources

Marsha and Bill thought they were doing very well. Both attorneys, their practices were thriving and their reputations and bank accounts were growing rapidly. They didn't see each other until late in the evening, but their adolescent children seemed to be very successful in school despite a family that was operating on automatic pilot. One day, Bill received a call at work from the school, informing him that his sixteen-year-old son Ron had returned to school after lunch quite drunk. At first, Bill dismissed this as an adolescent lark, a one-time occurrence. But he was smart enough to check further by calling the parents of some of Ron's friends. What came to light was that Ron and a few of his friends had developed a serious alcohol problem. Indeed, a check of liquor cabinets and a smart visit to a family counselor revealed that Ron was a sad young man who felt unloved. As he had often seen his parents do, he sought solace in alcohol and developed a dependency on it. He had even considered suicide.

Marsha and Bill were shocked. As loving parents, financial ruin would have been less of a blow than what they were experiencing. Their seemingly successful world had shattered in a few days' time. Both felt terribly guilty as well, guilty that they had contributed to their son's difficulties and that they had been so blind to the symptoms. They cancelled their weekend plans and made reservations for the whole family at a mountain resort where all there was to do was walk and talk and be together. The next day at work, Bill and Marsha set about the difficult task of referring new cases to others in their firms. In addition, Bill decided to bring a younger associate into his practice, a move that would cut his total financial gain but allow him more flexibility and much more time at home.

The resources that Marsha and Bill lost were their sense of family well-being and their son's actual health and welfare. They might have lost Ron. Like most parents, they loved their children dearly. Yet work pressures and the need to succeed had distorted their priorities. They experienced a significant loss, but they were lucky enough to be given a second chance.

Ron's drinking was really a cry for help. He wanted to be caught in order to gain his parents' attention. Marsha and Bill were serious about making the changes they realized were necessary. They continued in family therapy once a week for fourteen months. Their daughter went too, for though she was coping better than her brother, she had become increasingly distant from her family. Dinner was still late sometimes, but about four nights a week everyone ate together. Bill and Marsha frequently took off work to see Ron play on the basketball team. (He played the bench much of the time, but did score a key basket once. He looked directly over to his parents when he did.) Ron and his dad also played golf most Sundays with another father-son pair (Bill's friends did not feel comfortable including Ron in their golf outings).

Today, both parents work fewer hours, earn about 20 percent less, and often visit their children at college. The children also come home regularly. They bought a small cottage in the mountains where the family frequently goes on weekends and holidays. Bill and Marsha have not enlarged their practices even though the kids are now away at college. They spend the extra time together. Sex has never been so good, and after many years of hardly communicating, both feel that they have a best friend as well as a spouse and lover.

Failure to Gain Resource Return

Tony and Chris were members of a different kind of dual career family, what is called a blended family: Tony's children from a previous marriage lived with them part of the time and were frequent visitors, and Chris's children from a previous marriage lived with them full time. Tony worked in insurance sales and Chris was an office manager for a local firm. Chris had married at nineteen and had spent the years of her first marriage raising her two daughters. She wanted to go back to college, but when her daughters started school the family needed extra money, so she went to work. For Chris and Tony, a blended family meant that much of the financial burden fell on them for all four children. Chris's ex-husband was a poor provider, his child-support contribution being low and sometimes nonexistent. With no way to advance at work, Chris had been feeling increasingly frustrated. Her boss was clearly less bright and capable than she, and Chris spent much of her time covering up his mistakes and taking care of their department's problems. Given the financial pressures of their family situation, there seemed to be no end in sight.

Where is the problem here? COR theory says that when individuals invest their resources—their time and energy—they expect a reasonable payback in terms of gains of other resources. Chris, however, was employed well below her level of ability. Despite her excellent job performance, she (like many women in her situation) received little reward for her labor. She was poorly paid and seldom complimented on her efforts. Eventually, Chris and Tony decided that the best solution was to cut their spending until the following September, when Chris would return to the university, finish her B.A. (she had a year to go), and then enter the Master's of Business Administration program. She also won the support of the vice president of her division in this venture; her excellence had not gone unnoticed by him. The firm would pay her tuition and keep her in a new position half time for three years. The vice president hoped that she would then choose to remain with the firm.

We cannot tell you the conclusion of this saga, for the story is still unfolding. Chris now feels excited when she gets up in the morning, and is enjoying both work and school. The whole family pitches in more with meals and laundry (the house is a bit messier than before, but sometimes something just has to give). They can't afford to build the planned addition on the house, and the kids will be two to a room for a long while. Tony's and Chris's cars together have 150,000 miles on them; they may trade one in for a used car, but no new car is in the forecast. Chris's education will take a year longer to complete than originally planned, because there were signs of strain when she tried to mix part-time work with full-time school. Resources can only stretch so far!

If you've read these examples carefully, you should have a pretty clear understanding of COR theory and why stress occurred in each of these dual career families. You should also understand how worse outcomes were avoided, even in the case of Bill and Marsha and their son's alcoholism. Human beings seek to increase their resources and avoid their loss, yet all they have to ensure resource gain and prevent resource loss are those same resources. In other words, we must use our resources to protect our resources. For example, just as we invest time and money in a business to make more money, we invest time and love in our relationships to enhance love and affection. Our children are a resource we dearly value, and we must invest other resources to ensure their physical and psychological health. These families experienced different kinds of loss or failure to gain resources, but reappraising their circumstances and investing their resources more wisely helped them put their lives back on a steadier, surer course.

RESOURCE SPIRALS

Another important aspect of COR is the notion that gains and losses of resources occur in ascending or descending spirals. You usually do not gain or lose a single resource. Events affect numerous resources simultaneously. Moreover, when you lose resources, you have fewer resources available to offset future challenges. This makes you more vulnerable to further loss.

For Marsha and Bill, problems at work or with their daughter might easily have followed upon their difficulties with their son. They could have turned their attention away from their daughter because her problems seemed less critical, thereby causing them to worsen. After all, the same situation that caused their son's crisis was also fueling their daughter's growing alienation from the family. When it rains, it pours. If their daughter's situation had in fact worsened, either Bill or Marsha might, in turn, have become severely depressed, reducing their ability to cope. Ultimately, this might have undermined the marriage, and the family might have fallen apart.

These spirals often accelerate at such a pace that, like a tornado, they lay waste to everything in their path. The extent of the ensuing damage sometimes makes repair and rebuilding difficult, as each loss of resources tears at the fabric of the total resources available, leading to greater and greater depression, anxiety, and despair.

The good news is that gain spirals also occur and they, too, build on themselves and gather momentum. Each gain increases our confidence that we can continue to cope successfully and improve the quality of our lives. In addition, as resources are gained, we broaden the array of resources that we can call upon to offset the effects of future losses.

The trick is to make those first gains, especially following an initial setback. As Sandra began to make a success of her business, her and Tom's marital relations improved in response. Sandra's heightened self-esteem helped her to shed the twenty extra pounds that she had carried since her last pregnancy. Their daughters responded to the reduction in family tension and to the wonderful role model that Sandra provided; their grades improved and they experienced a greater identity and closeness with their mother. Tom had a brief period in which he found his wife's success threatening. Their increased intimacy, however, helped him overcome this, and he grew with the experience and came to understand that Sandra's venture was a shared success. He also found that their greater financial security enabled him to reduce the part-time consulting he did for extra income; they spent the additional free time on themselves and on the occasional rendezvous at a luxury hotel downtown. Again, one success led to another, increasing the potential for future gains and advances.

Your resources are like a golden chain. Gaining resources adds to the number of links in the chain and to the thickness and resiliency of each link. Losses weaken the chain and make the links brittle and easily broken. Keep this symbol in mind, to help remind you of the need to work toward preserving personal and family resources and the strength of your resource pool.

By successful resource investment and management, you not only survive in a dual career family but actually thrive. Loss spirals can be avoided or quickly halted. Gain spirals are not beyond your reach. Surely the demands on the dual career family are great, but the potential rewards for the family and its members can also be enhanced by working together, building resources, and making the dual career family succeed.

Chapter 3

Cultivating Your Personal and Marital Resources

Investing resources might make you think of financial planning, but that would lead you astray from our point. Financial planning sounds cold, and we think it is also too simple compared to the complexity of successful dual career life. When you think about evaluating resources and watching them grow, think instead about the farm family working the soil together to produce crops for the next year. You must have seeds to plant and a plan for all the phases of preparing the soil and planting, growing, and harvesting crops. You must nurture the soil from which your crops emerge and the life that grows from it. In a family, each person must know his or her role and be flexible enough to help out when bad weather or blight threatens. Close your eyes and imagine holding the rich soil in one hand and the life-giving seed in the other. These are the resources of which we speak: As the farm family is tied to the land, so are we tied to the sustaining resources we have and will need for our own and our family's resource-filled future.

As a dual career family, you are concerned with your own resources and with those of your partner, your children, and the family as a whole. Yet, in family therapy we often see couples who have lost sight of their resources by pursuing purely financial or individual goals, to the detriment of other resources that they may actually value much more. They wonder why they feel so empty and how they lost touch with their spouses, their children, and their own mental and physical well-being. Because work dictates much of how you use your time and resources, it is all the more critical that you establish your priorities and learn how to nurture your key resources and watch them grow.

What are your key resources? This would seem to depend on the individual. Are our resources the same as yours? Surprisingly, they are to a large extent. We value our health and the health of our children. We value our love relationships, feeling good about who we are, having a stable income, a little extra money for a vacation, a roof that doesn't leak, and a car that runs. Most likely, you and your partner work for similar goals. Psychology and the media have emphasized individual identity so much that we have lost sight of the fact that, for all our differences, we are all very similar. Indeed, in the study of other cultures, a foremost finding is that people from very different cultures have many common values.[1]

That we desire similar resources is a way of saying we want the same things out of life. Of course, we are different from each other as well, but it is the values we share that allow us to develop a list of central resources as a common starting point. Identifying our resources helps us determine how to guide our resource investments—which crops and flowers are important, when to plant, and how to nurture the soil so that we can reap a rich harvest. The particular value you place on your resources, as an individual and as a couple, is also important, but it is helpful to establish that we are playing on a common field. It is even somewhat comforting to know that we are part of a larger

WORK WON'T LOVE YOU BACK

community of people who share our goals, values, and aspirations. Especially when it comes to the most valued resources, we are more or less of one mind.

In this chapter we present a way of evaluating your resources by means of the COR-Evaluation, or COR-E. We and other counselors and therapists have used this method with great success in our work with dual career families. It will provide you with a resource profile that will be of great help in guiding your dual career decisions.

To further convince you of the merits of this approach, we briefly discuss the scientific evidence (honest, we'll make it brief and interesting) that confirms its worth. We hope your desire to change your life and ensure your dual career future is strong enough that you will take an active role and complete the suggested tasks and exercises. That is the best step you can take to thrive in a dual career family. Your time and energy are two resources that will always be in short supply, but you must invest them when the potential gain is great. Just reading our book should prove valuable, but completing the exercises and discussing the material with your partner is the best way you can choose to lower dual career stress and enhance your lives.

CREATING THE COR-EVALUATION

How did we arrive at the seventy-four basic resources that make up the COR-E? We had groups of people from different walks of life (folks like you) discuss among themselves what they most valued and how they succeeded in obtaining what they most valued. For example, if they valued health, in and of itself, they would include health in their list. If they did not value money in itself, but did value the things that money brings, money would also be listed. After making its list, each group then evaluated the lists of other groups. At this point, they could add to the combined list or delete items from either list that they thought really were not very important. We did this with some thirty groups, until no new resources were added that another group did not delete.[2] (One individual did insist that playing the tuba was a resource, but the group's will prevailed, and tuba playing did not appear on the common list of central resources.)

Later, we had four groups of some fifty psychologists and health professionals in Holland create their own list using this method. After

Resources from COR-Evaluation

Personal transportation (car, truck, etc.)
Feeling that I am successful
Time for adequate sleep
Good marriage
Adequate clothing
Feeling valuable to others
Family stability
Free time
More clothing than I need
Sense of pride in myself
Intimacy with one or more family members
Time for work
Feeling that I am accomplishing my goals
Good relationship with my children
Time with loved ones
Necessary tools for work
Hope
Children's health
Stamina/endurance
Necessary home appliances
Feeling that my future success depends on me
Positively challenging routine
Personal health
Housing that suits my needs
Sense of optimism
Status/seniority at work
Adequate food
Larger home than I need
Sense of humor
Stable employment
Intimacy with spouse or partner
Adequate home furnishings
Feeling that I have control over my life
Role as a leader
Ability to communicate well
Providing children's essentials
Feeling that my life is peaceful

WORK WON'T LOVE YOU BACK

Acknowledgment of my accomplishments
Ability to organize tasks
Extras for children
Sense of commitment
Intimacy with at least one friend
Money for extras
Self-discipline
Understanding from my employer/boss
Savings or emergency money
Motivation to get things done
Spouse/partner's health
Support from co-workers
Adequate income
Feeling that I know who I am
Advancement in education or job training
Adequate financial credit
Feeling independent
Companionship
Financial assets (stocks, property, etc.)
Knowing where I am going with my life
Affection from others
Financial stability
Feeling that my life has meaning/purpose
Positive feelings about myself
People I can learn from
Money for transportation
Help with tasks at work
Medical insurance
Involvement with church, synagogue, etc.
Retirement security (financial)
Help with tasks at home
Loyalty of friends
Money for advancement or self-improvement (education, starting a
    business, etc.)
Help with child care
Involvement in organizations with others who have similar interests
Financial help if needed
Health of family/close friends

a much briefer period, they produced a list that contained fifty-six of the seventy-four resources on the COR-E, and they included no resource not on the COR-E. Their list was shorter, but that was probably because of the shorter time frame. This suggests that the items really are a basic set of agreed-upon resources. Of course, that does not mean it is a list of all the resources you might value. Nevertheless, it can be considered comprehensive, if not exhaustive.

RESEARCH ON THE COR APPROACH

To be read with your favorite coffee and a small sweet to make it even more interesting!

COR theory and the COR-E are distinguished from other strategies available to the public by the great deal of research that supports them. This book is not the place to present a research report, but we feel that if you are to trust us and consider our advice, you should have the benefit of knowing more about the soundness of our methods.

First, it is important to note that the items in the COR-Evaluation were created by persons such as yourself in a process designed to elicit the greatest range of resources. Many tests, in contrast, are designed by clinicians or researchers and are based on their professional experiences or insights. There are merits in both approaches, but we feel that ours has the decided advantage of representing what people themselves think is important. Research and clinical training provide excellent insights, but they can also be a hindrance in that experts are apt to create tests that are biased by that same professional training.

COR theory and the COR-E help people to evaluate the stress in their lives and how to find a personal way to overcome or avoid it. Reports on the use of our methods in scientific journals, with their rigorous standards, support this claim. However, if reading about research studies is not your cup of tea and you simply wish to trust what we say, skip the next few paragraphs and proceed to the next section.

Researchers at the Medical University of South Carolina's Department of Psychiatry have tested how well the COR-E predicts the effects of disaster.[3] Using the COR approach, they examined people's resource losses following Hurricane Hugo, which devastated Charleston in 1989, and later after the Sierra Madre earthquake, which hit Los Angeles County in June of 1991. Such disasters are even more stressful than dual career family life! In both cases they found that resource loss predicted the psychological distress of those exposed to the disasters. It was also the best available predictor of distress. Most interesting, loss of resources was related both to severe psychological problems, for which drug treatment or hospitalization would be advised, and to less severe levels of psychological distress. This is an important finding because many approaches predict either severe disorder or midrange problems, but few predict both.

A group of organizational stress researchers led by Dr. Mina Westman at Tel Aviv University examined how the loss and gain of resources affected Israelis in the work force.[4] Israel has been called a stress laboratory, and we therefore thought it would be an excellent place to examine COR—imagine that many of these people lived in Israel *and* had dual career families. Dr. Westman and her colleagues used the COR-E Hebrew version and found that people who experienced resource loss were higher in anxiety than those who were relatively loss-free. They also found that those who failed to make resource gains were the most vulnerable to burnout at work. Symptoms of burnout include emotional exhaustion, detachment from the job, tension and feelings of helplessness at work, and general irritability. This is an interesting finding because loss had not necessarily been incurred by those who developed burnout. Rather, the mere fact that resource gains were not made led to an emotional problem. This also had a financial cost to employers, as burnout severely interferes with job performance and often causes employees to change jobs or even careers.

Stevan used the COR approach and COR-E to examine how stress affected adults in a variety of settings.[2] He and his colleagues found that most of the concerns of young adults were related to individual resources such as personal accomplishment, a stable work environment, and a solid income. For adults with families, health and family concerns, as well as finances, were increasingly important. This shows that resource profiles change during different life stages, as we would expect. More surprising, perhaps, was that those who lacked resources or experienced more recent resource loss had the highest levels of anxiety and depression, although most respondents were experiencing only everyday stress. A few of these individuals were so anxious or depressed that they probably would have benefited from professional treatment, but most were experiencing psychological distress equivalent to a serious case of the blues. Such ongoing negative feelings take the pleasure out of life and can make dual career family life a drudgery.

These are only a few of the research findings based on COR theory and the COR-E, but we hope that they convince you of the validity of the approach. We can further attest to its usefulness in our own clinical work with individuals, couples, and families in therapy. Here we also find that the method serves as a valuable guide in our work, often providing us with insights into why some individual or family is experiencing greater difficulties than one would expect. It is certainly not the only tool that we use, but its research value is further supported by our clinical work. Also testimony to our method, perhaps, is the fact that we rely on it in making judgments and decisions for ourselves and our family. We have a policy of leaving work at work, but this is one method that we trust enough to use on our greatest resource—our family.

THE COR-E AS A TOOL FOR YOU

We hope you are satisfied that the COR approach is worth a sincere effort of resource investment on your part. We are confident that in using it you will become convinced of its value.

The seventy-four resources in the COR-Evaluation are presented in no particular order. It might, however, be helpful to think about them in terms of the four resource categories that we discussed in Chapter 2: objects, conditions, personal characteristics and skills, and energies. Hence, object resources include "necessary tools for work," "personal transportation," "adequate clothing," and "housing that suits my needs." Condition resources include "loyalty of friends," "personal health," and "status/seniority at work." Personal characteristics and skills include "sense of optimism," "feeling that I have control over my life," and "ability to organize tasks." Finally, energy resources include "time for work," "free time," "money for extras," and "adequate financial credit."

We provide identical versions of the COR-E questionnaire—How Important Are These Resources to Me? To What Extent Do I Have Them—for each partner, so that both of you can fill it out indepen-

Partner *1*

*How Important Are These
Resources to Me?
To What Extent Do I
Have Them?*

COR RESOURCE	Importance	Extent
1. Personal transportation (car, truck, etc.) . . .		
2. Feeling that I am successful		
3. Time for adequate sleep		
4. Good marriage		
5. Adequate clothing		
6. Feeling valuable to others		
7. Family stability		
8. Free time		
9. More clothing than I need		
10. Sense of pride in myself		
11. Intimacy with one or more family members .		
12. Time for work		
13. Feeling that I am accomplishing my goals . . .		
14. Good relationship with my children		
15. Time with loved ones		
16. Necessary tools for work		
17. Hope		
18. Children's health		
19. Stamina/endurance		
20. Necessary home appliances		
21. Feeling that my future success depends on me .		
22. Positively challenging routine		
23. Personal health		
24. Housing that suits my needs		
25. Sense of optimism		
26. Status/seniority at work		
27. Adequate food		
28. Larger home than I need		
29. Sense of humor		
30. Stable employment		
31. Intimacy with spouse or partner		
32. Adequate home furnishings		
33. Feeling that I have control over my life		
34. Role as a leader		

35. Ability to communicate well . . . . _____ _____
36. Providing children's essentials . . . . _____ _____
37. Feeling that my life is peaceful . . . . _____ _____
38. Acknowledgment of my accomplishments . . _____ _____
39. Ability to organize tasks . . . . _____ _____
40. Extras for children . . . . _____ _____
41. Sense of commitment . . . . _____ _____
42. Intimacy with at least one friend . . . . _____ _____
43. Money for extras . . . . _____ _____
44. Self-discipline . . . . _____ _____
45. Understanding from my employer/boss . . . _____ _____
46. Savings or emergency money . . . . _____ _____
47. Motivation to get things done . . . . _____ _____
48. Spouse/partner's health . . . . _____ _____
49. Support from co-workers . . . . _____ _____
50. Adequate income . . . . _____ _____
51. Feeling that I know who I am . . . . _____ _____
52. Advancement in education or job training . . _____ _____
53. Adequate financial credit . . . . _____ _____
54. Feeling independent . . . . _____ _____
55. Companionship . . . . _____ _____
56. Financial assets (stocks, property, etc.) . . . . _____ _____
57. Knowing where I am going with my life . . . _____ _____
58. Affection from others . . . . _____ _____
59. Financial stability . . . . _____ _____
60. Feeling that my life has meaning/purpose . . _____ _____
61. Positive feelings about myself . . . . _____ _____
62. People I can learn from . . . . _____ _____
63. Money for transportation . . . . _____ _____
64. Help with tasks at work . . . . _____ _____
65. Medical insurance . . . . _____ _____
66. Involvement with church, synagogue, etc. . . _____ _____
67. Retirement security (financial) . . . . _____ _____
68. Help with tasks at home . . . . _____ _____
69. Loyalty of friends . . . . _____ _____
70. Money for advancement or self-improvement
    (education, starting a business, etc.) . . . . . . _____ _____
71. Help with child care . . . . _____ _____
72. Involvement in organizations with others who
    have similar interests . . . . _____ _____
73. Financial help if needed . . . . _____ _____
74. Health of family/close friends . . . . _____ _____
75. _____ _____
76. _____ _____
77. _____ _____

Partner 2

How Important Are These Resources to Me? To What Extent Do I Have Them?

COR RESOURCE	Importance	Extent
1. Personal transportation (car, truck, etc.) . . .		
2. Feeling that I am successful		
3. Time for adequate sleep		
4. Good marriage		
5. Adequate clothing		
6. Feeling valuable to others		
7. Family stability		
8. Free time		
9. More clothing than I need		
10. Sense of pride in myself		
11. Intimacy with one or more family members .		
12. Time for work		
13. Feeling that I am accomplishing my goals . . .		
14. Good relationship with my children		
15. Time with loved ones		
16. Necessary tools for work		
17. Hope		
18. Children's health		
19. Stamina/endurance		
20. Necessary home appliances		
21. Feeling that my future success depends on me .		
22. Positively challenging routine		
23. Personal health		
24. Housing that suits my needs		
25. Sense of optimism		
26. Status/seniority at work		
27. Adequate food		
28. Larger home than I need		
29. Sense of humor		
30. Stable employment		
31. Intimacy with spouse or partner		
32. Adequate home furnishings		
33. Feeling that I have control over my life		
34. Role as a leader		

35. Ability to communicate well . . . . _____ _____
36. Providing children's essentials . . . . _____ _____
37. Feeling that my life is peaceful . . . . _____ _____
38. Acknowledgment of my accomplishments . . _____ _____
39. Ability to organize tasks . . . . _____ _____
40. Extras for children . . . . _____ _____
41. Sense of commitment . . . . _____ _____
42. Intimacy with at least one friend . . . . . . _____ _____
43. Money for extras . . . . _____ _____
44. Self-discipline . . . . _____ _____
45. Understanding from my employer/boss . . . _____ _____
46. Savings or emergency money . . . . _____ _____
47. Motivation to get things done . . . . _____ _____
48. Spouse/partner's health . . . . _____ _____
49. Support from co-workers . . . . _____ _____
50. Adequate income . . . . _____ _____
51. Feeling that I know who I am . . . . _____ _____
52. Advancement in education or job training . . _____ _____
53. Adequate financial credit . . . . _____ _____
54. Feeling independent . . . . _____ _____
55. Companionship . . . . _____ _____
56. Financial assets (stocks, property, etc.) . . . . _____ _____
57. Knowing where I am going with my life . . . _____ _____
58. Affection from others . . . . _____ _____
59. Financial stability . . . . _____ _____
60. Feeling that my life has meaning/purpose . . _____ _____
61. Positive feelings about myself . . . . _____ _____
62. People I can learn from . . . . _____ _____
63. Money for transportation . . . . _____ _____
64. Help with tasks at work . . . . _____ _____
65. Medical insurance . . . . _____ _____
66. Involvement with church, synagogue, etc. . . _____ _____
67. Retirement security (financial) . . . . _____ _____
68. Help with tasks at home . . . . _____ _____
69. Loyalty of friends . . . . _____ _____
70. Money for advancement or self-improvement
    (education, starting a business, etc.) . . . . . . _____ _____
71. Help with child care . . . . _____ _____
72. Involvement in organizations with others who
    have similar interests . . . . _____ _____
73. Financial help if needed . . . . _____ _____
74. Health of family/close friends . . . . _____ _____
75. _____ _____
76. _____ _____
77. _____ _____

dently. Or you may wish to make a number of copies of this questionnaire and the other COR-E and self- and family evaluation tools, so that you and your partner can go back and use them in different ways.

Although our research and experience suggest that we have captured a comprehensive picture of people's key resources, we may have missed a few that you feel would personalize your list. In all of the COR-E questionnaires we have left space for an additional three such resources. Write them in at the bottom of the questionnaire and use them as you would the other seventy-four resources listed. You may think of extra resources now or later on, so feel free to insert them whenever you do. If three spaces are not enough, go ahead and add an additional sheet for yourself, as it may help you to express something that you feel we missed.

We suggest that you and your partner independently complete this and all the other questionnaires in this book. Then discuss them. Listen carefully to what your partner has to say. Next, take some time to think about what each of you has said, and follow this with further discussion. Although we provide ways of scoring most of the questionnaires, don't get hung up on numbers; the general impressions you receive are most important. Regular discussions about major aspects of your lives should be a part of your routine, and if we are able to catalyze this process you will gain a critical resource for your relationship.

Now, as a first exercise, go through all of the items in the questionnaire and rate their importance to you. Mark the ratings in the column entitled "Importance" from 1 to 5, where

1 means not at all important

2 means important to a small degree

3 means important to a moderate degree

4 means important to a considerable degree

5 means important to a great degree

Thus, if you think financial stability is important to a great degree, give it a 5. If you think it is only important to a moderate degree, give it a 3. Don't dwell on any one item, as time is a valuable resource. We want you to complete these tasks, but there are probably children who need a ride somewhere, work to accomplish, and resources to build and sustain. It is a good idea to read while commuting to work, but not if you are driving!

Now, in the "Extent" column, rate how much you feel you possess each resource, where

1 means not at all

2 means to a small degree

3 means to a moderate degree

4 means to a considerable degree

5 means to a great degree

Thus, if you think you don't receive the affection of others at all, give this a 1. If you possess affection from others to a great degree, give it a 5. It is critical that you be honest with yourself, or your scores will have little meaning and will be of no help in making future resource decisions.

DO YOU POSSESS THE RESOURCES YOU WANT?

Compare the ratings in the two columns. Circle the resources for which there is a discrepancy of more than one point between the two ratings. For example, if support from co-workers is considerably important (a score of 4), but you feel you lack such support totally because you do not work outside the home (a score of 1), you have a discrepancy score of −3. In contrast, if you have all the furnishings for the house that you want (a score of 5), yet you don't value this highly at all (say, a score of 1), you have a discrepancy score of +4. In other words, a negative discrepancy results when you have less of a resource than you value that resource, and a positive discrepancy results when you have more of a resource than you value that resource.

Resource Deficiencies

Let's look more carefully at these two kinds of discrepancies. In the first case, you rate a resource as important but lacking. You do not have enough of this important resource. We call this kind of resource discrepancy a resource deficiency. The following anecdote illustrates such a situation.

Helen and Dave recently moved so that Dave could open a business. He had been very successful managing a department in a large retail chain, and felt he could do better for himself and his family by striking out on his own in the same kind of business he had managed so well for someone else. This entailed a move to a new community, far from Helen's family and friends. Helen had been a full partner in the decision to move and open the business, and the new location actually improved her opportunities for finding work in her field. Nevertheless, she had become very angry and agitated immediately following the move, but did not know exactly why. We used the COR approach in marital therapy to help her understand her feelings.

The business was already succeeding, their home was nicer, and the local schools were great, but Helen rated intimacy with friends very highly. In their previous home, she had developed a close circle of friends that had been a treasure to her, because Dave's employer had moved them six times in the previous ten years, each time disrupting her friendships. Now the absence of friends was aggravated by the initial coldness she felt from her neighbors. In addition, Dave was working long hours getting his business started, and where she would normally have enjoyed his companionship, he was now unavailable for support. The resources that she found important— friends, family, and intimacy with her partner—were all lacking. Hence, she felt very angry over these critical resource deficiencies.

If you are like Helen and Dave (remember, this is both their concern, not just Helen's problem), you too have resource deficits that are troubling you. You may not be feeling extremely angry, which was Helen's way of showing stress. The two of us, for example, are vulnerable to back pain, overeating, and, when things are especially bad, anger and withdrawal. You may experience some of these stress signs yourself. Or you may simply have a general feeling of dissatisfaction with your life, marriage, or work. It is also common for stress to show itself in an absence of highs. In any case, research on stress makes clear that you will be vulnerable to some sort of negative stress response if you are experiencing resource deficits.

Resource Surplus

The second kind of discrepancy occurs when a resource is unimportant but in great supply. We call this a resource surplus. This is akin to when in junior high all the wrong members of the opposite sex liked you! Many people either ignore these surpluses or consider them bonuses, icing on the cake. In our experience, this kind of discrepancy can be positive, because it gives you some extra resources to fall back on. However, it may also be a sign of problems.

How could a resource surplus lead to problems? This is an illustration of how COR theory can help you find the underlying causes of stress that you would otherwise overlook or, worse, try to increase. Let's look more closely at what a resource surplus means. To create resources that you have more than enough of but are not very important, you invested other resources, such as time, energy, money, or work. In the process, you may also have forfeited opportunities to create and maintain other resources. These resource surpluses did not come out of thin air but are the results of your resource investments.

Elena was a high-powered executive who had fallen into the trap of accumulating "things"—a bigger home, a sports car, expensive clothing, the right watch, membership in the proper country club. This led to an increasing need to earn more and more money and set up bigger and better deals. At first her husband and children were caught up in her whirlwind, but eventually the family began to fall apart at the seams. Their daughter was running with a rough crowd and doing a lot of drinking, and their son had quit his sports teams and stopped earning good grades. Their daughter's pregnancy was the event that brought them all into family therapy.

Elena couldn't understand that it was her chasing after material things that was having a negative effect on the family. She claimed that she didn't value those things very much, but that she valued her family greatly. However, all of her time was invested in work. As a result, she had a surplus of resources she valued less and a deficit of resources she valued more.

What kinds of resources typically accumulate into surpluses? We would be surprised if you had a surplus of health or affection from others, because you probably consider these resources to be very important. For that reason, you could not develop a surplus of them. However, many people rate financial assets and a luxurious home and clothing as less important. Have you developed surpluses in these resources at the expense of other resources? Did the addition to the house come at the expense of companionship with your partner or time with your children? Did the house and extra clothing mean time spent working or shopping instead of investing that time in other resources that you feel are more critical? Did overspending in some areas undermine your overall financial stability? Clearly, if you possess high levels of the most important resources, the gain of less important resources will be a bonus. But if you invested unwisely, it will create deficits of critical resources.

HOW DO WE COME TO OVERINVEST IN LESS CRITICAL RESOURCES?

We have often seen families in therapy whose individual and financial resources were more than adequate but had come at the expense of social and family resources. Often this occurs as a result of seeking financial or career success, but it may also have a loftier reason, such as the desire for a sense of accomplishment or a commitment to an important cause. Traditionally, men have been the culprit in this kind of problem, but with women entering careers in greater numbers, and at higher levels of employment, it has become common for them as well. Let us not forget, however, that you are not in complete control of where your resources are invested, and you may have a very resource-demanding job. As one woman put it, "My employer has adopted flextime; I can work any 80 hours a week that I want."

How can you detect this kind of resource profile? There are two ways to determine from the COR-E whether gains in your individual resources have come at the expense of social and family resources. The first is when you have rated such resources as sense of accomplishment, finances, or feeling independent as important, and you have also given your possession of these resources a high rating. In contrast, resources in the social realm, such as intimacy with a friend or with family members, companionship, or time with loved ones, are lacking. Such a discrepancy between personal and professional resources and social resources spells trouble.

However, you may be so deeply involved in promoting resources concerned with accomplishment that you have developed a blind spot when it comes to the social realm. In that case, you may be so absorbed in work that you can only recognize a problem by looking at your partner's ratings. If your partner has indicated that he or she lacks resources of either the personal and professional type or the social type, it may be because you are absorbing his or her time and energy and that he or she is working hard to fill gaps left by you in your quest for resource gains. Women often complain that their husbands' work and hobbies pull them from their families. Men are likely to say that their wives spend too much time with their extended family (parents and siblings). Once again, however, such trends are largely a product of the tendency of men to be drawn away from home and social life because of their careers, while women are left to care for home and hearth. With women increasingly entering the workplace and pursuing careers, however, we suspect that men and women will be equally likely to overdraw on the resource reservoirs of their partners and families.

Lauren and Tom were both career-oriented. Lauren was chief nurse in a department of surgery. Tom was a school principal. Both rated sense of accomplishment and feeling successful as very important and both felt that they possessed those resources. Finances were not a problem, and they had excellent medical and retirement benefits. Tom felt that they did not spend enough time with each other or with their children, and Lauren felt that she lacked a sense of purpose in her life, despite her accomplishments.

*When each saw what resources the other felt were lacking, it was
as if a flashbulb went off; the illumination was intense and shocking.
After discussing their careers, they decided that extensive after-hour
meetings and the work each brought home were encroaching on
home life to a destructive degree.*

*Lauren and Tom's teenagers were semi-independent, so no prob-
lems had been apparent there. However, their discussions revealed
the possibility that their kids might be independent because they
lacked parents on whom to rely. They were raising wonderful children but perhaps had deprived them of the family life they still
needed. Teenagers still need a guiding, loving hand.*

Tom and Lauren were not having problems with their children, so
maybe we are lifting rocks that are best left unlifted. However, we fear
that problems are likely to crawl out from under those rocks if the
couple's resource discrepancies are not addressed. Otherwise, more
and more of their resource investments will be out of balance, and the
ultimate price they will pay will be much greater than the cost of making tough decisions now. We would also emphasize that had they not
shared their resource evaluations, they would not have uncovered
their problem at such an early stage. Taken individually, each of their
resource evaluations is below the threshold where concern is war-
ranted. Together, however, they show a serious problem brewing.

What choices would you make in their place? Would you make the
tough choices or try to wait until clearer problems emerged? Would
you make minor adjustments or think it was time for a major over-
haul? These are hard decisions and ultimately they can only be made
by you, as a dual career couple and family.

BUILDING HEALTHY INTERDEPENDENCE

It is hard for both partners to get what they need when they face so
many pressures and demands. A foundation for receiving what you
need is a healthy interdependence. The dependent couple totally relies
on one another. In an independent couple, neither partner relies on

the other. Interdependence lies somewhere between these two extremes. Each partner can act independently to a degree, but also relies on his or her partner for guidance, love, compassion, material resources, and help with tasks. In our striving for independence as a society and the related emphasis on individual identity, dependence has gotten a bad name, with independence being considered the equivalent of mental health. Research on intimacy suggests that interdependence is the preferred mode.[5]

This notion of interdependence can best be understood by looking at your resources. Your current resources are a product of the investments made by you and your partner. Similarly, the maintenance and future growth of your resources depend on both of you. Few good marriages or relationships endure otherwise. The catch is that if these resources are mainly produced by only one of you and not the other, resentment can follow.

Think about where your resources come from. The source of your medical insurance may be your spouse's work, your source of companionship may be your spouse, and even your self-discipline may be derived from the reminders and encouragement of your partner. Perhaps most important, from where do you receive love?

If you are feeling resentment over how much you have given versus how much you have received, then your relationship may not have a healthy interdependence. If, in contrast, you have a sense of equal partnership, then your relationship is probably based on interdependence. It is time to examine these feelings more fully.

Throughout their fifteen-year marriage, Martin had pursued his career and Pam had been a homemaker. Both felt that the other's contribution to the family was enormous. Neither thought for a moment that the other was not totally committed to the marriage and the family. Martin made a good income and considered it to belong to him and his wife equally. They discussed all large purchases together and planned their budget for small things with equal input. They had good friends and close family ties. Pam was the mainstay in this arena, planning family gatherings, getting dinner on the table, trans-

WORK WON'T LOVE YOU BACK

porting the children to tutors and friends, and helping Martin's aging parents with shopping and figuring out medical bills. Martin and Pam felt good about being interdependent. The balance between them was very traditional, with Martin operating more in the work domain and Pam more in the home domain, but it was what each of them wanted.

Now they were about to experience a transition, because Pam planned to take a job outside the home. Their only child was entering high school and they felt they needed more money to send her to college. Also, although Pam loved being a mother and homemaker, she was beginning to feel that this was demanding less of her time and was less fulfilling now that their daughter was older. The plan was for Pam to return to teaching after finishing some required refresher courses. She and Martin realized that the transition would change many things about their lives, but their past sharing of resource investment decisions led them to be optimistic about their new life-style.

For another couple, such a situation could be a source of conflict. But Pam and Martin had an agreed-upon value system and their plan to enrich their combined and individual resources was mutual. They depended on each other for some things and acted independently in other ways. Pam and Martin's success was related to their knowing what they wanted, rather than worrying about what others expected of them. It is common to develop uncomfortable feelings of dependency or overindependence if you rely on others' notions about what is best for you. This danger is illustrated in Angela and Nick's situation.

Angela and Nick came from very traditional families. Their parents often told them what they and their religion expected of them. Men were to work hard and provide financially for the family. Women were to be homemakers. Men did not clean house, cook, or change diapers, and women did not earn income, purchase cars, or mow lawns. These rules were not written down, but it was almost as if they were etched in stone. It was also apparent in the cold looks Angela received from their parents if the house was not 1950s' spick-and-span perfect when they came to visit.

This model might have worked if Angela and Nick had not been exposed to experiences that led her to adopt decidedly different notions. She had done extremely well in college. She was an officer in her sorority and was considered a born leader. She was also an athlete who had played competitive tennis. Angela worked for four years before she and Nick had their first child, after which she accepted the role of homemaker with open arms, believing it was what she wanted.

Now Angela felt she was lacking in critical resources, and she was growing jealous of the satisfaction that Nick derived from both work and family. Her sense of independence was very low, her feeling of being a leader almost nonexistent (Lord knows, the kids never listened), and her sense of accomplishment was laid to waste by a house that never stayed clean. You just started over again on one end when you finished the other. A perfectly clean bathroom was a simple target for a two-year-old with bad aim.

Nick was supportive of Angela, but his love and caring could not provide her with a sense of accomplishment, leadership, and independence. He initially resisted Angela's attempts to talk about the problem, but she pressed on until they were able to discuss it openly. They realized that they were playing out their parents' script. Nick liked Angela's being home, but he was open (or at least willing) to change if it was what she wanted. The hardest thing for them was facing his dad and her mom with the changes they intended to make. Both were hesitant and Nick was a bit apprehensive about the whole arrangement, but probably due to Angela's tennis-learned tenacity, they managed to press ahead with their new program.

In the cases of both Pam and Martin and Angela and Nick, resource investment was critical. Money, a nice car, seniority at work, and a sense of accomplishment are very different kinds of resources. They can all be obtained, however, by means of an independent, dependent, or interdependent relationship. When resources are obtained through interdependence in an agreed-upon arrangement, overall satisfaction is likely. The money earned by one partner may be used by the other, but unless both partners are interdependent in the plan for creating resources, that resource may be devalued. Each must have a full sense of partnership.

This would all be easier if parents, commercials, the media, the women's movement, and the workplace were not placing pressure on us to behave in certain ways. We are influenced by the world that exists around us, and to believe otherwise is a fantasy. Furthermore, because the world is in transition, conflict is all the more likely. We know ardent feminists who became homemakers for a period of years and we know very traditional couples who have active dual careers. We are a generation of life-style pioneers; perhaps no other generation has been as free to make so many choices about how to conduct their lives. If the last one or two generations experienced the great rise of the middle class, with greater economic freedoms, now we are experiencing the greatest rise in life-style opportunities. When we think about the varieties of work and home life available to individuals and couples, we are dazzled by the possibilities for resource gain and loss. Even if we begin our quest in one direction, there is no guarantee that our notions about how we run our lives might not change over time.

How do we decide how to invest our resources? Which crops do we choose to grow and which flowers do we wish to have flourishing in our garden? In the next section we discuss resource investment strategy and how it operates. This general introduction will help to guide you when you consider such problems as whether both of you should be working outside the home, how to invest in the home if you both decide to go to work, and how to ensure that your children receive the maximum investment of resources. Applying the principles we will be developing could bring you rich fields of barley and gardens full of multicolored flowers.

DUAL OR DUELING COUPLES

Now we can delve deeper into the interactions between you and your partner. Are you sharing each other's resources? Do you share resources when one of you is experiencing resource loss or gain? What do your partner's resources represent to you? These are important questions that indicate how you interact. Two people can work very hard, but if their labor is in opposite directions their lives may be torn apart. If they coordinate their efforts, however, they can build things of wonder.

Balanced Resource Profiles: Good Ones and Bad Ones

What's mine is yours and what's yours is mine is an admirable ideal for marriage and intimacy. Such positive sharing of resources depends on a few conditions, however. You might find it helpful to sit down with your partner and your COR-Evaluations, or just get a cup of coffee and find a quiet place to talk about these issues if that feels more natural. Dealing with things that concern you as a couple requires your combined effort and attention.

GOOD BALANCES

Is each of you receiving the resources that you view as important? If the answer is yes, you have found a good balance in your relationship and are sharing your resources. This probably comes from love, hard work, and dedication to your family. Perhaps you are reading this book to ensure the continuation of this favorable state, but up to this point, at least, things have been going very well indeed.

You do not have to have every resource, either. What is critical is that you have a balance of the resources that are important to you. If you *both* have strong resources in the areas of intimacy, companionship, and marriage, but resources are lacking in the financial or achievement categories, you still have a positive balance. This is especially true as long as you don't overvalue the financial and achievement areas of life. If, despite some financial and work-related problems, you are also optimistic, it is probable that your personal and relationship strengths are providing a positive balance. You are giving each other love, support, and compassion and this is fueling a positive view of life, despite any obstacles relating to work and finances.

BAD BALANCES

Perhaps your balance profile indicates that you both have adequate financial, work, and accomplishment resources. Unfortunately, a balance in these spheres will not sustain resources in the love and companionship sphere. Even if both of you are experiencing job satisfaction and financial success, a lack of love, companionship, and affection is likely to be a sign of potential problems in your relationship. Many couples who are having relationship problems bury themselves in their private and work lives. This does not necessarily mean that they have outside romantic involvements. Rather, their true love becomes their work or their golf game or their friendships, and their partner is excluded.

In such a situation, both partners share financial and work success and lack relationship success, so their resource profiles balance. However, it is a bitter balance that draws them away from their home and family. Sometimes the love of both partners for their children is their only common bond. However, it is more common to see children suffering from the growing distance between their parents. External demands on each parent's attention draw them away from their children, despite the genuine love they may feel. Your resources will grow where they are nurtured; if they are nurtured away from home, that is where your garden will grow.

———

Lavomme and Edgar had been together for four years. Lavomme's two children from her first marriage lived with them, and Edgar's child lived with his former spouse. Lavomme was a successful architect and Edgar was a small building contractor who was having great business success despite the regional building recession. Thankfully, the lack of money to buy homes meant that those with a little money wanted to add a room or remodel a kitchen. They both were very dedicated to their children, and each treated the other's children lovingly.

They felt that things could not be better when it came to their personal accomplishments and financial resources. They were from working-class backgrounds and their home had more bathrooms than their childhood homes had rooms! They also felt good about their children and were grateful for each other's commitment. However, both felt they were lacking in intimacy, mutual support, and a good marriage. This was no surprise, because they had talked about going to a marriage counselor but until now had balked at the idea. Once they made an appointment but had cancelled it because of other pressing matters.

For both Lavomme and Edgar, financial security and success were powerful goals. They wanted to give their children all that they had lacked when growing up. They were the first in their families to have an education and financial success, and their families had very high expectations of them.

They danced around the issue of intimacy for a while, figuring that maybe they wanted too much, that passion was reserved for new relationships, and that mutual understanding was the important thing in long-term relationships. They might have ended the conversation at this point, but Edgar decided to take a risk. He tentatively stroked Lavomme's thigh and said, "I know you love me, but I miss your loving me." Lavomme began to cry. Now Edgar took a bigger risk. He asked Lavomme what she felt and what she wanted from him. Never before had Lavomme heard him ask about her feelings. Both spoke of their loneliness. They made love that night (twice) and Edgar called for an appointment with a marriage counselor the next morning. Lavomme sent him flowers at a construction site, and his gruff crew kidded him about those flowers for two years thereafter.

Lavomme and Edgar had a balanced resource profile in that both shared resources in the financial domain and lacked resources in the area of intimacy and affection. Perhaps because their professional and financial goals were so strong, they had almost ignored their emotional needs. However, they were able to confront their difficulties, because both saw love, intimacy, and sharing as important. They still loved each other, and though they were not providing each other with much love, it was all that was needed to motivate them to solve their marital problems. Marital therapy was a good choice for them, because it was not clear what was keeping them apart. True, work was getting in their way, but they were allowing that to happen. A good marital therapist would probably want to explore this question in depth. Lavomme and Edgar had both already experienced one bad marriage and their current marriage was in jeopardy. One might simply conclude that they shouldn't let work interfere with their relationship, but that might not solve the underlying difficulties.

Unbalanced Resource Profiles: Good Ones and Bad Ones

Just as balanced resource profiles can be either good or bad, unbalanced resource profiles can also be a sign of either strength or weakness in a relationship. By considering the nature of the balance, you can arrive at clues about your own relationship. When one spouse derives more from a relationship than the other, COR gives us insights into how to divide resources more fairly and provides hope for a brighter dual career future.

Unbalanced resource profiles can be good when both partners are willing to share resources in order to work toward correcting the imbalance. Indeed, such a willingness can be the key to creating increased intimacy and commitment. The imbalance may be in the work-related economic domain, in the personal domain, or even in the relationship domain. In any case, it is important for the two of you to discuss the imbalance, how it came about, and what can be done about it.

The period in which a couple tries to correct resource imbalance is a delicate one in a relationship, because the partner who is lacking resources may not fully believe that the situation can be reversed. How much of his or her resources will the other partner give? However, this kind of imbalance does not necessarily mean serious trouble if a better balance promises to be forthcoming.

BAD IMBALANCES

This couple's situation is an example of a bad imbalance.

Stu and Judy both worked outside the home, Stu in sales and Judy as a secretary. They made a fair income, but bills at the end of each month always strained their budget. Still, they felt that they had most of the things they needed for themselves and their family.

Stu's work involved travel and Judy worked closer to home so that she could attend to the children's needs and be home in time to prepare dinner. She accepted this but felt that Stu should be available to her and the family on the weekends. Stu devoted much of his free time to his favorite hobby, golf, but felt that this was part of his work because most of his games were with clients. Judy felt that playing golf and watching football were luxuries that Stu had to limit. She wanted some free time on the weekend for herself, she wanted more time with Stu, and she wanted Stu to spend more quality time with the children.

At this juncture Judy is angry because she feels that she is getting the short end of the stick. She would like more exciting work and better pay, but this would mean additional commuting and longer work hours. Stu also worked very hard, and golf and TV on the weekends were ways for him to relax. Whether or not Judy and Stu resolve their imbalance depends on Stu's willingness to change. If Judy gives in, she will only become angrier. In the current situation, she works eighty-hour weeks and thirty-two-hour weekends. Stu is also working hard, but is trying to live like his buddies whose wives don't work outside the home. The imbalance is in his favor because he has added work satisfaction and leisure time, at the total cost of fewer work hours, when you consider Judy's investment in household labor. Possible compromises include Stu's playing only eight holes of golf every other Sunday, limiting himself to watching only one sports game per weekend, and taking over the responsibility at home for some period over the weekend so that Judy can have some time for herself.

Stu resisted meaningful change, however, arguing that he worked hard all week, brought home most of the money, and needed ways to

WORK WON'T LOVE YOU BACK

relieve himself of work pressures. He suggested that Judy not work if it was so hard on her. But he knew that was unrealistic, given their financial situation and the fact that Judy wanted to contribute financially and have money that she felt she had earned.

Given their resource imbalance and Stu's unwillingness to devote his resources to a resolution, this couple is likely to experience further estrangement and increasing marital conflict. Judy's anger will not just go away, although it may be channelled into increasing depression. Meanwhile, Stu is angry too, but he channels his anger into an increasing alcohol problem and more and more time spent away from the family.

GOOD IMBALANCES

Stu and Judy's situation stands in striking contrast to that of Larry and Michelle. They, too, have a resource imbalance, but it was planned from the beginning and both partners know how to deal with it.

Larry and Michelle have lived together for five years. Although they have felt no need to get married yet, they are very committed to each other. Neither had entered the relationship with appreciable financial resources, and both had started work without finishing college. Michelle, however, had been an excellent student and was close to graduating when she and Larry met. She returned to college while Larry continued working, then attended law school and ultimately obtained an excellent position in a local law firm. Larry felt both pride and a tinge of jealousy over Michelle's success. Overall, however, his love, commitment, and pride in her were by far the stronger feelings.

Michelle's success allowed the couple to start the long-awaited second stage of their plan. Larry was a sculptor whose occasional success at art shows suggested real talent. He worked with metal and hoped that opening a fancy-ironwork business would allow him to make a living and sculpt as well. It was a touch-and-go operation, and for the first two years profits were slim.

Recently, however, Larry had received a few sculpture commissions for office courtyards and his name was also beginning to be known in the ironwork world. Michelle sustained his experiment with her growing income and he had excellent legal counsel to boot. Larry sometimes felt insecure that he was not doing his share, but they talked regularly, and Michelle always gave her full support. She reminded him that he had worked as a welder for five years while she was going to school. Michelle also mentioned that she was pregnant and had worked out a deal with her employer that would allow her to work at home for six months after their child was born. Larry sculpted a graceful pregnant woman with heavy books in hand for his next courtyard commission.

Larry and Michelle showed unusual flexibility. They had few preconceptions about how men and women are "supposed" to behave. Either of them could be the main wage earner, and it was okay to experiment with untried ways of doing things. In many ways they could be described as a nontraditional couple. However, they had both retained one key tradition from their families: You support your spouse fully. Support means showing encouragement, believing that together you can succeed, and knowing that love comes from sharing. Sometime in every relationship there are resource imbalances, but commitment to a long-term balance of resource investment and gain is part and parcel of a relationship.

Research by Dr. Margaret Clark at Carnegie Mellon University indicates that this give-and-take does not occur on a tit-for-tat basis.[6] You don't check your hand for change after each exchange. You should not expect a return on each and every investment. That is the nature of good business relationships, not good love relationships. Rather, Dr. Clark describes close relationships as being *communal*. What is given is really put into the joint resource reservoir, not received by one individual. Because both partners are active in giving and receiving resources, the relationship benefits. When a resource imbalance continues, however, one or both partners are likely to feel resentful and begin watching the accounting more closely to ensure that he or she gets as much as he or she gives. Dr. Clark calls this an "exchange relationship," as opposed to a "communal relationship," because the emphasis is on the marketlike exchange of resources. Such careful attention to the exchange of resources makes it hard to appreciate the relationship for itself, even after the imbalance is wholly or partially corrected. A relationship is not a business, even if it is a partnership.

RESOURCE STRATEGY

In this chapter we have begun the process of exploring your resource profile. Perhaps you have learned more about your resources and those of your partner. We have discussed the research basis of COR theory and the COR-Evaluation method, and we hope that you have participated (or will participate) fully in the exercises we propose. Some of these discussions with your partner, or confrontations with your own resource picture, may have been difficult for you. However, the more difficult they were, the more likely this book will be valuable for you.

We looked at resource profiles from a number of different angles. As an individual, it is important that you either possess the resources you feel are most important or feel optimistic about making important gains. We would emphasize, however, that few individuals have all the things they desire. What is important is to receive enough of the re-sources you need. How much is enough is hard to judge, and we cannot tell you what is enough for you. Nevertheless, we have pro-posed clear guidelines for judging your resource reserves in order to help you find the answer for yourself.

We also discussed your resources as a couple. Your resources, like your relationship itself, should be interdependent. Your relationship requires both the communal qualities of sharing and the individual qualities of personal initiative and accomplishment.

The best relationships are those in which both partners share the burden of resource investment as well as the joy of resource gain. When one partner has to give too much or receives too little, problems ensue. We also emphasized that both partners must recognize that the overall expenditure and gain of key resources should be fair and represent love and caring. We want you to thrive, not just survive. We want your marriage to be like a rich land, flowing with milk and honey.

Chapter 4

*Her Career
Investment and
His Reactions*

Now that we have considered your overall resource profile as an individual and as a couple, it is time to think about what a dual career life-style requires and what it offers you. We have framed this chapter in terms of "her" decision to also work, because that is the overwhelming trend in our society, as increasing numbers of women move from homemaker to career roles. Still, we recognize that sometimes the male partner stays home and that women in some families have worked outside the home for generations. You may also be in a situation where both of you must work, or you may already have a dual career family. Whatever the case for you, it is important to consider what you may lose or gain in a dual career life-style. For readers who are considering a dual career life, this chapter should help you make a more informed choice.

If the truth be known, neither staying home nor working outside the home is all that it's cracked up to be. Staying home entails manual labor, meeting children's demands, coping with endless hassles, and tying up loose ends that keep untying. When we ask a woman if she works, what we really mean is whether she is employed; we should be fully aware that staying home is work, too. If you have stayed home with children for a week, you know exactly what we mean. If you have young children, a single day is sufficient for this stress test. If two are in diapers, four hours when they are not napping is all the weak at heart can endure.

Likewise, having a career usually means getting up early, getting everyone out the door, performing tasks that are not always the most fulfilling, taking guff from bosses and clients, waiting in traffic, and having too little time to do too much. Even those who have "ideal" jobs do not find their work ideal all the time. Otherwise, it wouldn't be called work, and you would pay to do it.

It is also absurd to think that satisfaction can't be found in employment outside the home or in being a homemaker. Both roles can be fulfilling, and many of us would not have it any other way than the way we have it. For some women, and for an increasing number of men, the home is a source of pride and satisfaction, too. This may be hard to admit in an age when everyone is so excited about the joys and fulfillment of a career, but nonetheless it is the case. Staying home provides a valuable service that would require great amounts of money to replace.

Even for families in which both partners would like to work, the high cost and abysmal state of day care and the costs of replacing the stay-at-home partner's labor may encourage one partner to stay home. Just as economic pressures result in some couples having to work outside the home, financial considerations may force other couples to have one partner remain at home. When one partner has a job that virtually ensures that he or she be away for more than fifty hours a week, or that entails frequent overnight trips, legitimate concerns about adequately supervising and providing love and nurturance for children become additional issues.

We cannot kid ourselves—or you—however, that men and women are on an equal footing when it comes to making these choices. If someone has to stay home, it is almost always the woman. This fact is virtually independent of whether or not she could make more money than her partner, whether she has a career or not, whether she wants to or not, and whether she enjoys the homemaker role or dreads the very thought of it. It is a choice that is too often based on a man's pride, rather than on a woman's opportunity to be proud of what she does. Many men are changing and are truly valuing their wives as full partners. If you men are embarrassed about your wives' working, then you better have a house full of servants, because staying home is hard labor. When a woman stays home for a man's selfish reasons, she is denied equal status in the family and as a person. Thankfully, we find that most men are coming to a better understanding of this fact.

In this chapter we look carefully at both the merits and costs of dual career life. We consider the resources that are gained and lost by working outside the home. We feel strongly that both partners must decide whether one of them should seek employment or be a homemaker. In a good relationship, no decision of this magnitude is taken without considering the serious counsel and interests of one's partner and family. Ultimately, however, it is still a personal decision. When either partner presses the other into a role against his or her will, the basis of their interdependence (see Chapter 3) and trust in the relationship is undermined. Think about it; this is the question of what someone you love will do for much of his or her life. Work very much defines our identity, and we must not deny our loved ones the right to choose what they wish to be.

GAINS FROM STAYING HOME

Regardless of your current situation, it is important to consider the resource gains that may result from staying home. If you value the homemaker role, staying home is an important source of accomplishment. No one would deny that success at home is a challenge, and succeeding at a challenge has many rewards. It enriches self-esteem, provides a sense of inner peace, enriches your sense of identity, and can be a source of hope for your and your family's future. When someone stays at home the house is likely to be cleaner, laundry is more likely to be folded and properly put away, and dinner is more likely to get to the table at something close to dinnertime. We would emphasize here, however, that if you do not particularly value this role for yourself, research shows that you will not find these contributions to be meaningful.[1]

A homemaker also contributes financially because money does not have to be spent on day care, babysitters, and housecleaners. Few couples would have chauffeurs if both worked, so don't be unrealistic and figure that the homemaker will save your family that cost. However, many people who work do hire household help for other domestic chores. The practice of leaving unattended children with a handkerchief filled with opium, as was done during the Industrial Revolution, is no longer in vogue, so the cost of day care and babysitters may be a consideration. We should add that many other families who turn to a dual career life-style do not hire outside labor and simply find ways to make do with less.

Having someone at home sometimes means better supervision of children and more time to nurture them. Especially when children are young and day care is not ideal, some parents feel that a stay-at-home parent can provide the love, affection, attention, and stimulation that their child needs (see Chapter 9 for a detailed discussion of this issue). Children may also enjoy more varied activities when someone is available to drive them to after-school functions. We discuss the issue of children in depth in a later chapter, but for now it is important to note that this is why some parents want to stay home.

THE STAY-AT-HOME WIFE AND WHY SHE IS LESS AND LESS COMMON

With all the advantages of homemaking, why are fewer women and only a handful of men choosing it? Two trends are contributing. First, in order to improve, or at least maintain, their standard of living, it has become necessary for both partners to have paid employment. The material demands of the middle- and upper-middle classes have also increased. We know few individuals who live in a home that is not larger than the one in which they were raised. New cars cost more, and the old one is upscaled each year with whistles and bells because people want more. This desire for more material goods often translates into the need for both partners to receive a paycheck.

Second, women increasingly are demanding participation in every aspect of society, including employment. As long as the homemaker role had major financial value, it was reasonable for women to desire it. When women were making clothing, canning, churning butter, quilting blankets, and tending home gardens, they were doing highly valued work that the family could not afford to purchase. High infant and child mortality and the need for more hands to tend the farm were also incentives to have larger families. Women were performing jobs that could not have been purchased had they worked elsewhere. Today women are more likely to stay home in the interest of their children's healthy development, for example, rather than for financial reasons. Chickens were not only unavailable in the prepared food section; they came with feathers, and that translates to an hour a chicken just to dress it for the pot.

Women remaining at home for ideological reasons (and raising good kids is not a bad ideology) is mainly a post–World War II phenomenon. Their venture into "leisurely" home life was encouraged in order to reabsorb soldiers returning from the war, and the men came home in the millions. A strong postwar economy allowed this trend to continue for longer than it otherwise might have. Now that it no longer affords optimum financial value, however, women are seeking new opportunities. When you add to this the fact that physical strength or size is seldom a factor in modern employment, there is little to stand in the way of women working outside the home.

Hence, financial pressures and the desire for work that is rewarded have combined into a powerful force moving women out of the home and into the workplace. That this occurred is as inevitable as the continuing demands by women for equal status at work. We all want the things we do to be valued, and when those things are in the workplace, that is where we will seek it, especially if we can still keep the home fires burning.

COSTS OF STAYING HOME

There are costs in financial, social, and psychological resources that result from staying home, and these should be considered both separately and together.

Financial Costs

The most straightforward costs of staying home are financial. Yet even these are misunderstood. Let's dispel some myths associated with home economics.

There is no financial gain in doing housework that you would not otherwise pay to have done. We already mentioned chauffeuring as an example. For many, hiring outside household labor is not feasible, so don't assume that staying home will save you money unless you would actually pay someone to replace your lost labor.

There is no financial gain in doing a job twice. Many household chores are done over and over because they stare you in the face. When you are working, either you don't notice them or you turn away and slowly count to ten; your standards of cleanliness adjust to the time you have available.

There is no financial gain in doing housework "better." The difference between "good enough" and "better" is an endless quest. No doubt your home can always look nicer, but that does not amount to a savings that you lose by working outside the home.

Other financial myths concern the costs of child care versus the amount the homemaker would make by working outside the home. These arguments are almost always used to dissuade women from working outside the home. True, day care can be expensive. However, usually it is expensive only for the few years when children are very young. Moreover, relatively inexpensive alternatives are often available. Given the high rates of depression among mothers who stay at home with young children, therapy costs may need to be factored in as well. With depression rates for this group as high as 25 percent among those at home, this is not an exaggeration.[2, 3]

Too often people consider only the short-term financial value of both partners being employed and try to balance it against child-care costs. However, every year spent outside the labor market reduces an individual's earning potential and every year spent working increases it. In the business world and the professions, extended breaks may not be forgiven, even when the woman returns to work with full dedication. Later on, those who took no breaks will look more desirable when their résumés are compared with those of women who stayed away for a number of years to raise their children. Furthermore, retirement benefits, medical benefits, sick leave, and vacation time add up for as long as you work without interruption. These benefits are financial and should be considered in your calculations. Finally, if the break is long enough, refresher courses and relicensing requirements may take up to a year of full-time schooling for reinstatement. This says nothing about feeling out of touch with all the advancements in your field.

The most long-term cost of dropping out of the work force is lost wages in later years of employment. Most of your savings are usually accumulated in the last ten years of employment, when college and other children's expenses are out of the way and the home is fully paid for. Where will you be on the pay ladder in your last ten years of work?

Stevan had an interesting experience that suggests that men may be even less likely than women to be forgiven for a career break. When Ivonne had to fulfill her obligation to the Air Force, she was sent to an Alaskan base as a captain and psychologist. Stevan interrupted his budding academic career to (perish the thought) follow Ivonne. There were no academic positions available in Anchorage, so he worked as a clinical psychologist in private practice. Even after years of academic success, this gap in his record has been suspected on a number of occasions of indicating a lack of seriousness about his career or an inability to "cut it" in academia. Perhaps it was a double sin that he deviated from the accepted career track and the expected sex role by deferring to his wife's career needs.

It is a good idea to get out a worksheet and actually calculate the pluses and minuses of working versus staying at home. Call up a local day-care center and talk to other families about how they care for their children and how much they pay. Consider all the costs and pay-offs. Project them forward at least five years, as the first year may provide a misleading picture. Look at last year's taxes and calculate how a higher income will affect your tax bracket.

On one hand, the last money in the pot gets taxed higher. Be aware that dual career families also get certain tax advantages. Check into these as well. Also, once the bills are paid, the extra money means extra savings or extra luxuries. In this way, the last money in the pot is the most fun. Finally, compare your net gain with some of your big-ticket expenses. An additional $150 per week is substantial—it can equal your grocery bill. Two car payments might be made with, say, $500 to $600 per month. An additional $5,000 per year may not sound like a lot if your partner is earning many times that amount, but saved up it would pay for a nice education for two children.

Personal and Social Costs

There are many emotional costs involved in staying home. Unfortunately, there is almost no research on the effects on men of staying home. We will have to settle for examining what we know about women who stay home and try to extrapolate that to men where possible.

Staying home with young preschool-age children places women at high risk for depression.[2] Studies by Professor George Brown of the University of London found that such women are more prone to both bad cases of the blues and major depressive episodes. Other studies show that women who stay home are more likely to be depressed than women who work outside the home, even when employment conditions are stressful. One study, for example, found that women who stay at home are more than twice as likely to be depressed than women who have low-stress jobs and 50 percent more likely to be depressed than women who have high-stress jobs.[4]

As women began to seek employment in greater numbers, some feared that their physical health might suffer. However, once again studies show that it is homemakers who are at the greatest risk. Again, this is exacerbated when there are young children at home. Although employment does introduce additional strains, something about staying home has a negative effect on health.[5] This is true despite the fact that employed women usually do housework when they get home and so work more hours per week than unemployed women. It is also possible, however, that some women who are less physically healthy stay home, but in any case, the stress of outside employment does not appear to have a deleterious health effect on women.

Social scientists are searching for explanations for why staying home can be so hard on women, and are beginning to wonder how it might affect men as well. Let's explore the facts from the COR perspective, which emphasizes what resources are lost by staying home.

*Marla decided to stay at home with her and her husband, Mark's,
two young children, only one of whom was in school. She dressed
quickly in the morning to get Joey ready for the school bus. Joey was
a dawdler, always running late. The rest of the morning was spent
cleaning the house and caring for Maura, her two-year-old. Whatever she cleaned, Maura tore asunder.*

*Joey came home from kindergarten at noon, and Marla prepared
a hot lunch. In the early afternoon, they all went shopping and ran
errands. Later, Marla juggled Maura's nap with Joey's Cub Scout
meeting, soccer game, or visit with a friend. At 4:30 she began dinner
and tried to use the TV as a babysitter.*

*At 6:30 Mark came home and dinner was on the table. Mark
worked in the city and the commute took a lot out of him. Still, he
helped by clearing the table and loading the dishwasher while Marla
bathed the kids, read them a story, and popped them into bed. After
that she finished the laundry, tidied up odds and ends, and tried to
watch the news. At 10:30 she collapsed in bed, exhausted.*

If you are thinking that Marla's and other homemakers' problem is
work load when at home, think again. That does not seem to be the
answer. Marla does not work as hard as most women who are employed and also have families, although she does work very hard.
Rather, she daily experiences a number of losses, threats of loss, and
failures to make gains.

The job of a homemaker is akin to that of a factory worker on a
circular assembly line. She rarely sees the product of her labor, and
worse, most of it has only a temporary effect. No sooner does she clean
a room than the room turns into a major disaster area. She may be a
loving mother who takes the time to read to and play with her children, and this will have long-term positive effects. But if you have
children, you also know all about the short-term payoff.

*Ivonne was able to spend last Saturday one-on-one with our youn-
gest child, Jonathan. They played miniature golf, went bowling, and*

had a snack. Jonathan had his mother's undivided attention. On the way home, Jonathan complained, "I'm bored. There's never anything to do around here."

Ivonne should consider this a great success. After all, the kid was excited for as long as three hours and was willing to spend his precious time with her rather than with a friend. Instead, though, parents tend to feel frustration in such situations, as if their investment of energy and resources means nothing. Marla's love and attention do not ensure that Maura will not cry and make incessant demands. Nor does her dedication to Joey's afternoon activities mean that Joey will not call her "the worst mommy in the world" the moment she says "no" to one of his demands. This is the way normal children behave, but it can still create feelings of inadequacy in moms.

Marla's tasks lower her self-esteem because they seem simple and are not valued in our society. Her sense of mastery is diminished because she does not see the positive result of her efforts, only the repeated need to do it all again. Her husband contributes to these feelings by expecting the children to be cleaned and neatly packaged by the time he gets home, wondering what she does all day.

Marla and other homemakers also report feelings of loneliness and isolation. Seeing other women who have young children during the day can help reduce these feelings, but most of the work is still isolating. Napping schedules and chores also limit the possibility of social interaction. Moreover, if Marla "plays" with her friends during the day, much of her justification for staying at home—that she does it for the children, not for herself—will be lost. Because she does not earn a salary, she feels she is freeloading unless she is constantly working hard.

Studies also show that homemakers are more strongly affected by parenting and marital difficulties than are employed women. Because they do not have a work identity that could provide a sense of self-worth and accomplishment, nothing exists to balance out marital or family problems. We all have good and bad days at work and at home. When you have a bad day at work, you may have a good day at home, and vice versa. This provides a balance. The homemaker role does not provide this safety valve. Marital or parenting problems can get blown out of proportion because you lack a job that might reduce domestic strains and put things in perspective. Of course, if you are employed you can have a bad day both at work and at home, but chances are the bad days spread themselves out.

Overall, you can see that homemakers experience losses in self-esteem, mastery, and social support. These are three of the most critical resources that we have. As the homemaker becomes more vulnerable to the negative effects of stress, the risk of depression and health problems grows. Research suggests that these negative outcomes are especially likely when the woman would prefer to be employed. However, even women who have chosen to be homemakers are at risk.

You may find it helpful to know how other couples are affected when the woman is a homemaker, but how do their experiences relate to you? If you are a single career family, first get a sense of your own situation by means of the COR-Evaluation questionnaire presented here: What's Best—Homemaker or 9-to-5-er? Again, each partner should complete the questionnaire separately and then compare lists.

If you feel that having a partner at home adds to a resource for you, write a plus sign in the "One Partner at Home" column. If you feel that having or being a homemaker causes a loss of the resource, write a minus sign. If you feel it has no effect, write a zero in the column. According to COR theory, minus signs are bad, but zeros can be bad, too, because we feel under stress when our life-style does not increase our resources. If you have many minuses and zeros, staying at home may not be the best choice for you or your family.

Although we know more about how staying home affects women, more men than ever before are now choosing to remain at home, at least for awhile. If you are one of them, you can evaluate your own situation using the COR-E questionnaire in this chapter, but you'll find few men to compare it with.

GAINS FROM WORKING

Just as staying home has certain advantages and disadvantages, working outside the home is a mix of positives and negatives. Here, too, you should consider the financial, social, and personal sides of the picture.

Financial Advantages

We don't need to say too much about the financial gains of working, as in discussing the financial costs of staying home we were in large part discussing the financial gains of working. To restate our main point, employment should be considered in terms of short-term, midterm, and long-term gains. The cost to a career of frequent or long interruptions should not be underestimated.

Jane and Bill decided that Jane would take a few years off to stay home and care for their six children, from her one and his two former marriages and from their current marriage. But when the bills began to mount, Jane decided it was time to return to work. However, they hesitated for a year because they believed that day care was expensive, and the secretarial jobs Jane saw in the paper were low paying. Eventually, after the economic tension had begun to threaten their marriage, Jane found a job at a law firm.

Jane and Bill found day-care arrangements in a local church for half the cost they'd expected, and Jane's new employer paid medical and dental benefits, reducing their yearly outlay by about $500. After only three months on the job, Jane proved such an asset to the law firm that she was promoted to office manager and given a 25 percent salary increase. She was also allowed to set aside money for day care from her salary, making it almost completely tax deductible. She also gained modest retirement benefits.

Jane and Bill were back in the black in fourteen months. It turned out they had underestimated Jane's potential financial contribution. We have often noted in marital therapy this tendency to underestimate what a woman can earn. Perhaps this is a reflection of the general tendency in our society to undervalue women's contributions. In any case, it is absolutely necessary that you actually test the waters and make all the short- and long-term calculations.

Financial gain from work affects more than your bank account. There is also the feeling associated with producing income. People who earn a paycheck also gain a feeling of ownership over their money.

Partner *1*

HOME/WORKPLACE

+ = adds to this resource
− = loss of this resource
0 = no effect

*What's Best—
Homemaker or 9-to-5-er?*

	Expected Rewards and Costs	
COR RESOURCE	One Partner at Home	Both Partners Employed
1. Personal transportation (car, truck, etc.) . . .		
2. Feeling that I am successful		
3. Time for adequate sleep . . . . ;		
4. Good marriage		
5. Adequate clothing		
6. Feeling valuable to others		
7. Family stability		
8. Free time		
9. More clothing than I need		
10. Sense of pride in myself		
11. Intimacy with one or more family members .		
12. Time for work		
13. Feeling that I am accomplishing my goals . . .		
14. Good relationship with my children		
15. Time with loved ones		
16. Necessary tools for work		
17. Hope		
18. Children's health		
19. Stamina/endurance		
20. Necessary home appliances		
21. Feeling that my future success depends on me .		
22. Positively challenging routine		
23. Personal health		
24. Housing that suits my needs		
25. Sense of optimism		
26. Status/seniority at work		
27. Adequate food		
28. Larger home than I need		
29. Sense of humor		
30. Stable employment		
31. Intimacy with spouse or partner		
32. Adequate home furnishings		
33. Feeling that I have control over my life		
34. Role as a leader		

35. Ability to communicate well . . . .   _____ _____
36. Providing children's essentials . . . .   _____ _____
37. Feeling that my life is peaceful . . . .   _____ _____
38. Acknowledgment of my accomplishments . .   _____ _____
39. Ability to organize tasks . . . .   _____ _____
40. Extras for children . . . .   _____ _____
41. Sense of commitment . . . .   _____ _____
42. Intimacy with at least one friend . . . .   _____ _____
43. Money for extras . . . .   _____ _____
44. Self-discipline . . . .   _____ _____
45. Understanding from my employer/boss . . . .   _____ _____
46. Savings or emergency money . . . .   _____ _____
47. Motivation to get things done . . . .   _____ _____
48. Spouse/partner's health . . . .   _____ _____
49. Support from co-workers . . . .   _____ _____
50. Adequate income . . . .   _____ _____
51. Feeling that I know who I am . . . .   _____ _____
52. Advancement in education or job training . .   _____ _____
53. Adequate financial credit . . . .   _____ _____
54. Feeling independent . . . .   _____ _____
55. Companionship . . . .   _____ _____
56. Financial assets (stocks, property, etc.) . . . .   _____ _____
57. Knowing where I am going with my life . . . .   _____ _____
58. Affection from others . . . .   _____ _____
59. Financial stability . . . .   _____ _____
60. Feeling that my life has meaning/purpose . . .   _____ _____
61. Positive feelings about myself . . . .   _____ _____
62. People I can learn from . . . .   _____ _____
63. Money for transportation . . . .   _____ _____
64. Help with tasks at work . . . .   _____ _____
65. Medical insurance . . . .   _____ _____
66. Involvement with church, synagogue, etc. . . .   _____ _____
67. Retirement security (financial) . . . .   _____ _____
68. Help with tasks at home . . . .   _____ _____
69. Loyalty of friends . . . .   _____ _____
70. Money for advancement or self-improvement
    (education, starting a business, etc.) . . . . . .   _____ _____
71. Help with child care . . . .   _____ _____
72. Involvement in organizations with others who
    have similar interests . . . .   _____ _____
73. Financial help if needed . . . .   _____ _____
74. Health of family/close friends . . . .   _____ _____
75.   _____ _____
76.   _____ _____
77.   _____ _____

Partner 2

What's Best—
Homemaker or 9-to-5-er?

COR RESOURCE	Expected Rewards and Costs	
	One Partner at Home	Both Partners Employed
1. Personal transportation (car, truck, etc.) . . .		
2. Feeling that I am successful		
3. Time for adequate sleep		
4. Good marriage		
5. Adequate clothing		
6. Feeling valuable to others		
7. Family stability		
8. Free time		
9. More clothing than I need		
10. Sense of pride in myself		
11. Intimacy with one or more family members .		
12. Time for work		
13. Feeling that I am accomplishing my goals . . .		
14. Good relationship with my children		
15. Time with loved ones		
16. Necessary tools for work		
17. Hope		
18. Children's health		
19. Stamina/endurance		
20. Necessary home appliances		
21. Feeling that my future success depends on me .		
22. Positively challenging routine		
23. Personal health		
24. Housing that suits my needs		
25. Sense of optimism		
26. Status/seniority at work		
27. Adequate food		
28. Larger home than I need		
29. Sense of humor		
30. Stable employment		
31. Intimacy with spouse or partner		
32. Adequate home furnishings		
33. Feeling that I have control over my life		
34. Role as a leader		

35. Ability to communicate well . . . .   _____ _____
36. Providing children's essentials . . . .   _____ _____
37. Feeling that my life is peaceful . . . .   _____ _____
38. Acknowledgment of my accomplishments . .   _____ _____
39. Ability to organize tasks . . . .   _____ _____
40. Extras for children . . . .   _____ _____
41. Sense of commitment . . . .   _____ _____
42. Intimacy with at least one friend . . . .   _____ _____
43. Money for extras . . . .   _____ _____
44. Self-discipline . . . .   _____ _____
45. Understanding from my employer/boss . . . .   _____ _____
46. Savings or emergency money . . . .   _____ _____
47. Motivation to get things done . . . .   _____ _____
48. Spouse/partner's health . . . .   _____ _____
49. Support from co-workers . . . .   _____ _____
50. Adequate income . . . .   _____ _____
51. Feeling that I know who I am . . . .   _____ _____
52. Advancement in education or job training . .   _____ _____
53. Adequate financial credit . . . .   _____ _____
54. Feeling independent . . . .   _____ _____
55. Companionship . . . .   _____ _____
56. Financial assets (stocks, property, etc.) . . . .   _____ _____
57. Knowing where I am going with my life . . . .   _____ _____
58. Affection from others . . . .   _____ _____
59. Financial stability . . . .   _____ _____
60. Feeling that my life has meaning/purpose . . .   _____ _____
61. Positive feelings about myself . . . .   _____ _____
62. People I can learn from . . . .   _____ _____
63. Money for transportation . . . .   _____ _____
64. Help with tasks at work . . . .   _____ _____
65. Medical insurance . . . .   _____ _____
66. Involvement with church, synagogue, etc. . . .   _____ _____
67. Retirement security (financial) . . . .   _____ _____
68. Help with tasks at home . . . .   _____ _____
69. Loyalty of friends . . . .   _____ _____
70. Money for advancement or self-improvement
    (education, starting a business, etc.) . . . . . .   _____ _____
71. Help with child care . . . .   _____ _____
72. Involvement in organizations with others who
    have similar interests . . . .   _____ _____
73. Financial help if needed . . . .   _____ _____
74. Health of family/close friends . . . .   _____ _____
75.   _____ _____
76.   _____ _____
77.   _____ _____

This does not mean that you have to make as much as your spouse. Your spouse may produce five times your income, but if the twenty-dollar bill in your pocket is the fruit of your own labor, you will hold it with a greater sense of pride.

Personal and Social Advantages

In a society that esteems having a career and earning money, employment certainly has advantages over staying home in the personal and social resource realms. Employment increases the size of your social support system and allows you to speak daily with people who are over three feet tall and who use big words. Both women and men who work outside the home report that their careers give them a social boost. Friendships are forged at work, and we know many of the people with whom we socialize directly or indirectly through our jobs.

It is interesting that the social support gained at work usually does not derive from talking about problems at home. This might be another reason why employment eases domestic stress. Studies show that social support has both positive and negative effects. The positive effects are a product of the increased resources that such support provides (see Chapter 3). The costs are related to what has been called "the pressure-cooker effect." When Stevan and his colleague, Dr. Perry London, studied women in Israel whose husbands, brothers, and sons were away at war, they found that the more the women talked about their problems, the worse their problems became. This has also been found to be the case with homemakers, who tend to talk constantly about their problems at home. As a result, the pressure from those problems increases. In the pressure-cooker effect, the more you discuss a problem, the more the pressure increases, which makes you want to talk more about the problem.[6] Sharing your concerns with a confidant is important, but having a place where you can get away from your problems can help ease stress as well.

Having a job eases the pressures of home by diverting our attention not just to the pleasures of work but also to its difficulties. We complain about our colleagues, our boss, our pay, and the department down the hall. By three in the afternoon, we look forward to going home and getting away from all that stress. When we work well, our colleagues increase our self-esteem and sense of identity. They tell us when we have succeeded and provide thanks for a job well done. Just the fact that they work with us confirms that we are not only husbands, wives, and parents.

Having a career multiplies the rewards of work. Careers can mean advancement, more responsibility, greater knowledge, and higher pay. This is not only the case for high-powered attorneys, physicians, and business executives but for secretaries, artists, and plumbers as well. The growing demand for productivity means that productive people are being rewarded more highly on the shop floor and at the office. A career, therefore, can provide that critical sense of mastery—the feeling that you can successfully manage tasks and positively influence your life.

People derive much of their identity from work. People place their degrees after their names and their diplomas on the wall. You say, "I'm an engineer" or "I'm head of food services" because that says something about who you are. The name plate on your desk or door is a sign of your identity. It raises your self-esteem and announces your existence to the world. Our oldest son Ari made a pen holder for Ivonne engraved with the title "DR. MOM." She proudly displays it on her desk. It shows her dual identity for all who enter her office to see.

Given the prejudice against women in the workplace and the difficulties they encounter rising to senior positions (the glass ceiling), one might think that women would find work less rewarding than men. However, women actually derive equal or even greater rewards from work. Some sociologists believe that this may be because women expect less from work than men do.[7,8] Men are historically more likely to see work as central to their identity and as the measure of success. Women have a more balanced view. They are less likely to expect to become the president of the firm and more likely to be satisfied with simple gains. Hence, women are more likely to be fulfilled by their jobs, despite having more obstacles to overcome.

Go back to the What's Best—Homemaker or 9-to-5-er? questionnaire. What resources do you expect to gain from working? Write a plus sign under the column headed "Both Partners Employed" if you think you are likely to gain a resource by working. Afterwards, talk your answers over with your partner. In what ways did the two of you differ in your expectations of dual careers? Of course, the partner who

WORK WON'T LOVE YOU BACK

already works outside the home will expect to gain different things than the partner who is thinking about doing so. If one of you expects fewer potential gains, is it because you are trying to sabotage the plan before it gets off the ground? Trying to be protective? Or are you just less optimistic? Talk about your reasons.

COSTS OF EMPLOYMENT

It is not our intention to place work on a pedestal and promote it as all things good. Employment has some decidedly negative aspects.

Increased Work and Stress

Employment increases the amount of total time you invest in working. On the average, the total work load of men whose wives are employed increases only modestly, if at all, so the cost to men should be calculated accordingly.[9] However, women who work outside the home increase their total work load by ten to fifteen hours per week by most estimates. Some couples can afford to have someone clean the house one day a week, but others cannot afford this luxury. Even if you are able to afford some household help, remember that laundry, kids, and dinners will remain.

Employment can sometimes be a major source of additional stress. Earlier findings by sociologists suggested that men were affected more negatively than women by problems at work. This was explained by women's weaker identification with and involvement in their employment. The thinking was that for women it was a job, not a career. However, the most recent studies by the Wellesley College Center for Research on Women have found that women are now bothered by work stress.[7] Hurray for social progress! As more women enter demanding careers, there is an added price to pay in work-related stress. Bosses can be overly critical, skills can be underutilized, advancement may be blocked, and gender or ethnic prejudice may be present.

Women are also discussing sexual harassment more openly now. Although most women say they are not currently being sexually harassed, it is common enough that it occurs sometime in most women's careers.[10] Indeed, lifetime rates of sexual harassment are alarmingly high. When sexual harassment does occur, it is a very stressful experience that can color a woman's feelings about work and her sense of confidence for years thereafter. Employment opens the door to problems as well as solutions.

Social and Personal Costs

Men seem to do a better job than women of separating their work and home lives. When they work, their minds are at work, and when they are at home, their minds are at home. In Dr. Robert Weiss's interviews with men, they talked about the importance of separating work and home.[11] Many referred to the drive to and from work as the time when they "beamed up" and "beamed down" between the two.

Women may experience more leakage between work and home. This has been attributed to the superwoman syndrome. The superwoman is able to be all things to all people, and at the high energy level appropriate to a superhero. Whereas men are often "assistants" at home (What can I help you with, dear?), women are usually in charge, even when they have full-time employment. If the house is not picture perfect, who will feel that others have been let down? If dinner is not hot and nutritious, who will feel guilty? If a child is sick, who will either stay home or feel guilty at work? If the answer is both of you, you are sharing the burden in an unusual way, because such responsibilities typically fall on the woman.

As long as men had capable managers—wives—at home, they were free from worry about daily domestic hassles. With both partners working, someone has to be concerned with the connection between home and work.

Judge Babbit saw her babysitter coming up the driveway and so she exited out the back door, in a hurry to get to a meeting. Two-year-old Anthony was asleep upstairs. Three miles from home she chanced to see her babysitter driving in the direction of her house! She immediately made a U-turn and raced home, breaking all possible speed limits and traffic laws. Anthony was asleep in bed. The mystery car had probably been using her driveway to turn around. Although used to high pressure, the judge broke into a cold sweat at her mistake.

WORK WON'T LOVE YOU BACK

At home, dual career partners are likely to feel they are not serious enough about their careers. At work, they feel guilty about not being good enough parents at home. At one time it was believed that such feelings were more intense for women than for men, but that gender difference is diminishing.[12] In any case, if you are a dual career parent, you have probably had these feelings.

———

Evelyn returned to the office after ten years at home. She was an accountant and her skills were in demand, despite her long absence from the job market. She had kept current with computers and the law, and numbers were still numbers. For her, the hardest thing about working was missing her kids' performances at school. Her children were disappointed that mom could no longer come each and every time. Although they now enjoyed extra spending money, ski trips, and name-brand gym shoes, they still made their mother feel guilty for not being at their beck and call. Evelyn felt torn, like someone had knifed her in the stomach, when they looked at her with their sad eyes.

When women first began to enter the work force in large numbers, some feared that their dual role would produce overload.[13] The theory went something like this: If the homemaker role was demanding and the job role was demanding and the parent role was demanding, then women were in for triple trouble. This theory in no way suggested that women were weak. It just predicted that this triple juggling act was beyond human endurance (note that Superman kept his social life to a minimum!).

More recent studies, however, find that in dual career families the overall pressure on women from both work and home is reduced. Compared to homemakers, dual career women consistently have an advantage in terms of social and personal resources.[13] Employed women with families have higher self-esteem, a greater sense of mastery, and better social support—the three key personal and social resources. Studies also suggest that employed women are more satisfied with their relationships with their children.[14] We address the issue of children in greater detail in Chapter 9, but for now suffice it to say that the children of dual career families not only are not suffering but actually seem to do better in many ways.

Now complete the last column of the questionnaire. Write a minus sign under the column headed "Both Partners Employed" after all the resources you expect to lose as a result of your or your partner's becoming employed. Write a zero if you expect neither to gain nor lose a resource. Write a plus sign if you expect to gain in this resource. Talk to other dual career couples and get their input as well. Again, both of you should do this independently and then talk about your responses. Do you get the feeling that one of you is trying to influence the decision by exaggerating or minimizing expected losses? The closer together the two of you are on your expectations, the smaller the chance that one of you will later have recriminations of "I told you so," and the more likely that meeting future challenges will be a common concern worthy of both your efforts.

MEN'S REACTIONS TO WOMEN'S WORKING

There has been much less research on how men react to their wives' working outside the home than on how women themselves respond to going to work. We think that those of you who are deciding whether to become a dual career family will find the studies that do exist very interesting. We will also present insights from our work with couples and families that shed light on this issue. We give you the punch line right up front: Success depends on the man's support as a partner and friend.

Are Men Helping?

Look back at the questionnaire. What resources do you think you would need from your partner if you went to work outside the home? There are four resources that seem critical: intimacy with your partner, help with tasks at home, help with tasks at home, and help with tasks at home! Once again, it is usually the woman who leaves the homemaker role to enter the workplace,[9] and this mainly applies to that situation.

Women with children at home put in about seven and a half hours of labor per day if they are not employed. If they do not have children, they labor about six hours a day. In either case, this is more or less equal to a full day's work for the average man, who puts in about seven and a half hours a day.[9] When the woman obtains outside employment, this household labor must be absorbed.

Who picks up the slack in housework when a woman goes out to work? If the man in your home is willing to take on this role, you are beating the odds, because in general, the husbands of working women do not meaningfully increase their household labor. In contrast, employed women work an extra one and a half to three hours per day compared to women who are not employed.[9] So the slack that is picked up is picked up by women, not by men. Remember, too, that these are averages, and the average working woman is employed sixteen to twenty hours a week. If the woman in your family is working full time, her total increase in hours worked is even more substantial.

Nevertheless, many men are beating the average and doing their full share around the house. When we see couples in marital distress, or working women who are depressed, we can often solve the lion's share of their problems by getting their partners to increase substantially their share of housework. Many men simply do not know what to do around the house. It is also not uncommon for some men to play dumb about this and hope their ignorance will go unchallenged.

Milt's wife left for a series of meetings that could not be rescheduled. It was Milt's responsibility to get ready for guests who were coming to dinner that evening. He read the paper until an hour before the guests' arrival. He then took the potato salad and coleslaw out of the refrigerator and put them on the table in their original plastic containers. He cut up the onions and tomatoes and left them on the counter, and took some old frozen buns out of the freezer and put them on the table in their wrapper. At this point he also realized that he'd better take the meat out of the freezer.

Milt was surprised when his wife was less than joyful when she walked in and saw that dinner was about two hours away from being ready.

Either Milt is being passive-aggressive and trying to sabotage his wife's career or he is simply underestimating what it takes to prepare for company. We see couples in which there is a little of both.

Many men are holding on to a little anger and discontent over their wives' working. This can happen even when they agreed with her decision to work and genuinely support the decision. Nevertheless, they may not have considered what the cost would be for them in terms of housework and responsibility. On a more mundane level, most men are not properly trained to do housework. It's not rocket science, guys; you can do it. However, it does take thoughtful planning and preparation.

Nor is it always easy for men to enter into the world of housework, because women sometimes block their entrance into what has been women's realm. Women can be ambivalent about allowing their partners to do "women's work." They will not allow their husbands to help, because he doesn't hold the baby quite right, doesn't bathe the kids like she does, and doesn't wash the pans like her mother did. Given that men are not terribly excited about these chores and wearing an apron in the first place, they often give up trying. Such discouragement is enough to douse whatever flame of interest they might have had in housework. Of course, a man used to his bachelor days of bohemian disarray might have a particularly long way to go, but it takes effort and patience on both sides.

Stevan's father was an excellent cook and baker, but once he burned a pie. His working wife never let him or others forget it. Dad learned his lesson and never baked a pie better than mom again. If a woman feels guilty about not doing the housework or is afraid of being replaceable, she may sabotage her partner's involvement. Each situation is a little different and you must evaluate your own circumstances and the gulf that needs to be bridged between his desire and ability to do housework and her need to accept his partnership in household labor.

We discuss how men can better meet this challenge in the next few chapters. For now, it is important to recognize that the first step is planning ahead. Milt should have made a list of everything he had to do from the very start. Then he should have checked what he needed to make it to zero hour. If hamburgers are the order of the day, where are they? Are the buns fresh and are there enough for the big eaters expected? Maybe in your bachelor days you ate soup out of the can (cold . . . yuck!) in your underwear over the sink so you wouldn't have to clean the kitchen or your shirt, but you still appreciate when the table is set nicely and the counters are clean. Now it's simply your turn to make sure the mission is accomplished.

Are Men Emotionally Supportive?

Men are more likely to be emotionally supportive of their working partner than to share chores equally. Indeed, this strange fact is one of the reasons we feel optimistic that things will change and that men will learn to help more at home. We just think their actions are lagging behind their feelings.

The general prejudice against working women is fading and men are accepting that their partners will be employed outside the home. Not long ago it was a common belief that women could not make tough decisions or make it in the workplace. Few men think this today, even though some may believe that a man can do some jobs better than a woman. But Israel had a woman prime minister who held firm in war in Golda Meir (she was raised in Milwaukee!), and few people are as tough-minded and strong as Margaret Thatcher, the former prime minister of Great Britain. The U.S. Supreme Court now has two women justices. As more and more men work with women both on the job and at home, the old myths are being dispelled, even if there is a ways to go before we have full equality.

In Stevan's studies of women's satisfaction with support they receive, few women or men said that the man was doing his share of the housework. However, most women felt that men were providing the necessary emotional support. In particular, women were satisfied with the overall support they received if their husbands provided emotional support and intimacy, even if they did not adequately help in the chores. If the men also provided support with chores, this helped further, but the emotional support was paramount. Emotional support means saying that you appreciate what your wife is doing, standing behind her when she makes decisions about how to balance work and family, and easing the guilt she may feel about not being there for every play and performance of your children. Men have more experience with working and being in a family at the same time, and can share this in the way of emotional support and encouragement.

When men do not provide heavy doses of emotional support, their wives become very dissatisfied with the marriage, and all of the stresses of work and home intensify.

Laura taught physical education at a nearby high school and coached the women's basketball team. Bill was an insurance salesman. They both had to work to afford to live in a community where their children could attend good schools.

Bill was willing to help around the house, but he repeatedly made disparaging remarks, especially in front of other people, about the house's appearance and that he couldn't get a good meal anymore. A common routine was for him to storm around in the morning complaining that he did not have an ironed shirt for work. When it was his turn to do the laundry, he left tissues and gum in pockets, mixed darks with lights, and left finished loads unfolded until the clothes were too wrinkled to be worn. When it was his night to cook he usually found a way to order out or took the family out to dinner.

Although Bill benefited greatly from Laura's working, he never told her how much he appreciated her contribution to the family. His income was higher than hers, but it depended on sales and was very unstable. Laura's income provided much-needed stability. She also had an excellent benefits package and had summers off when the children were out of school. But Bill both took her work for granted and criticized her for not being the perfect homemaker.

It is not surprising that Laura is angry. Bill is trying to contain his own anger about not being taken care of by Laura. He still expects a wife to be a homemaker, and the fact that she is employed does not fit into his scenario. Bill's mother was a homemaker, and she and his sisters did the housework. He helped outside with dad on the lawn, and that was all the division of labor he knew. Privately, he may also feel inadequate about not making enough money for Laura to stay at home. Laura, however, would not want to stay home even if she could. They are a dual career family, but each is living according to a different idea of how life should be. Both Bill and Laura have some difficult decisions to make, and their relationship is now in jeopardy as the current status quo pulls at the fabric of their marriage.

Ron is the more typical dual career man:

Ron supports Nancy in her career as a teacher and frequently acknowledges her hard work. In front of others he talks about how difficult teaching is and how teachers should receive more rewards and appreciation for their contributions. He describes her hard-won successes with special-education students. This is his way of letting Nancy know that he thinks highly of her work. When the kids complain that the shirt they wore yesterday is not clean and back in their drawer today, he tells them that mom is working hard and that they have plenty of other shirts to wear. Each month when he does the bills, he never fails to tell Nancy that they could not have gotten through the month without her contribution.

However, Ron does much less than half the housework. He cleans up after dinner and occasionally gives the kids their baths, but he usually has to be asked to help out. He himself says that he is "helping" Nancy out. Nancy is exhausted by the end of each day. Their main area of marital strain is about sex. By 10:30, when the kids are finally in bed, laundry is sorted, and lunches are made for the next day, Nancy is seldom motivated for a sexual encounter. She enjoys sex very much, but it's hard to get motivated when she is so tired.

As you can see, Ron is emotionally supportive of Nancy's working. Indeed, he expresses this more than many men. Even so, he is not contributing his share to the household's support. He still takes the role of assistant, as if the housework is Nancy's responsibility. Our research, discussions with friends, and work with families in therapy all point to this being the norm.

If you are a single career couple considering the move to dual career status, it is important for each of you to have clear expectations about how household chores will be handled. List all the work that has to be done and discuss who will do what. Start with things that you think need to be done. Then for about a week add to the list as things pop up. Chapter 7, which focuses on household labor, may be particularly helpful to you in this regard. You men must swear an allegiance to provide emotional support when your partner needs it. Also, be ready to help her overcome guilt about not being able to do everything perfectly. You can play an enormous part in making your wife's entrée into the workplace successful.

SO WHERE DO WE STAND?

Becoming a dual career family is a major decision. Some of you have little choice but for both of you to be employed. Others have done it for ideological reasons, because you believe it is right for women to be employed, or because life is more rewarding when you have both career and family.

We hope that we have dispelled a few myths. Many women today are finding satisfaction in being homemakers. The major factors in this decision seem to be wanting to be a homemaker and having the ability to live well on a single salary. Other women find great satisfaction in being employed. For women, satisfaction in a dual career family depends on their desire for a career, the degree of career stress they are encountering, and the support of their partners.

Both the single career family and dual career family are workable options in theory. Your life, however, is not lived in theory, and so you must consider how these different possibilities would actually affect you. Do you want to be employed or do you have to for the money? If you could stay home, would you choose to? Are you willing to support your partner's decision fully? Will you provide emotional support and a full share of household labor? These questions apply equally to men and women, and people are experimenting with all kinds of options.

We also hope that we have helped you understand that if you are a woman who has chosen to work outside the home, it is normal to feel guilty about not being either a perfect homemaker or a perfect career woman. Most women report feeling split over this. If you are a man and you feel bewildered about what to do about housework, you are also in good company. Most men feel the same way. If you are willing to learn to make simple, well-prepared meals, miss an occasional day of work to care for a sick child, and clean bathrooms so a health inspector wouldn't want to close down your household, there is a path to dual career salvation for you.

If, however, either of you is resistant to dual career life, you are likely to experience problems. Where this resistance is minor, there will probably only be minor flashpoints of conflict. If you have major reservations about your role in the dual career family, you are probably both in for stormy seas. Children of dual career families will do about as well as their parents, as children are a barometer of family harmony and satisfaction whatever choice you make.

One thing is certain: The transition to a dual career family is never easy. The homemaker's major job is smoothing out family problems and picking up the slack wherever it occurs. If there's a bruised ego to sooth or surprise guests to entertain, the homemaker rallies to the cause. When the homemaker goes to work outside the home, however, that ability to pick up the slack is lost, never to be heard from again. Everyone will have to do more to meet emergencies, and some things just won't be done as they once were. Other things won't get done at all. The financial payoff, greater self-esteem and sense of mastery, and increased mutual support will be ample compensation.

Chapter 5

Avoiding the Pitfalls of a Dual Career Life-Style

"*H old* on a second . . . we just need to get these two little ones out the door for the bus, then we'll be back with you. Really, this will just take a second. . . ." "No, dear, you can't take the hamsters to school in a plastic bag." "Honey, it's your office calling about your 8:30 appointment." "Where's the homework you did last night? It's due today." "Jonathan, those pants are ripped, you can't wear those to school, go change." "Honey, your secretary's waiting." "My briefcase was here just a minute ago." "Hey, who put this video game on the computer file with our manuscript?" "What *is* this sticky stuff on the desk, anyway?" "Are the cleaning people coming today?" "Honey, I think your secretary hung up."

O.K., now where were we? Oh, yeah! Dual career families must cultivate their resource gardens with both care and creativity. Dual career life is inherently stressful given all the demands and challenges that must be met daily. You cannot live a dual career life without stress, because both work and families produce stress. Put them together and both the resource advantages and resource disadvantages are increased manyfold. We find that the potential gains of dual career family life far outweigh the losses. However—and this is a big "however"—like a lot of big deals, when they fall apart, the consequences are enormous.

In this chapter we discuss how to prevent *severe* dual career stress and how to correct common, serious problems that dual career families experience. Avoiding stress altogether is a utopian dream, but we will make a set of recommendations that can be useful when serious stress arises. The more facets of this prevention plan you integrate into your life-style, the richer your dual career resources will become. On the other hand, the fewer parts of this plan that you have in place, the more likely you are to experience resource loss. Although some stress is normal and unavoidable, it is important to recognize serious sources of stress. Don't kid yourselves; some of these problems can lead to divorce, major health or psychological problems, and alienation of family members. Denying major difficulties when they arise will only fail to make them go away and allow them to get worse.   .

STEVAN'S WEDNESDAY NIGHT

Let's take a Wednesday night a few years back to illustrate a few points about how bad everyday stress can get. Stevan tells it in his own words:

As usual on Wednesday evenings, Ivonne was working in her psychology practice until 10:00, seeing individuals and families not able to make daytime appointments. That means I was left to my own devices at home with our three children. I am a dual career dad and a psychologist. I had been in the Israeli army. I could do it.

I had three goals for the evening, and this was to turn out to be two too many. I wanted to watch a special on PBS television, drain the hot-water heater as recommended in the instructions for home-owners, and survive the evening with the children. The latter included baths, homework, dinner, and the immortal task of getting them to bed at a reasonable hour. The plan seemed great because the water heater only needed to have its faucet opened and then closed a few hours later, and the PBS special would be on after the kids were to be in bed. Simple.

At 5:00, Jonathan, then seven, complained of a headache. I checked for fever and found none, so I gave him two children's aspirin-substitutes and sent him to bed. Then I descended to the basement and opened the valve on the water heater and shut off the household water. I was smug over my mastery of traditional male and female household tasks.

After chasing behind Ari, age twelve, I finally succeeded in getting him to begin his homework. Meanwhile, Sheera, age eight, decided she wanted to take her bath early. So I went back down to the base-ment and turned the water back on. I then went back up to the second floor to fill the bath, then went back down again to the basement to turn the water back off. Ari needed help with his home-work, so I headed off to see whether I could remember anything about algebra.

Sheera yelled that she needed a towel in the bath. I hadn't gotten to the laundry yet, so I got a damp towel—the cleanest one—and put it in the dryer for a few minutes. Ari began to nudge me about his homework, and I told him (still calm) to work on it himself until I could get Sheera's towel needs straightened out. Ten times up and down the stairs later, I headed for the bathroom with a dry towel. The door was jammed. I could not get in and Sheera could not get out. She began to cry because she was cold, while I held the warm towel in my hand. I went back downstairs to get some tools and pro-

ceeded to take apart the 110-year-old brass lock on the bathroom door of our old, old house.

Unknown to me, Jonathan had gotten up from his nap and gone to get a drink of water from the other upstairs bathroom. Of course, no water came out because it was shut off at the main. So, leaving the faucet open, he went back to bed. Soon after, I went back down to the basement and turned on the water for the house. Realizing that the pizza I had ordered an hour before had not yet arrived, I got on the phone to find out what gives. While I was on the phone, Ari came to me complaining that I wasn't helping him.

An hour later, I got back to Ari and his homework and told Jonathan and Sheera to set up the board game I had promised to play with them. They returned, asking why it was raining in the living room. I thought they meant outside the living room, but when they came back a second time, I had a flash—raining in the living room! Just then there was a crash. That's right, the living room ceiling collapsed under the weight of water from the upstairs bathroom where Jonathan had innocently left the faucet on. Just then, Ari made the mistake of asking when I was expecting to help him with his algebra!! I yelled that he might wake up and realize there were some slightly larger problems developing here.

We all went to see what had happened in the living room. We entered—water dripping, huge chunks of plaster everywhere, dust like thick fog. In unison, the kids said, "Boy, you're in big trouble with Mom!"

I somehow got dinner together, more or less keeping my cool (only three major outbursts) and began the task of making Ivonne dinner for her 10:15 arrival. I sat down to watch the last five minutes of my program. I then pan-fried a quick, elegant dinner for Ivonne and took out wine glasses and candles, arranging for her to enter through the back door. The sight of her living room, with its ceiling collapsed on the living room furniture (beige chairs and light blue carpet), would wait until after dinner and wine, which I would serve giving

no sign of the evening's travesty until I had succeeded in getting her
to increase her usual one glass of wine to at least two glasses.
And there was still Thursday and Friday left before the weekend!

Then there was the time we rushed from work to drive to a wedding in Chicago, only we found ourselves headed toward New York after trying to get the kids to do their homework in the van so they would be free for the weekend's festivities. But that's another story, and we think we've made our point. Dual career family life is stressful, and even well-seasoned "experts" can run into heavy seas. What is critical is that we watch over the healthy development of our important resources and nurture them. Problems will arise, but there is nothing as valuable as a good plan.

PREVENTION OF DUAL CAREER STRESS: UTOPIAN DREAMS AND OTHER FANTASIES

A stress-free dual career family could only be found in a perfect world. However, thinking about utopia can be helpful because we can adopt at least some aspects of utopia in our daily lives and be richer for it. Many people merely react to stressful circumstances. Like candles, they allow their flames to falter in the wind or to be doused by the rain. To succeed in a dual career family, you must nurture your sense of mastery. Research indicates that this is done by accepting challenges and meeting them.[1] Don't bite off more than you can chew, but don't underestimate your abilities either, as mastery is developed by meeting real challenges. Preventing dual career stress is just such a real challenge.

Flexibility

Incorporating flexibility into your schedule is a key advantage in dual career life. The very fact that both spouses are committed to their careers limits your freedom, but there are many things you can do to maximize what flexibility you have. Remember, there is no utopia, but these are the keys to creating some aspects of a perfect world in your life.

FLEXIBLE SCHEDULES

Work flexibility is critical. Choose a job that allows you to make your own schedule. A flexible fifty-hour week can be easier on a family than an inflexible forty-hour week. Can you start early, work late, or bring work home? Is it possible to work four long days or six shorter days? The more flexibility you have in your job, the easier it will be to manage children's schedules. This applies to vacations as well. Four weeks' vacation may not help much if you are not allowed to take it when the children are out of school.

Bill was traditional-minded when it came to his job. He worked from 8:30 or 9:00 in the morning until 5:30 or 6:00 in the evening, and he put in extra hours on the weekends. He did this despite the fact that he was allowed to fix his own schedule and was paid on commission. Eventually, Bill decided to try an unconventional schedule that would allow more family time. He went to work one hour earlier and worked until 3:30, eating lunch while working at his desk. He scheduled one evening when he worked until 8:00, which gave him a chance to meet with some clients for whom this was more convenient. He made lunch appointments after 1:00, when restaurants were less crowded and taxis more available. He limited weekend work to Sunday morning from 9:00 to 1:00.

These changes increased Bill's productivity because the phones were quiet during the early morning and lunchtime. He beat the rush hour in both directions, saving him frayed nerves and an additional two hours per week. He also picked up extra clients because he was the only one in the business with evening hours.

When Bill got home at 4:00, the children were still fresh. Sometimes he was just there while the girls were running in and out, and sometimes he helped with homework, ran the car pool, read with them, or played soccer in the backyard.

The arrangement also allowed Bill's wife, Francine, to work full time instead of a thirty-hour week. She gained a 40 percent salary increase and a full benefits package (part-time workers received none).

The biggest change was in intimacy. Bill had been outside of the loop with his daughters, and by changing his work hours he became a more immediate part of their lives. Francine noticed the difference and felt much closer to him in his new father role. She also felt closer because she felt the changes he had made showed a new commitment to her and acknowledged the importance of her work. He even took on some light cooking.

How did these changes spiral into such great resource gains? With traffic on his work schedule, Bill had been away from home for fifty-five hours a week. Now he was away about forty-eight hours a week—a seven-hour gain. Most important, when he came home it was not the end of the children's day, when families are at their most chaotic. Instead of coming home to the hurry-up-and-eat-dinner-do-your-homework-go-to-bed time, he had an opportunity for positive, close interaction. Before, he had felt like his wife and girls were part of a club, and he was an outsider. Now he was a member. These things were never spoken, but they were there and they were real.

How did this affect Francine?

Although Francine's hours at work increased, her work load at home decreased by about the same amount—resulting in no net change. However, she felt much better about herself, Bill, and the girls.

In the past, coming into the house had always been terrible for her. She entered through the back door, where the sight of the laundry and the mess the girls had made in the thirty minutes prior to her arrival filled her with dread about all she had to do to make it from 4:00 until 7:00, when Bill got home. She was often short-tempered and constantly felt behind schedule.

Now coming home was actually fun. Bill met her at the door, always had a pot of coffee ready, and she could—hooray!—ignore the laundry. Working full time meant she was taken more seriously, had

*a chance of promotion, and was off the "mommy track" that all part-
time mothers occupied at her company. She also lost the twelve
pounds that had plagued her for years and felt much sexier. Bill
seemed to respond to her better attitude and figure with an increase
in his own sexual appetite and a jogging routine targeting his extra
thirty pounds.*

LEAVE FROM WORK

What about your options for paid and unpaid leave? Oh, you say, in
your office this is all "pie in the sky." Well, that may be true where you
work, but if you shop around you will see that even many Fortune 500
companies have excellent leave policies. Check about the leave policy
offered by your company or the firm you are considering in regard to
children's illness, aging parents' illness (an increasingly common problem), maternity leave, and paternity leave. What if you decide to adopt
a child? With new family leave legislation, the opportunities for leave
will be expanding.

Don't confuse written policy and practiced policy. At a recent meeting of a group of academic parents, we heard of wide variability on this
score. Some universities had liberal written policies that were never
put into practice. Other universities had old-fashioned policies that
were uniformly ignored, where women were given ample time for paid
pregnancy leave, and men who wanted to take parental leave were
allowed it as well.

---

*Carolyn remarked that a women's college had been completely un-
supportive and had viewed her pregnancy with suspicion, whereas
when she moved to a traditional men's engineering college, she was
treated with respect and encouragement. Other faculty members
covered her courses and she was given administrative work to do at
home. Not a day's worth of salary was lost.*

Before choosing an employer, consider its policy and practices by
talking to people who work there.

At many places, especially small businesses and large employers where few women have held the kind of position you occupy, policy regarding time off is nonexistent and you will be a pioneer. Save the stories to tell your grandchildren; they will be very proud of you.

Megan remarked that she was the first woman in her department at the university to become pregnant while employed there. Other women had had their children before coming to the department or chose not to have children. She talked about how everything she did was a first. Sometimes she encountered resistance and at other times she received support. At each step, however, she had no idea what to expect.

LOCATION, LOCATION, LOCATION

Flexibility is also a product of where you live. If you have a long commute, your flexibility is cut considerably. Choose a short commute if at all possible. When talking to a group of dual career executives in New York, we found that most understated their actual commute, only counting the time they were actually on the train. Real commuting time is door to door. We visited a friend who spent fourteen minutes a day on or waiting for his building's elevator (we timed it), but he did not include this in his commuting time. Who is he kidding!

If you cannot live in the perfect location—and many people can't—be creative with your commuting time to increase flexibility. One fellow we know walks the mile between the train and work each day rather than taking the shuttle. This is a peaceful time in which he enjoys his thoughts and his Bob Dylan tapes—and gets some good daily exercise as well. An attorney friend bicycles in London, rain or shine. This means he arrives at work faster than he would by car or the tube (subway train), and he feels like he's still in college, to boot.

Can you work while commuting? We spoke to a book publisher who commuted from Philadelphia to New York twice a week. She was able to work on the train, and this was considered work time because she was paid for product, not time at her desk. The long train ride meant no phone calls and a solid period of work. She entered her office with a dictation tape full of letters for her secretary to type. By commuting only four days a week, instead of five, you may save two hours a week that can be devoted to other tasks.

BUILDING FLEXIBILITY

Find or create work that provides windows of flexibility midday. Children inevitably get ill or have a play they really want you to see. If you can free yourself up every once in a while at midday and finish up the day's work later on at home or back at work, you are way ahead of the game. Often this is a matter of attitude, as many individuals who have this option don't use it because of their ideas about what work should be—even if they own the store.

A man called Ivonne about therapy for his child, who was in rather bad shape. The father had two possible hours available over the next month for an appointment, which he then cancelled due to a last-minute engagement. Ivonne told him very simply—she could only see him if he made the time to be seen. The son began to get worse quickly, and the father made time. Chances are that if he had been more flexible earlier, things would not have reached such a serious level.

Flexibility is often a product of two factors—risk and excellence. Low-risk jobs are often inflexible. Jobs at public institutions are often of this type. The large bureaucracy means there is a carefully watched time clock and a boss whose only role is keeping underlings in line. Opening a private practice can be riskier than working with a large office of attorneys or accountants, but being the boss means you can set your own schedule. Even in a large firm, walking into your boss's office and asking for flextime or taking your pitch to the human resources committee of your university is risky. Still, nothing ventured, nothing gained. The individuals we know who have achieved flexibility in their work have often taken risks to win these advantages.

This is where excellence comes into play. If you are not performing well at work, you are not in a position to take a risk. You may want to avoid attracting attention. However, if you have been an excellent employee, the chances are that your request for greater flexibility will be received positively.

Nancy was an attorney at a large, conservative law firm and had a sound income. She often worked sixty-hour weeks and made junior partner in six years. She and Dave had held off having children until she was almost forty because she wanted to firmly establish her career first. Now she was pregnant and feared that she would have to leave the firm if she demanded even the three months' leave that she dearly wanted in order to stay home with her baby.

Nancy did not even consider that her 100-attorney firm would grant her paid leave. No other partner had ever been pregnant, and while a secretary could be replaced for three months, how could they replace an attorney with a heavy caseload?

When Nancy tendered her request for three months' leave, her request was denied. Rather, the senior partners made a counterproposal: up to one year of paid leave from the office, but she would come in one day a week and be available for occasional critical meetings. During the first three months they would use her mainly as a consultant and assign her cases out. After that she would work full time at home, using a computer, fax machine, and courier services. Further, when she returned to her regular job, her salary would increase by 15 percent. Although she felt like fainting, Nancy managed to pull herself up to her full height of five feet and said, "Yes," and that she appreciated the offer.

This offer was not made because Nancy's firm had liberal policies. Rather, the senior partners were seeing to their own self-interest. Nancy was a brilliant, hardworking attorney who they knew could get a position with another firm if she was disgruntled with their response to her request. She had a large, growing clientele and had developed excellent contacts with a growing group of clients—businesswomen. They also felt confident that she would be productive during the year of paid leave, so there would be little or no cost to them. The 15 percent incentive was based on their assessment of her value, and they hoped it would persuade her to return to a full in-office work schedule before the year was out.

Family Stability

It may seem odd that the resource of family stability is largely dependent on flexibility. They seem so opposed. How can you maintain a flexible family that is still stable? The answer to this question is one of the many keys to a successful dual career family.

There are some basic forms of stability that every family needs. First and foremost, love must be stable. There must be no question but that those in the family are consistently loved and cherished. We often see couples in therapy who use love as a weapon with which to threaten each other. In many subtle and not so subtle ways they convey the message that "my love for you is conditional." Inconsistent love undermines family stability, and little can be built on this weak base.

Regular family rituals also create a sense of stability. These are times and ways of doing things when the family is together. Sunday dinner with grace being said is one such ritual. A family walk is another. A favorite board game played on rainy Saturdays is still another. Mealtime is an essential part of stability. A number of meals a week should be eaten together as a family. The TV should be off and everyone should be around the table. This is a time to catch up on news, talk about family matters, and share each other's thoughts, plans, and gripes. Every major religion builds the family meal into its traditions because of the importance of this aspect of family life. The communication that goes on at such times creates a sense of belonging and caring. Children should be seen *and* heard.

Other rituals also contribute to family stability: Sunday afternoon for family outings, Friday night for family TV watching, a monthly family touch football match or Trivial Pursuit contest. These are occasions for weaving the fabric of family togetherness. Togetherness develops not only from the interactions themselves but also because you can *count* on those interactions. It doesn't matter whether it's a nightly walk, a weekly trip to a favorite ice-cream parlor, or a family poker game. What is important is the combination of regularity and togetherness.

Family vacations are also important for stability. These are times when everyone is together and doing things as a unit. It may be an expensive vacation in Europe or a long weekend hanging around the house—the cost does not matter. What matters is that the family learns to look forward to being together, to sharing fun, and to getting to know one another.

Larry and Betsy were both very busy with their careers. Indeed, perhaps they were too busy, but there was a lot of love in the family, which was a comfortable and stable one. Vacations were key for them. Larry and Betsy took off three weeks a year and all the long holiday weekends. For one week they went away with their two children, and one week they went on a cheaper vacation at a lakeside cabin. The third week they went away with the family if they had money or they stayed home doing things with the kids if they didn't. Long weekends were also times for going to movies, visiting art shows, and looking at local historical sites.

For Larry and Betsy, regular vacations were enough to make up for the busy times in between. Weekdays were especially chaotic, and either one or the other was out of town on some weekends. The couple also ensured stability by never being out of town at the same time. There they drew the line at both their jobs. On weekends at least one parent was fully available to the children.

Schedules and rules enhance the solidarity of the family. These may not be adhered to with complete strictness, but they can provide general guidelines about who does what and when. A simple rule about homework time helps children get their work done when they know you are available to help them if they run into problems. Partners who know each other's schedule are saying that they care enough to keep one another informed. Many people tell us that nothing angers them more than when their spouses fail to call and let them know when they will be home. You would never do this with a business associate unless he or she was your subordinate, and even then it would not be courteous. When you keep your partner in the dark, you are implying that he or she is subordinate to you and your schedule. Children are especially vulnerable in this way. They are easily disappointed and may shut you out if they feel your schedule does not take their needs into account. Similarly, reasonable rules let family members know what is expected of them.

Judy was quickly climbing the corporate ladder. She developed the bad habit of calling home on the car phone when she was already late. Allen never knew when she would be home, and the children were often disappointed over yet another broken promise. At home, she was typically distant, more likely to pay attention to a work-related phone call than to a child's need to talk or pick up some school supply.

Her daughters became increasingly distant from her and combative with each other. Laura, the oldest, rebelled at school. If her mom cared above all about her grades, she would be damn sure her grades were awful. She was taking many sexual risks, but so far this was not known to her parents. Tamara, the youngest, drew closer to her dad and developed a long list of psychosomatic medical problems. She also developed a lot of fears—of the dark, strangers, school—that caused her to become panicky.

When Judy became undependable at home, the family became increasingly dysfunctional. Her husband filled in as best he could, but he was not able to make up for all the disappointments she caused. He could not create a stable, loving home when her behavior threw all the family's boundaries and rules into doubt.

This brings us full circle to stability depending on flexibility. If you are flexible, loved ones will know that you can be counted on to be reasonable. If you are flexible about changes and pressures in their lives, you are providing stable love and understanding. In contrast, if you are rigid about rules and schedules, you are saying that the rules exist for their own, and not your family's, sake.

Finally, being available at times of crisis is essential to family stability. Know when your partner or child really needs you. If you disappoint your loved ones at these times, they may feel they are operating without a safety net. When Stevan was in the Israeli army, he was home on leave one weekend when our daughter, Sheera, was very sick. There was no way to communicate with his commanding officer, so he went AWOL for twenty-four hours until he knew she was not going to need hospitalization and was successfully keeping down food. He could have left this for Ivonne to handle alone, but this was a time when both she and Sheera needed him. The event also served to remind Stevan that the family comes first. (No, he didn't get the stockade, but it was close.)

Overextending Yourself

We are always amazed at the way many dual career parents overextend their commitments. You already have your job and your everyday family demands, so cut down on other commitments wherever possible.

Parent-teacher organizations, church and synagogue groups, and community organizations depend to a large degree on voluntary efforts. We are not telling you to avoid all such commitments, but be judicious. You cannot compete with your nonemployed neighbor in cookie production for charities. Don't even try. You cannot be the weekly lunch monitor at school, and you cannot volunteer to direct the church choir. Well, perhaps you can do one of these things, or even two, but then you must learn an important word: "No." Say it three times in a row. Do it in front of the mirror so you can see how forceful and convincing you are. Say, "No, I would like to help but I'm already overcommitted during that time (to my children and my partner)."

Think of creative ways to fulfill commitments without overextending your family's resources. If your neighborhood is having a block party, volunteer the whole family. You should probably talk to them about it first, but if you can convince the whole gang to do it together, then you will succeed in contributing to your community and your family at the same time. Call other families and get them to co-host the event.

If you must volunteer, then volunteer to coach or assistant-coach your child's team. This way you can be with your child as you contribute to the community. We like the assistant-coach role because we never really learned the rules for soccer and this places us in a position of great contact with our children without taking on too much responsibility. We just toss off occasional motivational cheers (Go team! Great job! Terrific effort!), pick up children with little bruised bodies and egos, and carry them off the field in our arms when they get the inevitable hit in the nose with the ball.

We are asked to speak for different community organizations on a regular basis. We plan these engagements carefully and avoid evening and weekend commitments, because they come at the expense of family time. We could make more money working more evenings, as there are never enough psychologists available for evening appointments. Once a week is the limit we set. There are so many pulls toward making more and more commitments that you can risk losing all your family and personal time. Instead, just say no.

Maximum Quality and Nonquality Time

You have probably read a lot about quality time. Time with your family is one of your most critical resources and one that is constantly threatened by outside demands. Quality time is time spent interacting with your child or partner. It means talking, loving, eye contact, touching, and doing things together. Possible ways to spend quality time are too many to list. They include everything from making love with your partner to throwing a ball with your child.

Sharing quality time is a wonderful generator of resources for you, your partner, and your child. It eliminates feelings of guilt for working outside the home. That guilt is a powerful obstacle to resources, because it is hard to have a sense of accomplishment or self-esteem when you feel that it comes at the expense of your children.

When you spend quality time with people, you send them a message about who they are and what their relationship to you is. You are saying that they are important, loved, valuable, and successful, and that they have a stable, valued role in the family. If they did not, why would someone as important as you be spending time with them?

———

Randy was an adopted child. Five years after his adoption, his parents had a child of their own. He remembers losing his father's attention and being told it was only because right now Bobby, his baby brother, needed it more.

But the attention never returned. Dad always had more time for Bobby and always seemed to favor him in family arguments and decisions concerning the two boys. Now, thirty-five years later, dad lives close to Bobby, but hardly sees Randy or knows his children. His father refuses to acknowledge that he treats his sons differently, but he avoids visits. In therapy, Randy is dealing with his chronic lack of self-confidence, his inability to trust other men in friendships, and his difficulty being close to his own sons.

The other day, Randy described an event that stood out in his mind. As a boy, he had worked on his batting skills because sports were important to his dad. In this particular game, he hit a triple in the sixth inning. Dusting himself off at third base he looked up to where his dad was sitting in the stands, but his dad was nowhere to be found. After the game he learned that his father had left because Bobby was bored with the game. For Randy, this was a defining event in his life.

Quality time is no less important for you than it is for your partner and children. Their wanting to spend time with you is affirmation of your role and who you are. You are a mom or dad or partner who is loved and cared about. If you have a teenage child who wants to spend time with you, you're really scoring points. Many dual career parents live lives full of excuses to their partners and children. "There was an unexpected meeting" or "I just had to do some extra paperwork." You will pay a price for this, and so will they. No one looks back at his or her life and says, "Gee, I wish I had spent less time with the kids."

This emphasis on quality time may seem to suggest that less concentrated time together isn't worth the trouble. Not so. There is value in just watching television together, being available to help with homework for fifteen minutes, or being the one who runs the car pool. All these activities contribute to others' sense of who they are and what their importance is to you. Touch your children every time you pass them in the house. Stroke their hair or their little shoulders. You'll add a million touches in their lifetime. When other people's children are standing apart from them in line at the movies, yours will be leaning against you, comfortable with the sense of love and contact.

Nonquality time also opens windows of opportunity for quality time. You cannot always schedule quality time. But if you take a child grocery shopping, an important discussion may ensue—or it may not. Children won't always tell you about their day on command. However, they may offer you bits and pieces about their little lives when something reminds them of what they have done.

Fair Division of Household Labor

Chapter 7 is devoted to the division of household labor, but because it is an integral part of dual career utopia, we want to mention some important points here. Fair division of household labor does not mean that both partners do an equal amount. If only it were so simple! If one partner works full time and the other part time, it is reasonable for the part-timer to do more. The division of household labor should take other labor into account as well.

Problems arise when labor is divided according to traditional gender roles. Women are not genetically endowed with a flair for laundry, and men do not have a lawn-mowing chromosome. Forget sex roles; you are in this together. Consider your other responsibilities and divide up the home labor accordingly. Divide the monotonous jobs and the more interesting ones. Share the child-rearing tasks so that both of you have contact with the children, even when they want mom to do something because she does it best. Tell them mom is working hard to pay for their roller blades, and dance lessons, and soccer camp, and. . . .

Some chores, such as shopping, draw you away from home. If one partner is home more with the children, he or she will probably enjoy the break. We find that men tend to be the grocery shoppers when their partners work. This may be a sign that they find it hard to rejoin the family after being in another gear at work. Best to dive in head-first—the kids need dad's attention as much as they need mom's.

Avoid "cherry picking." Because most household labor has been considered women's work, men often see themselves as glorified assistants, picking the jobs they want. Well, it's better than not helping at

WORK WON'T LOVE YOU BACK

all, but it creates resentments. Instead, let the man take primary responsibility for one of the big, bad jobs, such as cleaning the bathrooms. We both dislike doing laundry, so we switch back and forth. That is another solution.

FINANCIAL RESOURCES: SOME ODD WAYS OF DUAL CAREER ACCOUNTING

Dual career families have more income than they would if only one partner were employed. However, this potential gain is cancelled out if you just increase spending. Keeping fixed expenses down makes your money more flexible, and that is critical for most families.

As psychologists, we hear more than most accountants about family financial problems and their effects. One accountant friend tells us that he makes it a strict practice not to discuss family problems. But how, then, can he discuss money? People often turn to us for help when financial problems have resulted in psychological distress and family difficulties. Here is what we have figured out.

Your regular expenses are your home and its upkeep, utilities, cars, insurance, child-care or school costs, and credit-card debt. We find that couples who generate extra income quickly spend it on their fixed expenses. They buy a new home, add a room, get a fancier car, send their kids to a private school, and buy, buy, buy. They also increase their food expenses by eating out more often and at more expensive restaurants. Some of us earn more and some less, but we all seem to overextend ourselves financially.

Extra money can lead you into the trap of materialism, a resource that may be important to you but not as important as intimacy, love, time with your children, or a sense of mastery. When your money rules you, you must work harder to keep up with expenses, and you may start to feel like its slave. We see wealthy executives who feel like pawns in their own lives because of financial pressures.

Where should you put your money instead? Invest it in building resources. How could you better use your money to increase the COR resources you value? Maybe an accountant will tell you to increase your savings, and that is never a bad idea. Since you probably thought of this on your own anyway, we will move on to other suggestions.

Dual career families need more vacation time together. Vacations take money. Do you want fancy clothes or time at the seaside with your kids before they are too old to want to go with you? Take an extra week during the summer at a cheaper cottage rather than a fancy resort. Take an extra day for a long weekend of skiing. Our children always talk about our past vacations. We think they remember them because those were special times when we all had fun together, instead of working and hassling with our regular schedules.

Purchase household labor. We never bought a lawn mower; a lawn service does the job. It takes them one hour a week; it took us three. Pay for it by driving a car a notch below what you can afford. Household labor is not cheap, but it relieves you of chores when you are home. This increases quality and nonquality family time and makes you feel more like coming home at the end of the day. If you "only" have to make dinner and throw in a few loads of wash when you get home, your stress level goes down and everyone benefits.

Full-time help is a luxury, but it may be a luxury that you can afford. If so, do it. We actually worked it out at a time when our income was quite low. For two years a young woman from Denmark lived with us. She wanted to see the country and take a break from her small-town life at home (yes, she was legal, so we can still run for office!). The cost was less than a full-time babysitter for two young children would have been at that time. During two other years we had a wonderful, warm woman working for us from 7:30 until 4:00, taking care of the kids and preparing dinner. We would come home to hot ethnic food and contented children. Even the darn dog was happier. The cost was about the same as a double dose of full-time day care. To pay for it, we waited an extra two years to buy a new car and held off on some much-needed redecorating. Believe us, it was worth every nickel sacrificed. A student couple we know (who earn below the poverty line) have a third student live in their home and trade day care for food and lodging. Our point is that assistance is not only a matter of money, even if money helps.

In the summer, girls from the countryside often want to experience the city. Consider this if it fits your needs. It's a great relief to know that your children have someone around, and you can go out at night with your spouse, which really feels wicked, but fun. Even if you are struggling financially, try not to scrimp on a babysitter for Saturday night. You need a break together. Brown-bag lunch, but hire the sitter. Go to a two-dollar movie and a deli instead of a more expensive night out—but go. You need the time together and the respite to develop your intimacy resources and refuel your tanks with talk and affection.

If you remove most processed foods from your shopping cart and substitute raw products, you can save about $150 per month for a family of four. Have salads twice a week to save time on preparation. Stir-fry rather than bake to save more time. Now . . . hire the babysitter for Saturday night.

THREE KEY RESOURCES

Research and our clinical work with couples and families suggest that there are three critical resources you should have. Not only are these three resources critical in and of themselves, they also give rise to many others. They are

- Feeling that my future success depends on me
- Positive feelings about myself
- Intimacy with my spouse or partner

Mastery

"Feeling that my future depends on me" has often been called sense of mastery or self-efficacy in the psychological literature. Work by such well-known psychologists as Dr. Albert Bandura[1] and Dr. Suzanne Oulette Kobasa[2] suggests that sense of mastery, or self-efficacy, is a key resource in stress resistance. Those who have a good sense of mastery have fewer stressful experiences, because they manage their lives more effectively. When they encounter everyday stressful events, they tend to see them as a challenge rather than a threat. Like knights on horseback, they meet the challenge willingly and head-on. When major stressful events occur, people with a sense of mastery are more able to rally their full armament of resources to overcome or withstand stress's onslaught.

Development of a sense of mastery is a lifelong process. Children who are encouraged to accept and conquer *reasonable* challenges develop a sense of mastery. In adulthood this process continues. Learn to look for and accept reasonable challenges. Try not to exaggerate or underestimate what you can accomplish—then go for it. In a dual career couple, each partner is a key resource in creating and sustaining mastery. You and your partner should encourage and reward each other's attempts at success. Believe in what your partner can do and encourage him or her to try to succeed. If he or she stumbles along the way, emphasize the right steps, not the wrong ones.

This can be as simple, or as complicated, as balancing a checkbook:

Anne took over responsibility for the checkbook from Tony. Tony had always complained that she was uninvolved in their financial affairs and that she overspent. Anne began to pay the bills, budget for the month, and make sure there was enough money in the account. However, whenever she made an error or a decision that Tony did not agree with, he was quick to point it out and was harsh in his response. This made Anne feel both angry and incompetent. One night she threw the checkbook in his face and broke down crying. Tony thought that her response was exaggerated.

Anne's response was no more extreme than Tony's attempt to retain control. If he had understood that he was undermining Anne's sense of mastery, one of her most critical resources, he might not have been so severe. If Anne could not keep the family's accounts, how could she perform competently on her job, where she was responsible for a department? Tony not only failed to confirm her mastery, he denied it and so caused her to question herself. She was angry at him for not believing in her.

As a couple, you have an opportunity to nurture each other's sense of mastery. Mastery begins with success at small things, and there are many opportunities for small wins in a dual career family. As success with larger problems increases, your sense of mastery develops in its wake. It is a process that you can build on as a couple.

Self-Esteem

"Positive feelings about myself" is a resource that is generally referred to as self-esteem. Why should self-esteem be a resource for stress resistance? Our research suggests that those who are high in self-esteem do not interpret stress to mean that they are of less value. In contrast, people low in self-esteem think stress means that they are guilty, that they have failed or are unworthy.

Joe is low in self-esteem. When he is under stress, he blames himself. To him, each stressful event indicates that he is no good and that everything he touches turns to ruin. He has the opposite of the Midas touch. When his children have school trouble, it is because he is a bad parent. When his wife is not happy, it is because he is an inadequate partner and lover.

Compare Joe with Janet:

Janet is high in self-esteem. When stress occurs, she looks at the situation and considers how she can do better. She does not make the link "this thing happened so there is something wrong with me." When something is her fault, she does not dwell on it, but instead acts to improve the situation. When her children have trouble in school, she thinks about how she can help them do better. She also tells them they are loved and important to her, even if they have not done well in this particular instance.

Because of these differences, people who are high in self-esteem tend to be much less negatively affected by stress. They are less likely to become anxious, depressed, or angry. Their response is to try to solve their problems rather than blaming themselves or others. This allows them to avoid the cycles of loss that follow the initial losses brought about by stressful situations. In contrast, the individual with low self-esteem deals poorly with the initial stress and is more likely to experience follow-up losses.

Like mastery, self-esteem is a personal resource that develops early in life. Parents who value a child for who he or she is and who emphasize acceptance and reward, rather than criticism and rejection, raise children with high self-esteem. Teachers who highlight what children do well, rather than what they do not know, contribute further to this process. However, the development of self-esteem does not end in childhood. How we are regarded by our families, by colleagues at work, and by our communities affects our self-esteem throughout our lives.

You can encourage self-esteem in your partner by expressing love and affection. Criticism crushes self-esteem; compliments nurture it. This is especially true when a compliment concerns some aspect of your partner's nature. Just praising his or her cooking is not enough. Who does your partner want to be, and how do you respond to him or her in that role? Showing that you want to be with your partner and expressing a desire to share time together are further paths to enriching self-esteem. Call up the babysitter, and plan a date, even if it is not what you normally do. "If you want to be with me, then I'll understand that I am valuable."

Intimacy

A feeling of "intimacy with my spouse or partner" is the third key resource. Intimacy is the sense that you are close to your partner, that you can rely on each other, share personal feelings, and support each other.

In recent work, Stevan and one of his doctoral students, Rob Gallagher, found that pregnant women who had a stronger sense of intimacy with their partners were less likely to experience depression following pregnancy. Women who lacked a partner were especially vulnerable to depression at this time. However, even with a partner, if they lacked intimacy they remained vulnerable to depression.[3] Many studies of couples suggest that intimacy and the support provided in intimate relations are the key to maintaining psychological well-being when stress strikes.[4] Since we know that stress is part and parcel of dual career life, this makes intimacy a key resource. Better get some!

Many couples get into trouble because they no longer feel close to each other. After meeting all the demands of work and doing all the chores, they are either too guilty to leave the kids with a sitter or too tired to go anywhere. Getting out together is like everything else. If you don't make arrangements and set aside the time for each other, you will run out of time and energy. Sometimes finding a good babysitter can be a problem, especially with younger children. One time we went through nine of our ten babysitters before we could find one who was free for our regular Saturday night date.

Feel guilty about leaving your children after a long week? Make dates with them, too, because otherwise they will be busy when you are free. Then make plans for later on with your partner. Just go out for a drink or a cup of java at 10:00 if that is all you can squeeze in. Two hours of one-on-one talk will keep you in touch and add to your sense of closeness. Hold hands across the table, look into each other's eyes, and recite good lines from old Bogart movies. "Here's looking at you, kid."

Perhaps you can see that more intimacy is good, but you may be wondering how it helps in the face of stress. An intimate partner first and foremost increases our self-esteem. If we are loved and cared for, we must be valuable. Why else would someone love us? An intimate partner also helps guide us in our decisions. This not only means that they give us advice, but also that they serve as a sounding board for our ideas. Here, again, by listening to us they are saying that we are of value. An intimate partner also assures us that we are capable of withstanding stress and accomplishing our goals. This, in turn, increases our sense of mastery.

An intimate partner provides caring and affection. There is something about the touch of someone you love that is soothing. It sends a message that all is not lost, that you are together on this roller-coaster ride of life, and yes, again, that you are valued. Sexual intimacy tends to calm us. There is surprisingly little research on the effects of sex on stress, but we believe that the closeness provided by a romantic involvement is somehow more sustaining than the few seconds of orgasm alone, exciting as they are. This even applies to stress as extreme as that experienced in bloody combat. Military personnel who come home to an intimate partner are able to avoid negative stress reactions and return to civilian life more quickly and completely than those who lack such a partner.[5] If it's good enough for combat, it's good enough for dual career marriage. (We could describe some specific get-the-kids-off-to-school mornings at our own house that qualify as combat, but you probably have your own examples.) Intimacy is a critical resource.

Mastery, self-esteem, and intimacy: together, these three resources are the fountainhead of well-being in the dual career family. Nurture them and strive toward them in all that you do. Build them in yourself and sustain them in your partner.

A BALANCING ACT

Well, we really need to get back to home life now. It's Thursday, so we are in the homestretch before the weekend. We are out of milk (we hate it, but the kids love it when that happens because they get to have tea for breakfast), nothing is defrosted for tonight, and we swore to cut down on eating out and ordering pizzas. Ivonne needs to do her books for the month and to pay herself, but has opted to do something special with the two little ones instead. Ari, our oldest, left for a month of summer camp yesterday. He is usually a helpful babysitter, so we have to juggle our schedules a little more to make sure the two younger ones are supervised.

We are lucky in that both our schedules are very flexible. We work long hours, but can cut and paste our schedules to make sure that the kids and house are covered. We noticed a couple of weeks ago that we haven't had enough time lately just to talk, so we have been trying to set aside more time for that. Our fixed expenses, like yours, are too high and we are wrestling with how we can lower them. We bought a cheaper car, decreased our entertainment and clothing budget, and remortgaged our home at a lower rate. Because it has been such a busy year, we added a week of vacation this summer. Also, the whole family came to one of Stevan's conferences, giving us some extra family time and reducing expenses by mixing business with pleasure.

We had some possible offers for jobs in distant states that would have increased our income substantially. However, we held back because our current home provides location, location, location. Our commuting time is short and the children can be relatively independent about getting to their activities. Those jobs would have been good career moves but bad family moves.

All this is to say that we, like you, are engaged in a balancing act. Because we have followed much of our own advice, we feel that we are in a good situation and that our life-style does not create too much extra stress. Three kids, a marriage, and two careers are enough to

WORK WON'T LOVE YOU BACK

balance. We have to remember to reward each other, support each other's sense of mastery and self-esteem, and nurture each other. We have had some rough times, and now we are basically holding steady. It is a good time to build our resources so that we will be better able to withstand future storms—and storms will occur. Our dual career ship is at sea, and the sea is an unpredictable place. There are no safe harbors, only an able ship and crew.

Chapter 6

*Can We
Have It All?*

Having considered dual career utopia in the abstract, it is now time to work toward that utopia in your own relationship and family. Whatever your stress level, this chapter will help you make positive adjustments that will lower stress and increase satisfaction. We will help you make resource gains where you think they are most needed and alter those aspects of your life-style that are contributing the most to resource loss. In the last part of the chapter we discuss some typical problems that dual career couples encounter and suggest solutions based on COR resource strategies.

117

This chapter contains key exercises and suggestions that you should undertake as a couple. In fact, just trying will increase some of your most important resources, for instance, communication. Schedule a time to sit down together and talk. Go for walks together. Hold hands and hug when you hit hard parts and show your willingness to be supportive rather than critical. It is difficult to say no to a request when someone is building up your self-esteem. It is hard to say yes to a request when you have been demeaned and criticized.

BALANCING YOUR RESOURCES

The truly hard part is for the two of you to balance your careers with your mutual resource goals. Your dual career life-style should support both of you equally. You should work *together* to reach both your individual resource goals and your shared resource goals. Sacrifice of resources should be equal and the dividends should place you on equal footing.

To help you assess that balance and correct any imbalance that exists, complete the COR-E Balancing Our Resources questionnaire on your own and have your partner do the same. First circle your top ten resources. These are the resources that are most important to you. Now circle up to five more (perhaps using a different color ink) that may be less important but that are your top five work-related resources. For example, you may not have rated financial assets highly overall, but you may feel they are an important resource to gain from work. If you have not already done so, also circle the following resources:

- Feeling that my future success depends on me (mastery)
- Intimacy with spouse or partner (intimacy)
- Positive feelings about myself (self-esteem)

As we discuss in Chapter 5, these are critical resources in themselves, and they also underlie passage to many other resources as well.

In the appropriate column indicate whether you possess or lack each circled resource. Use a plus sign if you have it and a minus sign if you lack it. Put a check mark next to every circled resource that you feel you need more of from your partner.

Partner *1*

Balancing Our Resources

BALANCE

From my partner, I
+ = have this resource,
− = lack this resource,
✔ = need more of this resource

COR RESOURCE	Have It	Lack It	Need More
1. Personal transportation (car, truck, etc.) . . .			
2. Feeling that I am successful			
3. Time for adequate sleep			
4. Good marriage			
5. Adequate clothing			
6. Feeling valuable to others			
7. Family stability			
8. Free time			
9. More clothing than I need			
10. Sense of pride in myself			
11. Intimacy with one or more family members .			
12. Time for work			
13. Feeling that I am accomplishing my goals . . .			
14. Good relationship with my children			
15. Time with loved ones			
16. Necessary tools for work			
17. Hope			
18. Children's health			
19. Stamina/endurance			
20. Necessary home appliances			
21. Feeling that my future success depends on me .			
22. Positively challenging routine			
23. Personal health			
24. Housing that suits my needs			
25. Sense of optimism			
26. Status/seniority at work			
27. Adequate food			
28. Larger home than I need			
29. Sense of humor			
30. Stable employment			
31. Intimacy with spouse or partner			
32. Adequate home furnishings			
33. Feeling that I have control over my life			
34. Role as a leader			

35. Ability to communicate well . . . . _____ _____ _____
36. Providing children's essentials . . . . _____ _____ _____
37. Feeling that my life is peaceful . . . . _____ _____ _____
38. Acknowledgment of my accomplishments . . _____ _____ _____
39. Ability to organize tasks . . . . _____ _____ _____
40. Extras for children . . . . _____ _____ _____
41. Sense of commitment . . . . _____ _____ _____
42. Intimacy with at least one friend . . . . _____ _____ _____
43. Money for extras . . . . _____ _____ _____
44. Self-discipline . . . . _____ _____ _____
45. Understanding from my employer/boss . . . . _____ _____ _____
46. Savings or emergency money . . . . _____ _____ _____
47. Motivation to get things done . . . . _____ _____ _____
48. Spouse/partner's health . . . . _____ _____ _____
49. Support from co-workers . . . . _____ _____ _____
50. Adequate income . . . . _____ _____ _____
51. Feeling that I know who I am . . . . _____ _____ _____
52. Advancement in education or job training . . _____ _____ _____
53. Adequate financial credit . . . . _____ _____ _____
54. Feeling independent . . . . _____ _____ _____
55. Companionship . . . . _____ _____ _____
56. Financial assets (stocks, property, etc.) . . . . _____ _____ _____
57. Knowing where I am going with my life . . . . _____ _____ _____
58. Affection from others . . . . _____ _____ _____
59. Financial stability . . . . _____ _____ _____
60. Feeling that my life has meaning/purpose . . . _____ _____ _____
61. Positive feelings about myself . . . . _____ _____ _____
62. People I can learn from . . . . _____ _____ _____
63. Money for transportation . . . . _____ _____ _____
64. Help with tasks at work . . . . _____ _____ _____
65. Medical insurance . . . . _____ _____ _____
66. Involvement with church, synagogue, etc. . . . _____ _____ _____
67. Retirement security (financial) . . . . _____ _____ _____
68. Help with tasks at home . . . . _____ _____ _____
69. Loyalty of friends . . . . _____ _____ _____
70. Money for advancement or self-improvement
    (education, starting a business, etc.) . . . . . . _____ _____ _____
71. Help with child care . . . . _____ _____ _____
72. Involvement in organizations with others who
    have similar interests . . . . _____ _____ _____
73. Financial help if needed . . . . _____ _____ _____
74. Health of family/close friends . . . . _____ _____ _____
75.   _____ _____ _____
76.   _____ _____ _____
77.   _____ _____ _____

Partner 2

Balancing Our Resources

BALANCE

From my partner, I
+ = have this resource,
− = lack this resource,
✔ = need more of this resource

COR RESOURCE	Have It	Lack It	Need More
1. Personal transportation (car, truck, etc.) . . .			
2. Feeling that I am successful			
3. Time for adequate sleep			
4. Good marriage			
5. Adequate clothing			
6. Feeling valuable to others			
7. Family stability			
8. Free time			
9. More clothing than I need			
10. Sense of pride in myself			
11. Intimacy with one or more family members .			
12. Time for work			
13. Feeling that I am accomplishing my goals . . .			
14. Good relationship with my children			
15. Time with loved ones			
16. Necessary tools for work			
17. Hope			
18. Children's health			
19. Stamina/endurance			
20. Necessary home appliances			
21. Feeling that my future success depends on me .			
22. Positively challenging routine			
23. Personal health			
24. Housing that suits my needs			
25. Sense of optimism			
26. Status/seniority at work			
27. Adequate food			
28. Larger home than I need			
29. Sense of humor			
30. Stable employment			
31. Intimacy with spouse or partner			
32. Adequate home furnishings			
33. Feeling that I have control over my life			
34. Role as a leader			

35. Ability to communicate well . . . .   _____ _____ _____
36. Providing children's essentials . . . .   _____ _____ _____
37. Feeling that my life is peaceful . . . .   _____ _____ _____
38. Acknowledgment of my accomplishments . .   _____ _____ _____
39. Ability to organize tasks . . . .   _____ _____ _____
40. Extras for children . . . .   _____ _____ _____
41. Sense of commitment . . . .   _____ _____ _____
42. Intimacy with at least one friend . . . .   _____ _____ _____
43. Money for extras . . . .   _____ _____ _____
44. Self-discipline . . . .   _____ _____ _____
45. Understanding from my employer/boss . . . .   _____ _____ _____
46. Savings or emergency money . . . .   _____ _____ _____
47. Motivation to get things done . . . .   _____ _____ _____
48. Spouse/partner's health . . . .   _____ _____ _____
49. Support from co-workers . . . .   _____ _____ _____
50. Adequate income . . . .   _____ _____ _____
51. Feeling that I know who I am . . . .   _____ _____ _____
52. Advancement in education or job training . .   _____ _____ _____
53. Adequate financial credit . . . .   _____ _____ _____
54. Feeling independent . . . .   _____ _____ _____
55. Companionship . . . .   _____ _____ _____
56. Financial assets (stocks, property, etc.) . . . .   _____ _____ _____
57. Knowing where I am going with my life . . . .   _____ _____ _____
58. Affection from others . . . .   _____ _____ _____
59. Financial stability . . . .   _____ _____ _____
60. Feeling that my life has meaning/purpose . . .   _____ _____ _____
61. Positive feelings about myself . . . .   _____ _____ _____
62. People I can learn from . . . .   _____ _____ _____
63. Money for transportation . . . .   _____ _____ _____
64. Help with tasks at work . . . .   _____ _____ _____
65. Medical insurance . . . .   _____ _____ _____
66. Involvement with church, synagogue, etc. . . .   _____ _____ _____
67. Retirement security (financial) . . . .   _____ _____ _____
68. Help with tasks at home . . . .   _____ _____ _____
69. Loyalty of friends . . . .   _____ _____ _____
70. Money for advancement or self-improvement
    (education, starting a business, etc.) . . . . . .   _____ _____ _____
71. Help with child care . . . .   _____ _____ _____
72. Involvement in organizations with others who
    have similar interests . . . .   _____ _____ _____
73. Financial help if needed . . . .   _____ _____ _____
74. Health of family/close friends . . . .   _____ _____ _____
75.   _____ _____ _____
76.   _____ _____ _____
77.   _____ _____ _____

Now it is time to sit down and talk. We suggest a three-stage discussion. This may sound a little formal, but believe us, it will ease the way in the end.

First, discuss your circled resources. Tell your partner why each one is important to you. Talk about whether you feel that you have or lack this resource. Then switch roles and listen to what is important to your partner. Don't judge. Pretend it's your first date and you are just showing interest in the other person. We so often miss this kind of talk. When was the last time you talked about your dreams with your partner?

Now move on to your work-related resources. Many couples keep this private. Maybe you want to avoid bringing your job home, or perhaps you've had more than enough of work by the time you get home. Dual career couples have less time for friends, so you might as well let your best friend know what is on your mind about the place where you spend most of your day. Tell your partner what important resources you expect to derive from work. Are you getting them?

Now we recommend a twist. Instead of moving on to what *you need* from your partner, make some suggestions about what *you can do* to increase your partner's resources. Base these on what your partner just told you about important resources that he or she lacks. Try hard to volunteer ideas and do not be afraid to ask questions. Show appreciation for your partner's willingness to try. We find that women are especially likely to expect their partners to "just know" what they want. They are not satisfied unless their partners spontaneously offer support. Perhaps if more men had been raised to be in the nurturant role this would be a reasonable expectation, but that is not the case. Many men want to be more nurturing and enjoy this role, so you women need to offer encouragement.

Only now make suggestions about what you think your partner can do to help you out. Explain in terms of your dreams and desires. Explain in terms of your mutual plans. Be concrete. Just complaining that you need more help around the house or time to yourself is not nearly as helpful as asking your spouse to take over bathing the kids or running the car pool in the morning. Nor is housework the only help you can ask for, by any means.

Matt and Ellen filled out the COR-E Balancing Our Resources questionnaire and reached this point in their discussion:

Ellen said she wanted more help with dinner and laundry and Matt immediately agreed. But he had a request as well. He felt that whenever he did housework Ellen criticized him. His help was never up to snuff. He felt Ellen's attitude extended to his work as well. Ellen was always pessimistic about his plans, and this squelched any excitement and enthusiasm he might have had about sharing ideas with her.

He wanted to make an exchange—his labor for her optimism and warmth. If he left gum in a pocket of the kids' pants, so be it. He didn't want to hear about it for a week. If he discussed an idea from work, he didn't want Ellen to respond with a worst-case scenario.

Underlying Matt and Ellen's problem is a combination of Ellen's bitterness about Matt's not helping more at home and her general pessimism. Ellen is prone to depression and was often criticized as a child, especially by her dad. Her mom tended to be depressed as well, and while dad was a strong figure, mom stayed in the background. Ellen hated criticism but had incorporated it into her personality. Just as her parents had been critical of her, that is how she responded to her own family.

Matt and Ellen worked on their new roles. Matt did not find doing the laundry exciting, but it was more tolerable when he moved a radio into the laundry room. He also added a shortcut that Ellen did not like: He put the sorted laundry in baskets in the children's rooms for them to put away. Tough! It was his choice. If he could be a foreman at the factory, he could make major laundry decisions!

Ellen found that she often had to bite her tongue to avoid criticizing something Matt or the children did. But she liked her new self a lot better, and the children seemed to be changing, too. They spent more time around her and shared more of their lives through snippets of information divulged over dinner or while watching TV. She could see they were all less on edge.

They moved on to a new stage. Matt decided that he wanted to open his own business. He was bored at work and his plant was offering early retirement at age forty-five. Ellen was still naturally a pessimist, but three months of forced optimism had changed her somewhat. For the first time she was able to discuss Matt's plans and try to be more optimistic by taking a step back. She still voiced her reservations, but was beginning to learn to separate reasonable fears from outlandish ones.

By considering what resources they needed to bolster and taking appropriate action, Matt and Ellen were able to begin to build these resources and increase their marital satisfaction. Balancing resources is an ongoing task, and if you take it seriously this exercise should take some time. It is not one that can be completed in a single sitting. Indeed, discussions about these issues should take place in stages. First, talk freely on a number of occasions about your existing resources, the resources you wish to increase, and the problems that are resulting in the lack of resources and your plans to overcome them. The next stage is to try to implement those plans and provide each other with ongoing feedback about whether they are working. Then you must reevaluate your key resources and see whether the changes you want are occurring. At all times try to concentrate on what you can do, not on what your partner can do. The more you demonstrate a willingness to change and be supportive, the more likely your partner will reciprocate.

Connie and Jack began discussing their resources. Jack felt that his self-esteem and sense of accomplishment were way down. For years, he had put Connie's career before his own interests. He supported her through her last years of medical school and residency. When she got her first job, they relocated. Connie wanted Jack to stay home with the children or continue in an undemanding job, arguing that this would be better for the children and for her, given the long hours required of a specialist in her field. Jack had acquiesced.

Now Jack wanted to finish his degree in journalism. However, he felt that if he were to go to school, Connie would have to spend much more time at home. Often she left at 6:00 in the morning and was not home until 7:00 or 8:00 in the evening. On weekends, she did hospital rounds both mornings until noon. Jack was not willing to leave the children unsupervised for so many hours a week.

Jack resisted telling Connie what he wanted from her. Rather, he talked about what he was feeling and how going back to school was important. He wanted Connie to come up with a solution. Connie thought long and hard about this dilemma and discussed it with two friends who seemed to balance their medical practice and home life more effectively. She decided on a plan that she discussed with her two partners at work and her husband.

She and her partners would hire two young associates on a salaried basis. One of them would cover for her more than for the other partners, and Connie would reduce her work hours and her percentage of the partnership. She would usually be home by 6:00 and would avoid most weekend work. They would also hire a live-in housekeeper/babysitter. This was a heavy financial outlay, but they could afford it. Jack had to be convinced about the babysitter part of the plan, but was won over by Connie's willingness to accommodate his needs.

Connie and Jack made major changes in their lives, and the key to their success was that the sacrifices were made voluntarily. For Connie, the life-style change was one on which she thrived, and one reason the change worked was that she had engineered it herself. In the past, she had really believed that working all those hours was the only way to handle a medical practice. Physicians are often high on sense of mastery, which as we know is an important resource. The problem is that they may carry it to an extreme, believing that only they can do the things that need to be done. As a result, they become incapable of relying on others and delegating work and responsibility. Too much of a good thing in this case.

So what made Connie see things Jack's way? First of all, they had always had a very intimate relationship, and Connie strongly wanted Jack to realize his dreams, too. In addition, Connie could understand

WORK WON'T LOVE YOU BACK

the things that Jack wanted for himself. Her career was very important to her, and she did not believe that marriage and family gave you everything. Yes, they gave you the most important things, but career meant more than just money. It built self-esteem, commitment, and a sense of accomplishment. Although she had lost sight of Jack's need for these things, when he expressed it and she considered it seriously, she saw there was no other way but to change. She had truly feared that her medical practice would fall apart without her constant attention, but she came to realize that this was an extreme fantasy and that competent physicians could use a variety of methods to build a successful practice. There was not just one right way.

One year later, Connie and Jack's plan was in full swing. Their income had not fallen, because the new associates actually increased the practice's total billing by more than the added salaries. The housekeeper was a new expense, but she made their lives so much easier that Connie and Jack said they would go without shoes to keep her. Jack felt very odd being older than most of the other students, but he and two other older students banded together into a mini support group. His experiences made him a much better writer and he outperformed the younger students on all the writing assignments. Multiple-choice exams? Well, he was not so hot there, but three children did not increase one's ability to concentrate!

Your resources and what goes into building them are embedded in your life and are not easily altered. Be patient with this exercise. It is not a simple gimmick or technique, but a way to negotiate. Believe in your partner enough that he or she can adjust to your needs in his or her own way. If you keep in mind that you share and gain resources from each other, compromise and adjustments should come easier.

PROBLEMS AND RESOURCE SOLUTIONS

No dual career family can actually prevent stress. We all encounter difficult problems, some small, some large. We do not have perfect jobs. We do not have all the money we need to purchase household labor. We do not all live in ideal locations. For some couples, mastery is lacking. For others, intimacy is wanting. Let us explore some typical problems that dual career families encounter and discuss how to rectify them. Keep in mind that separate chapters later on address division of household labor, children, intimacy, and work. For now, we examine some of the other common problems that you may confront in your negotiations with your partner in balancing your resources.

In suggesting a few basic responses to rather serious problems, we don't mean to be superficial. Indeed, if you go through all the exercises in this book, you will probably have done more in-depth work on your relationship than most couples do in a year of marital counseling. Treat this section like the index of an encyclopedia; its purpose is to give you a little extra direction in special problem areas.

One Inflexible Schedule

PROBLEM

Often one partner's schedule is quite inflexible. He or she must punch a clock or be on the job during certain hours and those hours are long, inconvenient, or both. In the past, men were more likely to have this problem, but now, with women pursuing careers in greater numbers, it is increasingly a problem for them as well.

SOLUTION

The most straightforward solution is for the other partner to choose more flexible employment. You may have to give up some income in exchange, but you will probably also incur fewer child-care costs. One sticky point with this solution is that often a very heavy load falls on the partner with the more flexible schedule. This can be addressed by being sure that the partner with the highly structured work routine maximizes flexibility when not at work. If you have an inflexible schedule at work and insist on playing eighteen holes of golf every Sunday to unwind, you are stretching the family's resources. Be flexible with your weekends and try to remember that your partner is filling in for you a lot during the week.

Another drawback with this solution is that the combination of a very flexible job and major home commitments may impede career success. If one of you is not ambitious about a career, this is not a concern. However, for help when both of you are, see the discussion later on about one partner's feelings of underachievement.

Two Inflexible Schedules

PROBLEM

Two inflexible schedules are increasingly common in a world where jobs are more and more demanding and both women and men are taking their careers more seriously. Double inflexibility at work means double trouble at home. It can result in very high stress, and the consequences for children are often negative. As stress levels increase, tolerance decreases, leading to further problems.

SOLUTION

We suggest both short-term and long-term solutions to this dilemma. The short-term solution is to purchase services whenever possible. If you cannot afford to purchase services, trade them. Offer to run the car pool on weekends in exchange for weekday car-pool assistance. Limit nonwork commitments to near zero. Your family has little room for them. Make family time a high priority when you are not at work. Family bowling, family swims, and family picnics will be key for you. Location is also a major consideration, as cutting commuting time will add a degree of flexibility. Throw out your ironing board; no time for such frills for you! Seriously, this is a tough situation and will demand the greatest openness to creative solutions on both your parts to compensate for your unforgiving schedules.

In the long term, two inflexible careers bode ill for your relationship and your family. Think hard about how you might modify your careers. Can you trade off so that one of you goes into gear at work during summer and fall, and the other during winter and spring? Can you both cut some of your work commitments to increase flexibility? Can one or both of you work at home some of the time? Should one or both of you consider another job? Go back to school to gain better credentials? Even switch careers? These are major life decisions and we do not minimize the difficulty in making them. However, if inflexibility threatens to turn stress into depression, anxiety, drinking, marital strain, or children's problems, it is time for a major assessment of your career patterns.

One Parent Drawn More to Work Than Home

PROBLEM

After an exhausting week, many dual career families chase around doing a thousand and one chores all weekend. Given the stress of work, many individuals also pursue personal goals or leisure activities on the weekend that draw them away from their families. Many bring work home and bury themselves in it from Friday night through Sunday. All of this typically results in little family intimacy. Children learn to find interests outside the family. Marital and family satisfaction are likely to wane as well. We see this especially when one parent is often absent over the weekend.

SOLUTION

Minimize weekend commitments other than to each other and the family. Set a date with your partner for Saturday night and set play dates with your children. You may be the type who enjoys a tight schedule, so schedule your family in. Consider these times sacred.

You may also be overreaching in your career. If this is the case only for a brief period, it may be worth the investment. If it becomes your life-style, you are looking for trouble. Problems in your marriage or with your children will put you back every peg that your hard work puts you forward. Your work may have moved you up five steps, but you will go back down ten if serious family or personal problems set in. This profile is sometimes a sign of fear of intimacy, with people looking for ways to avoid closeness with their partners and children.

—■—

Tammy worked as an executive and was very successful. Dan had less drive than Tammy and chose to work closer to home in a lower-

paying position than his business degree qualified him for. With Tammy's rise in the business world, he increasingly adopted a more nurturing role in the family. He took off work for school plays and meetings, took parental leave after their second child was born, and prepared dinner most nights. He seldom brought work home and provided most of the quality and nonquality time the children received.

Tammy not only worked long hours, she took extra consulting jobs requiring that she travel more often. After work, she increasingly stayed downtown for social gatherings connected with work. On weekends, she shopped, had her hair and nails done, met women friends for lunch, and did some office work. Sunday mornings she either slept in or golfed with co-workers or clients.

Their two girls showed increasing problems. One did better by being home less and less and spending much of her time at the home of a friend's nurturing family. The other could best be described as sad and underachieving. She was in and out of therapy, but little seemed to really help.

This pattern is not untypical, although usually it is the father who becomes the workaholic weekend absentee. With more women entering careers, it is now becoming a risk for both men and women. Tammy is avoiding her family. She never felt very adequate as a mother but was very much reinforced in her competency at work. Dan was very comfortable with his more flexible schedule but was aware of Tammy's increasing distance. This is not an easy situation to rectify. Tammy may resist efforts at family therapy, especially if her competence as a parent is called into question. Often, it takes some kind of shock before a workaholic can be brought to deal with family concerns. If one of the children's problems becomes more serious or if Dan threatens divorce, something positive might happen. Usually, however, the more flexible, nurturing parent does double duty and the family continues in a state of managed dysfunction. Because Dan is so nurturing, the ultimate effects on the children may not be so bad. However, unless he can get Tammy to change her pattern of avoidance, the family is at risk.

One Partner Feels He or She Is Underachieving

PROBLEM

Although feelings of underachievement can happen with either spouse, it is more typically a problem that women encounter. Women are more likely to have taken time off for child rearing, worked to put their partner through school, and followed their partner's career moves. This may result in low self-esteem, lack of a sense of accomplishment and mastery, and little commitment to work.

SOLUTION

The best solution to this problem is to devise a plan to promote the partner whose career has taken a back seat—recall the story of Connie and Jack earlier in this chapter. Such a plan will entail the investment of financial, personal, and social resources by everyone in the family. Consider going back to school to further your career or making a move that suits your career rather than your partner's. You may need to take out a second mortgage on the house because the local nursing school, business school, or medical school is expensive, but it's a good investment.

It may be time for the partner whose career is more advanced to increase his or her work flexibility so that the other partner can increase his or her work commitment. More men and women are expressing a willingness both to spend more time with their families and share career success, so this may be your opportunity. If the kids are older, they may need to take on more responsibility around the house. Don't be surprised if it helps them feel more self-confident, and don't be surprised if they groan (loudly). We know many couples who received great support from their children when they included them in the whys and wherefores of their career planning.

Limited Communication and Affection

PROBLEM

Four resources tend to operate together in families:

- Communication
- Affection
- Companionship
- Commitment to the marriage or family

A whole litany of problems follows when these resources are lacking. Members of the family feel isolated and tend to seek more rewarding experiences away from home. They may look at work, in their friendships, in their hobbies, or in an extramarital romance. Because commitment to the marriage is low, the motivation to dedicate other resources to the relationship decreases. Why devote time, energy, trust, and love when there is no adequate return on your investment?

Patrick and Deborah had been married for twenty-one years. They often spent time at home, but seldom together. Patrick was always fixing something or watching sports. Deborah usually busied herself with cleaning, cooking, and running errands. They were both introverted and had few outside friendships. Their children were their common bond.

Problems began to arise when they both increased their career commitments at the same time. However, there was no mechanism for addressing those problems. What neither Patrick nor Deborah could see was that they both avoided communicating for fear that it would create the kinds of conflict they had experienced while growing up. They thought the best way to avoid conflict was not to speak about anything controversial or about which there could be disagreement. The result was that, with the children leaving home, they were drifting apart. There was little fabric in their relationship to hold them together. They received so little from each other that they lacked the motivation to do the hard work their marriage needed.

In a dual career family, or any family for that matter, problems will arise, plans will need to be discussed, and agreement will not always be possible. By avoiding conflict, Patrick and Deborah ended up avoiding each other. When two people have not spoken all day, it is very difficult for them to jump into bed and be passionate. The gulf between the silence and the passion is too wide to bridge. Just being in the same house and sharing household labor does not produce a sense of companionship. Companionship means being together emotionally, not just physically.

SOLUTION

Like the solutions to the other problems discussed in this chapter, the solution to this problem is very complicated. Schedule time together for discussing family matters, work matters, and whatever else is on your minds. If you are both reading this book, the various exercises we suggest can be very helpful to you. We delve into feelings and provide some structure so that you can do the same. We encourage negotiating your way through areas of conflict, and provide avenues for doing so. The exercises are designed to minimize serious conflict, giving you a sort of safety net. Conflict will still occur, but by moving on to the next exercise or discussion, you keep avenues of communication open.

Couples who have grown apart should work on "dating" each other. Make arrangements for just the two of you to do things. If you see a movie, be sure to stop off somewhere afterwards and talk about it. Go to restaurants with slow service so you are forced to talk. Perhaps sit on the same side of the table like in some old movie; your knees will touch and the only comfortable thing to do with your hands may be to hold your partner's. Think about fun activities you enjoyed together while dating, and try some of those tricks again. For many couples, isolation comes from lack of practice at being together and touching. Busy schedules draw people apart. Correcting the problem often entails exchanging old habits for new ones.

___

At the beginning, Patrick and Deborah felt awkward trying these suggestions. They complained that it felt superficial. At first they had little to talk about, but they persevered and found more and more to discuss. They felt closer and sex became more natural. They found that by dating at home on Saturday night when their daughter went out with friends, they could have less inhibited sex. Their years together had taught them that they could depend on each other, and although they had some underlying fears about closeness, they were able once again to overcome these, as they had early in their relationship.

Patrick made a major move by arranging a weekend for the two of them at a luxury hotel downtown. They were tight financially and never did such things, so this was very special. Deborah was really pleased that Patrick could be so romantic, and when she found a red rose on her pillow, well . . . (sigh).

Lack of Family Stability

PROBLEM

Some dual career families move from crisis to crisis. Everyone walks around on eggshells, wearing flak jackets and helmets. It feels like any little thing might set off a new explosion. Clearly, a sense of family stability is lacking. Family members cannot count on anything but the fact that there will be more crises. They are not sure of receiving emotional support, are not confident of being valued, and doubt if they will be rewarded for their contributions to the family. They may even encourage conflict in order to have some interactions. The high emotional levels are almost addictive, and this is the main glue that keeps the family together.

SOLUTION

The crisis family often evolves as a product of stress overload. Stress frays emotions and increases anger, especially in those who are anger prone. Chronic anxiety also can create a sense of panic that is contagious. What are your sources of stress? They may be at work, they may be at home, or they may be at the home-work interface. Discuss where losses are occurring in your lives and where you are failing to make resource gains despite considerable resource investment. Chaos and high-flying emotions are a danger to your family, making whatever real problems you are having that much worse. Try to eliminate the sources of stress and increase resources that may help you approach stress more effectively. If crises continue, professional help may assist you in developing healthier family patterns.

The Traveling Partner Dilemma

PROBLEM

A common problem in corporate America is the traveling salesperson, manager, or director who is gone for most of the week and arrives home late Friday night. Again, this profile is much more common among men, but it is becoming increasingly common among women as well.

As if the time away were not enough, the traveler often has to catch up on paperwork at home. These jobs are stressful, and travelers often become used to being without their families. As a result, pressures at home and the need to defuse after the week's work may drive them to remain isolated from the family over the weekend. By Sunday afternoon, they are already preparing themselves psychologically and physically for getting back on the road or in the skies. Maybe, if the traveler is lucky, he spent Saturday afternoon at his son's football game and maybe was able to have a romantic interlude with his wife on Saturday night.

The traveler's job places tremendous pressures on the family. If the stay-at-home partner also works, he or she must juggle the entire family's schedule, do the daily chores, balance the checkbook, supervise the children, and occasionally make the radical move to attempt sleep.

Chuck and Eileen had been married ten years and cared for five children, two from Chuck's former marriage and three from Eileen's. Chuck's job required extensive travel. Eileen sold real estate, which gave her flexibility. Chuck would call daily, never failing to mention the great restaurant he had eaten at or the golf game he had played with a client.

Eileen reported one of her typical days. Johnny, their youngest, woke up sick in the middle of the night. After cleaning up the mess,

Eileen returned to bed, worrying about what was going to happen later that morning and how she would arrange the following day with a sick child. She was up by 6:00 and on the phone by 7:00. She arranged for her oldest son's transportation to school and to his math tutor after school. The girls had an argument over the bathroom that stopped only slightly short of a fistfight. She called her secretary and told her to postpone her appointments. This meant that a critical house deal might fall through, but so be it.

Eileen received a call from the school at 10:00. One of the girls had taken her morning temper into the classroom. She scheduled an appointment with the assistant principal for Thursday—more rearranging with her secretary. She spent the day caring for Johnny and catching up on laundry and paperwork. She lost some of her papers and found them in the dryer, quite hot and yellowish.

With Johnny up and in front of the TV, she jumped to the store for some groceries and then began dinner. Lance, the second oldest, came home and asked her to drive him to a friend's house.

When Chuck called, she had been trying to learn three chapters of geometry (she hated math) so she could help one of the kids, trying to remember what the heck the past perfect tense was for another child's English homework, and trying to referee the latest round in the continuing fight between the girls—this time over who would wear which outfit on Wednesday. Now Chuck was complaining about his stressful schedule at the restaurants and on the golf course! It was too much. She put down the phone without a word and went back to the children. She was afraid of what she might have said to him.

SOLUTION

This is clearly a very difficult situation for all involved. With five children in their care and two more living with Chuck's first wife, Chuck and Eileen have enormous financial pressures that keep them working hard. Even with their good combined income, it will be difficult to pay for orthodontist bills, let alone college. Chuck and Eileen may be stretched beyond their resources. The family is showing signs of strain in too many directions. Smart kids are having problems at school, one daughter is having behavior problems, and the strain is increasing on the marriage. The best solution would be for Chuck to seek employment that allowed him to be home more, even if it demanded that he make some adjustments. He is definitely senior enough and qualified enough to find another job.

In the meantime, they can make some stop-gap resource adjustments. Chuck must devote all his energy on weekends to the family. He could also stop feeling sorry for himself. Eileen would trade in her pressures for his and he knows it; he also knows that he would never trade places with her. He must maximize his support of her in every emotional and psychological way possible.

At a minimum, Eileen must have some help at home. The children could be involved more in doing chores, and a babysitter would allow her to get out one night a week. Eileen and Chuck also need quality time together on the weekend. They must reestablish their relationship and rediscover the meaning of all their hard work. That meaning can best be found in their love for each other and in the support they provide each other.

Unless Chuck can find a job that entails less travel, the prognosis for Chuck and Eileen is not good. The demands on their family's resources are unusually high because of the number of children and because of problems from prior marriages that continue to affect them through their children. Even in families with fewer resource demands, the fact of a traveling partner will always cause a strain. However, by maximizing the physical resources of the other spouse and the emotional support of the traveling partner, a reasonable balance can be found. One thing is clear: The traveler's weekends must belong to the family; that is a minimum resource requirement.

Signs of Severe Physical or Emotional Distress

PROBLEM

Depression, debilitating anxiety, heavy drinking or drug use (including prescribed tranquilizers or relaxants), and such physical illnesses as ulcers, heart problems, significant weight change, or high blood pressure may all be related to stress. These are signs of serious underlying problems. There are many factors that may be affecting your condition, but self-help books or videos are not a good primary source of help in such cases.

SOLUTION

Given the severity of your symptoms, we strongly advise you to seek professional help. If the symptoms are mainly psychological, seek a referral to a mental health professional. If there are physical symptoms, consult with your family physician, who may also want to involve a mental health professional's aid. If your physician does not refer you to a mental health professional, seek one on your own. Your physician cannot provide ongoing counseling or psychotherapy and may minimize the psychological aspects of your problem because they are outside his or her experience. You can still use this book, which we think can be quite helpful as an adjunct to professional help.

You may be experiencing early signs of these symptoms as a result of dual career stress. Perhaps your symptoms are currently at tolerable levels. If you have tried the exercises in this book and your situation doesn't improve, it is probably time to consider marital or family counseling. Don't wait until symptoms become too serious to handle or have major debilitating effects. At this stage, short-term counseling can help you get unstuck. People who take the initiative for change benefit the most from counseling, and the fact that you're reading this book and working on your problems is a positive sign indeed. Keep going with our suggestions, but seek professional aid as well. It will benefit your resources in the long run, even if you are reluctant to ask for help right now.

CHANGE IS ALWAYS POSSIBLE

We have not met a dual career family that is free of stress. You work long hours, have family responsibilities, need exercise and personal time, and are part of a community. That means you will have considerable responsibilities in your life. There will be minor hassles, more serious problems, and major crises. This does not mean, though, that you cannot increase your marital and family satisfaction, your enjoyment of your career, and your sense of personal accomplishment. Consider carefully the suggestions that we have made and apply the ones that might work for you. Many of these suggestions will demand a major reallocation and investment of resources. We are not suggesting that moving to a new place, changing jobs, or altering work patterns are minor adjustments. But they will be worthwhile if they are part of the solution for your family. The payoff will more than offset the investment in the end.

Other suggestions require only a commitment to change. Supporting your partner's sense of mastery or self-esteem, showing love and appreciation, taking more responsibility around the house, and being more flexible about your leisure time are things you can do right now and carry on forever after. The irony is that so many partners hold back because they want to retain dominance in the relationship, punish each other for some past sin, or simply never saw these resources valued when they were growing up. Your family will benefit more from investing in these resources than in any others. You would be wise to ensure that these riches are found in your home.

Chapter 7

*Household Labor,
Or, I'd Rather See
a Handsome Man
Wash Dishes Than
Dance Naked*

"I'd rather see a handsome man wash dishes than dance naked" was the opinion of a vast majority of women in a recent phone survey conducted by a popular radio station in our area. One woman's slightly more glib answer was: "Well, I *would* like to see him dance naked, but *after* he did the dishes. Now that would be a turnon!"

Household chores are a mundane subject, but they may be the most difficult area of negotiation in your marriage. They are certainly one of the major drains on your precious resources. Besides the obvious fact that chores are a drain on time and energy, they can also drain you of a sense of mastery and self-esteem. When you fall behind or become exhausted with housework, or when the children tell you that you never do enough for them (What parent does?), you may start to feel increasingly out of control, inadequate, and guilty. This, in turn, can lead to anger and depression. Sometimes it all comes down to the ketchup bottle that for the thousandth time was not put away—but then fireworks start.

We hope that household labor is divided fairly in your home. In her recent book, though, Dr. Arlie Hochschild came to the clear conclusion that housework, which she calls the "second shift," falls mainly on women's shoulders.[1] She found that whether the woman was an executive or a laborer, and whether she earned more or less than her partner, the second shift—work waiting at home—inevitably fell mainly on her. The extent to which men participate in chores is a critical ingredient in dual career marriages. This appears to be true for families at all income levels. It appears to be true for couples who hold traditional ideas about gender roles and for those who are liberal-minded on the issue.

Studies across North America confirm these findings. As dual career families increased in number, it was thought at first that men would join in closer to half of the housework, but that has not occurred or at least not enough to reduce significantly the labor demands on women. The trends are in an optimistic direction, as men are making positive changes; maybe they are simply not big enough or happening fast enough. Perhaps, also, men are so overtaxed by increasing demands at the workplace that they, too, are exhausted and hard put to find the time to contribute a great deal more at home.

Taking it from a different angle, our work in counseling dual career couples tells us that sharing household labor is the sexiest thing men can do and that not doing so is one of the biggest turnoffs. That's right—the sex lives of couples are best when the man is doing his share at home. Maybe it used to be flowers and fast cars, but now laundry, dishes, and child care are ingredients of romance (Ivonne says, don't leave out the flowers completely, however). Reducing women's feelings to their sex lives may seem to trivialize the problem, but a healthy romantic relationship should have a closeness that includes mutual sexuality. When one or both partners lose the desire for sex, it is a barometer for greater problems in the relationship. In

WORK WON'T LOVE YOU BACK

resource terms, when the man doesn't do his share of the housework, he is indicating that he believes his time is more valuable than his partner's. When he ignores signals that she is exhausted and that she also has better things to do than housework, it means that he is disregarding her. We seek closeness with those who build our self-esteem and are angry when we expect them to do things and they don't.

In this chapter we champion the cause of fair division of household labor. We admit up front that this is going to be harder on most men than on women, because in most families it is the men who are not doing their share.

Guys, don't run for shelter too quickly. There is reason for hope. First, we think we can improve your sex life, which is good for both of you. If you apply our ideas you will probably lower stress levels in your home, which is good for the whole family.[2] Most important, you will build greater intimacy, closeness, and family stability. You will also get better Father's Day presents—no more of mom getting heart-wrenching handmade cards and lovingly molded pieces of pottery while you receive another cheap paisley tie.

We also target some problems more typical of women, so the heat won't only be on men. Women can sabotage men's efforts to help, criticize them for not doing jobs "correctly" (translation: their way), and become jealous when the children run to dad for nurturance on occasions and leave only footprints on her sneakers on their way past.

ASSESSING WHO DOES WHAT AND WHEN

Before reading on in this chapter, we would like you to rate yourself and your partner on the Who Does What? Household Labor questionnaire. First estimate the number of hours that you work outside the home. Be sure to include your commuting time. Enter this figure in the designated spot at the top of the questionnaire. Then estimate the amount of time that each task takes you per week. Now estimate the percentage of time you, your partner, or someone else (like a housekeeper or another family member) does each task. For example, perhaps you do 20 percent of the vacuuming and your partner does 80 percent. If your family has a special responsibility, such as caring for an elderly parent or a child who needs special care, include that at the end of the list. Now compare questionnaires with your partner.

Well, how did you do? How do your estimates compare with your partner's? Remember that if your outside employment is not equal, then your household labor should not be split fifty–fifty. As you read the rest of the chapter, keep your estimates in mind and reflect on ways to improve the fairness of resource demands in your household.

THE WAY THINGS ARE

If you are one of those men who are doing their share of household labor, we apologize for "preaching to the choir." Most men, however, are not doing a reasonable portion of household labor. As we mentioned earlier, men in dual career households do not do appreciably more household labor than men whose partners are homemakers. Nor do men do appreciably more if their partners are working full time rather than part time. Overall, men are doing somewhat more housework than they did thirty years ago, but the increase is about the same whether or not their partners are employed outside the home.[3]

There are five central areas of household labor: meal preparation, shopping, child care, daily housework, and meal cleanup. Women do an average of 60 to 80 percent of the work in each of these categories, whether or not they are employed outside the home. The only advantage employed women have over unemployed women is that they let some of the housework go. They also let some of their sleep go, as men sleep more than women in dual career families.[1]

In a recent study by Dr. Lisa Silberstein, both men and women reported that women did about double the household labor of their partners.[4] Moreover, the bigger the chore, the more likely it was that women would do it. For example, slightly more men than women made breakfast, but twice as many women as men made dinner. Women and men supervised children's homework about equally, but women stayed home from work to take a child to an appointment or to care for a sick child at a ratio of about three to one over men. Men in this sample did do about half the vacuuming, but, in this rather well-to-do group, 70 percent of the vacuuming was done by maids, so the men were really doing half of the 30 percent that was left over.

Men do more outdoor and car-related work. Their kingdom begins at the garage and extends out into the yard. Men did about three times more yardwork and household repairs than women did in

Partner *1*

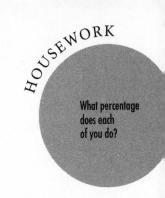

Who Does What?
Household Labor
Questionnaire

How many hours a week are you employed outside the home
(include travel time)? . . . . _____ hours

What percentage of these chores does each do at home?	I Say			Who Should? (Male, Female, Equal)	
	Me	My Partner	Some-one Else	I Think	My Partner Thinks
MEALS					
1. Prepares breakfast	_____	_____	_____	_____	_____
2. Prepares lunch	_____	_____	_____	_____	_____
3. Prepares dinner	_____	_____	_____	_____	_____
4. Plans meals	_____	_____	_____	_____	_____
CHILD CARE					
5. Awakens/dresses child	_____	_____	_____	_____	_____
6. Takes care of child alone	_____	_____	_____	_____	_____
7. Chauffeurs child/car pools	_____	_____	_____	_____	_____
8. Gets child ready for bed/bath	_____	_____	_____	_____	_____
9. Stays home with sick child	_____	_____	_____	_____	_____
10. Takes child to appointments	_____	_____	_____	_____	_____
11. Monitors child's homework	_____	_____	_____	_____	_____
12. Goes to school meetings	_____	_____	_____	_____	_____

CHORES

13. Does laundry   _____ _____ _____ _____ _____

14. Cleans up after meals   _____ _____ _____ _____ _____

15. Does major cleaning (e.g., floors, bathrooms, kitchen)   _____ _____ _____ _____ _____

16. Does other cleaning (e.g., dusting, sweeping)   _____ _____ _____ _____ _____

17. Does sewing and mending   _____ _____ _____ _____ _____

SHOPPING

18. Does grocery shopping   _____ _____ _____ _____ _____

19. Shops for child   _____ _____ _____ _____ _____

20. Makes household purchases   _____ _____ _____ _____ _____

ARRANGEMENTS

21. Takes care of bills, finances, insurance   _____ _____ _____ _____ _____

22. Arranges for babysitter, housekeeper   _____ _____ _____ _____ _____

23. Makes appointments for child   _____ _____ _____ _____ _____

HOME REPAIR, CAR, YARD

24. Arranges for/ does car repair   _____ _____ _____ _____ _____

25. Does home repair   _____ _____ _____ _____ _____

26. Does lawn and garden work   _____ _____ _____ _____ _____

SPECIAL CARE
(e.g., elderly parent)

27.   _____ _____ _____ _____ _____

28.   _____ _____ _____ _____ _____

Partner 2

Who Does What? Household Labor Questionnaire

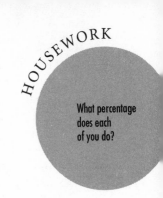

HOUSEWORK

What percentage does each of you do?

How many hours a week are you employed outside the home (include travel time)? . . . . _____ hours

What percentage of these chores does each do at home?	I Say			Who Should? (Male, Female, Equal)	
	Me	My Partner	Some-one Else	I Think	My Partner Thinks
MEALS					
1. Prepares breakfast	___	___	___	___	___
2. Prepares lunch	___	___	___	___	___
3. Prepares dinner	___	___	___	___	___
4. Plans meals	___	___	___	___	___
CHILD CARE					
5. Awakens/dresses child	___	___	___	___	___
6. Takes care of child alone	___	___	___	___	___
7. Chauffeurs child/car pools	___	___	___	___	___
8. Gets child ready for bed/bath	___	___	___	___	___
9. Stays home with sick child	___	___	___	___	___
10. Takes child to appointments	___	___	___	___	___
11. Monitors child's homework	___	___	___	___	___
12. Goes to school meetings	___	___	___	___	___

CHORES

13. Does laundry   _____   _____   _____   _____   _____

14. Cleans up after
    meals   _____   _____   _____   _____   _____

15. Does major
    cleaning (e.g.,
    floors, bath-
    rooms, kitchen)   _____   _____   _____   _____   _____

16. Does other clean-
    ing (e.g., dusting,
    sweeping)   _____   _____   _____   _____   _____

17. Does sewing and
    mending   _____   _____   _____   _____   _____

SHOPPING

18. Does grocery
    shopping   _____   _____   _____   _____   _____

19. Shops for child   _____   _____   _____   _____   _____

20. Makes house-
    hold purchases   _____   _____   _____   _____   _____

ARRANGEMENTS

21. Takes care of
    bills, finances,
    insurance   _____   _____   _____   _____   _____

22. Arranges for
    babysitter,
    housekeeper   _____   _____   _____   _____   _____

23. Makes appoint-
    ments for child   _____   _____   _____   _____   _____

HOME REPAIR, CAR, YARD

24. Arranges for/
    does car repair   _____   _____   _____   _____   _____

25. Does home repair   _____   _____   _____   _____   _____

26. Does lawn and
    garden work   _____   _____   _____   _____   _____

SPECIAL CARE
(e.g., elderly parent)

27.   _____   _____   _____   _____   _____

28.   _____   _____   _____   _____   _____

Dr. Silberstein's survey. However, note that yard work, car repairs, and household repairs are not among the five major chores, and we'd be surprised if they were for you. That is because home labor studies show that they do not take the time that the others require.

If you grew up in a mom-at-home household, it may have been legitimate for dad to expect mom to perform most of the household chores. If dad had been more involved with child care, he might have become closer to you, but at least he was strictly justified in terms of how much time he put in at work compared to how much time mom worked at home. Women who are homemakers work a high-stress job, but they work fewer hours than any other group. They work fewer hours than women who are employed outside the home and fewer hours than men, whether or not those men have wives who work outside the home.[3] Homemakers who do not have children work an average of less than six hours a day, and those who have children work under eight hours a day. In comparison, women who are employed full time work an average of closer to eleven or twelve hours a day.

We would also mention that since many household jobs are so monotonous and unrewarding, it may not be reasonable to count an hour as an hour. This was true for your mom if she was not employed and it is doubly true for women who are employed. Professional athletes cannot keep pace with a two-year-old child—studies have proved it! Whining can reduce an adult's nerves to mush in minutes. When you help your child with homework and he or she catches on, it can be very rewarding. On the other hand, our own children are usually still mad at us for not figuring out a way to help them understand things faster, better, and less painfully. After all, they are not exactly excited about homework in the first place; they say that if we didn't make them go to school, they wouldn't have any to do! We know a math professor whose children say their teachers know math better than he does (even though dad wrote the textbook!). So even these moments of joy are tempered by our children's perspective on reality.

Madison Avenue is trying to promote a certain image of the supermom. She looks like a mom from the 1950s, but in a dark suit. Her hair isn't mussed, and she carries a trendy leather briefcase and has an air of self-confidence. Women in our workshops tell it differently. They feel constantly frazzled. They run everywhere. Darlene, an executive secretary, says it this way:

I run to drop off the children, then I run to work. I run errands instead of eating lunch and after work I run to pick up kids. I run to pick up a few groceries and then I run to make dinner. When I'm not running, I'm rushing. I rush children to school in the morning and rush them home in the evening. I rush them through their homework, into the bath, and off to bed.

The only advantage women like Darlene have is that they can stow their high-heels in their bags and wear gym shoes when they are not at their desks, so they don't fall down when they're running and rushing.

WOMEN PAY TWICE:
WORSE JOBS, MORE HOME LABOR

Women used to do more housework because they were not working outside the home. Now more women are employed, but their lower status at work is sometimes used as a reason for them to do more at home. Michael, a foreman, puts it this way:

My wife works the same number of hours as I do, but I'm out there on the factory floor and it's a lot of stress. I also earn more than twice what she earns. It's not that I don't appreciate her work; we have a lot of extras that we wouldn't have if she wasn't working. I know that her boss can ride roughshod over her, too, sometimes. Still, it's my income that supports the family, and when I come home I just have no patience for the kids.

What Michael is saying is that his higher income and "more serious" job give him the right to be hassled less at home. Michael is like many other men who are appreciative of their partners but do not translate that into responsibility for housework. They believe that they pay all their dues to the family at the workplace.

Hal is a senior executive with similar attitudes, even if they are packaged in more liberal wrapping:

Jane works, too, but she is not as senior as I and she does not earn what I earn. I'm not saying money is everything, but without my income we would not have the family vacations we have, we could not send the kids to the colleges they want (and we want for them), and we wouldn't have the money we have for retirement. As a vice president I have less control over my time than the most junior clerk. I'm expected to be there first and be the last to leave. If there is a crisis, I'm expected to manage it. With all these pressures, I just can't have the house on my shoulders, too.

I support Jane's working, but I cannot be the one to organize the house; she's got to do that. Now with my mom being sick (early Alzheimer's disease), she lives with us. I just can't be the one to take care of her. My two brothers should help out more, but one is divorced and can't take care of her, and Jim and his wife still have three children of their own at home. I don't want to put her into care until we absolutely have to, and that will be soon enough, I'm afraid.

Michael and Hal base their arguments on their higher status and higher paying jobs. The problem is that women often land in positions of lower status by supporting their partners' careers. Women frequently short-circuit their own careers to follow their husbands' career moves or to care for the children. Women earn less, in large part, because they contribute to their partners' earning more. Women's lower status jobs are also generally more demeaning and more stressful than higher status jobs.[5] Since women hold lower status jobs than men on average, they may actually encounter more rather than less stress on the job.[5] Furthermore, women are usually paid less than men. This means that men get a bigger boost to their self-esteem than women from their paychecks. What do women get in return for lower status and lower pay? They get a greater share of the housework. Go figure!

In terms of COR theory, women experience greater drains on their resources at work. They also gain less esteem and financial resources at work. They are less likely to have union protection and job benefits such as medical insurance and retirement.[6, 7] In gaining fewer resources they also seem to lose power or leverage in the home. This results in their encountering still further resource losses at home, because the drains on their time and energy are greater. Often they translate the failure to receive help into a sense of not being valued by their partner or family.

Michael's wife, Peg, is rather traditional. Still, she feels overwhelmed with her share of the family load.

> I know that Michael works hard. I don't think that men should put on a frilly apron and cook or clean. A man should be a man. He can wait to do his jobs until the weekend, when he does the lawn and jobs like that. But I get exhausted every day and I feel like the days never end. If he would take just one of the big jobs, I would be satisfied. If he would just take over the laundry or the kids' bath- and bedtimes. I feel like a servant at work and a servant at home. Sexy? Ha! I feel thirty pounds overweight, haggard, hassled . . . [begins to cry a little]. I'd like to be sexier, but I just feel tired . . . no, not just tired, sometimes I get really mad, too. Like he's lord of the manor and I'm his maid.

Hal's wife, Jane, is more philosophical—and angrier. She has also developed shingles, a maddeningly itchy and painful stress-related disease.

> I put Hal through school and took time off to raise the children, because that is what we both wanted. But I have been working for fifteen years now and I have a good position. Now, just when my career really starts to go places, I have to take care of his mother. It's not fair. On the one hand, I can't be mad at Hal, because he didn't plan to have a sick mother and I understand what his job takes. His two brothers could help out more, but only Jim's wife [the wife of one of Hal's brothers] helps out and she has three kids of her own at home.

At least twice a week I wake up from nightmares where I'm trapped.
I feel like I have no control over my life and like I'm only on earth to
serve, serve, serve. [Jane apologizes for acting so angry.]

As you can see, women like Peg and Jane experience a drain on their resources. They lack reserves of energy and time, but more than that, they come to feel diminished and lacking in themselves. Michael may be doing less at home than the average man, but surveys of men suggest that they do even less housework than women say they do. Hal feels like he should do more, but he cannot find a way of balancing his high-pressure career with responsibilities at home. He and his brothers could actually do more, but they have learned that they can depend on the women in the family.

DO YOUR ATTITUDES KEEP THINGS UNEQUAL?

For many couples, beliefs and attitudes about men's and women's roles get in the way of a fairer distribution of jobs. Go back to the Who Does What? questionnaire. In the next to the last column, indicate whether you think men or women should mainly do the job listed on each line. If you think that mainly women should do a job, place a big W in that column. If you think that men should mainly do a job, place a big M in that column. Even if you have a *slight* tendency to think this way, place either the big W or big M in that column. If you feel a job should be done equally by men or women, write an E (for Equal). Now indicate what you think your partner feels about this in the last column.

When you have completed this exercise, sit down together and discuss your responses. Do you and your partner agree? Where is there disagreement, and why? How do your responses compare with what each of you thinks the other "should" do and what each of you thinks each of you is actually doing? For example, you may say that men and women should both cook, but in your house the man seems to have an allergic reaction to the stove. Many of these attitudes were acquired early in our lives. It is time to bring them out of the closet and discuss them.

Gender Roles and the Division of Household Labor

The best predictor of the division of household labor is society's general view of gender roles. Gender roles are the roles that men and women are expected to fill. You know: Women wear pink, iron, cook, clean, and provide nurturance, whereas men wear blue, fix cars, mow lawns, act tough, and throw the old football around.

Men and women can be divided among those who have traditional beliefs about gender roles, those who are transitional in their view of gender roles, and those who are egalitarian about gender roles. Traditionals are men and women who believe that men should be head of the household, that men should be the primary provider, that men should have the last say in family matters, and that women should have a more submissive, supportive, and nurturing role in the family. Egalitarians believe that men and women should be fully equal in all these matters. They should have equal status, equal say, equal work, and equal compensation. Transitionals are people who fall somewhere in between the two. Transitionals feel that men and women are more or less equal, but that there should be some differences between men's and women's roles. Transitionals are probably the largest category of people.

TRADITIONALS

If you feel that more than six of the indoor jobs (child care, cooking, cleaning, and so on) listed in the Who Does What? questionnaire should be done by women, or that the outdoor jobs should be done by men, you are probably a traditional. Traditionals are typified by the TV families of the 1950s. Mom does the housework, as long as it's inside the house. If she ventures into the yard, it's for flowers. Dad goes to work and gets a pipe and paper when he comes home. In terms of the dual career life-style, women come home from their job and do more work, and men still come home from their job and get a pipe and paper. Hmmmmmm! Traditional couples do not love each other less or value men more than women, they just feel that those roles are fair and appropriate. After all, some version of traditional gender roles has held societies around the world together for thousands of years.

Traditional men and women have the most obstacles to sharing household labor. Their attitudes can function as resource blocks because they subject the question of whether or not men should help to a kind of test. The test is whether a man or a woman is supposed to do a particular job. Traditional women feel threatened when their partners venture into the kitchen, don an apron, and do dishes. They feel their real work is in the home and they are working outside only because they have to. Their partner's presence in the kitchen is inconsistent with what they think men "should" be doing, and it may also challenge their authority. Traditional men feel uncomfortable doing what they consider to be "women's work." It challenges their sense of masculinity. They may wish to do more, but the jobs available do not pass the acid test—they're just not men's work.

EGALITARIANS

If you think all or all but one of the jobs listed in the questionnaire should be done by men and women equally, you are probably an egalitarian. Egalitarians also have major problems dividing household labor, but these problems are based in the outside world. Egalitarians are ahead of our society. We hear many such couples talk about being forced into traditional gender roles at work. They feel compelled to invest their resources equally in the household, but feel that outside forces inhibit their doing so.

For example, women are more likely than men to be offered parental leave or to have their boss's understanding (however grudgingly) if they have to take off work to care for a sick child. If a man has to entertain colleagues from his office, his wife is expected to prepare dinner. If a woman has to entertain from the office, she is in a bind. Other people's gender role expectations make it difficult for her. Even if her partner cooks, her colleagues may look askance at his preparing or serving the meal. The traditional men at the dinner table may even feel threatened that their partners will expect this of them. Women may experience the glass ceiling (an invisible blockade to upward advancement) at work if they admit to having family concerns, but men are treated even more harshly for dividing their attention between work and family.

Ricardo comes from a traditional Hispanic background. He feels very comfortable in the kitchen and has gone through a metamorphosis since finishing college and marrying Julia. When his family visits, however, there is a major uproar if he cleans up or serves dinner. At Julia's house the men pitch in, but with his family, it's as if you are breaking the Ten Commandments if a man so much as lifts a finger. At work he also finds that this is a sensitive issue. He says he's a "closet liberated man" because his sentiments are so unpopular in many settings in which he finds himself.

TRANSITIONALS

If you think one to five of the indoor jobs are best done by a woman, or that the outside jobs are best done by a man, you probably fall in the transitional category. This is especially true if you feel you are moving in the direction of thinking that men and women should divide household jobs equally. Transitionals are probably the most in sync with today's society, which is itself in transition. They feel comfortable sharing their resources for the household, but outside limiting forces do not bother them. They recognize the differences that still exist between men's and women's roles and are comfortable that they do exist.

Remember, our society is very much in a state of flux over these issues. We seem to want equal work and equal pay—but not quite equal. We want men to be more involved with their families, but we are not quite ready for the Scandinavian model, in which men and women can take time off for paternity and maternity leave. We want people to care for their families, but we also want to work longer hours to beat the foreign competition. If one partner is working a fifty-hour week, the other partner tends to be pressured into taking a less hard-driving job.

Transitionals are more able to go with the flow. The two of us are egalitarians, so do not think we are favoring transitionals. We are only saying that they are in sync with society. We are lucky to have maximally flexible jobs, and not to have to deal with the kinds of inflexible work demands and expectations that we are discussing.

How Powerful Are Society's Attitudes?

What might surprise you is that even couples who think that men and women should be equal tend to follow gender role stereotypes when it comes to housework.[1, 8] In this way, society's attitudes can be more powerful than our own.

Our society has an enormous influence on our thinking. Our oldest son called recently from camp and told us how much he missed his mom's cooking—this, despite the fact that dad cooks many of his favorite meals. Our youngest son once announced in the company of Ivonne and two women who he knew were physicians that only men can be doctors. Such attitudes are communicated so strongly in our society that even when children are brought up in families with a fair division of labor, they are still bombarded by very traditional gender role stereotypes. Sure, there are women physicians on TV, but it is their physical beauty and sexy bodies that catch our children's attention. When we were growing up, society held these traditional beliefs even more strongly, and we often find ourselves following them out of habit.

Mark and Marsha consider themselves to be egalitarian. They are both career-minded, and Marsha earns more than Mark. They have a two-year-old son, David.

Mark takes David to preschool in the morning so that Marsha can get an early start at work. Marsha works out in the employees' gym during her lunch hour. She leaves work at 5:00, even though she is the department head, and picks up David. She knows some colleagues say she is not completely devoted to work, but so far her promotions and pay indicate that her superiors think otherwise.

Mark plays racquetball in a league after work twice a week, but is otherwise home by 6:30. He tends to play the role of helper. He does odds and ends in the kitchen, odds and ends in the laundry room, and odds and ends with David. When there are programs on TV that he wants to watch, he does, whereas Marsha feels guilty if she

takes time off for a personal need. Mark gets David ready for bed if
Marsha asks and will throw some loads of clothes in the washer if she
asks—but she has to ask. Marsha considers herself lucky because she
knows that Mark is much more of a help than most of the husbands
among their friends, and he is a world ahead of most of the men at
her job. However, she still feels that Mark should take more responsi-
bility at home.

Three things are keeping Mark and Marsha from equally sharing the housework. First, Marsha's colleagues may look askance at her early departure from work (other department heads leave only after their staffs have left), but Mark's employer would not tolerate his doing so. Second, Marsha has taken on the role of supermom. Even when she has a chance to just sit down and relax, she doesn't, because it makes her feel guilty. She is away from home and from David all day, and her feelings of guilt build up as the day goes on. Mark, in contrast, feels no guilt when he takes a break. In fact, he has the opposite reaction; when he helps around the house he feels proud to be such a liberated kind of guy. He knows he does more than most men, and each bit of house-work is like a gift to Marsha. Third, Mark simply does not feel re-sponsible for the housework. He sees himself as an able and willing assistant. These three obstacles are the remnants of thousands of years of strict gender roles.

Does the Supermom Syndrome Prevent Your Getting Help from Clark Kent?

Expectations of the supermom, able to complete all tasks with bound-less energy, is another major obstacle to sharing household labor equally. Here's an example from our own abode.

―――――

It's a typical evening. Stevan has come home before Ivonne so that
she can stay to counsel a few families who could not make it earlier
in the day. He has prepared dinner, thrown in a load of clothes, and
played a little football with the kids in the backyard. When Ivonne

arrives, dinner is on the table and everyone sits down to eat. Ivonne is supposed to clear the table when Stevan cooks, but she gets involved with our daughter, Sheera, so Stevan asks Ari to help him clear the table and load the dishwasher. Although Ari argues that he has to do his homework immediately, Stevan refuses to take the bait and our son is forced into twelve minutes of labor.

The kitchen cleaned, Stevan gets involved in a board game with Jonathan and Sheera. Ari goes to do his homework. Ivonne hangs around the board game, but then goes to help Ari with his homework. Stevan is also willing to help, but not the way his son wants it. Ari wants a parent to sit and do his homework with him. He tries to make both of us feel guilty if we refuse, but only supermom takes the bait. This can mean two hours over the course of an evening.

The same thing with bedtime. It is only good the way mommy does it, and mommy responds (and likes it). Dad comes in for a final tucking in and hug, but is less willing to let bedtime drag on. Mom may even encourage this a bit. She has been devoting herself to other people's lives all day, and this is her chance to be close to and enjoy her children.

Now the kids are in bed, but there are lunches to be made. The kids like the way mommy tailors their lunch to their every whim. Daddy makes generic lunches. He forgets that Sheera doesn't like turkey sandwiches with lettuce because the lettuce gets soggy. She likes the lettuce in a separate bag. Jonathan likes his lettuce in between two slices of (thin) turkey so the bread doesn't get soggy. Salami, peanut butter, and cheese all have their own specific routine. Dad would be willing to devote the fifteen minutes it takes to make streamlined lunch, but he's not hired for the job. It's another way for mom to be closer to the children, because she does the half-hour specialized preparation menu.

This typical evening of ours illustrates a big difference between moms and dads. Supermom has to do it all. She has a hard time saying no, especially to the children. Dad has no guilt to assuage. He feels that everything he does that his dad didn't do is a gift to the family. Stevan, as a more modern father, does do much more for his children than his dad did for him. But mom is doing less than her mom did for her. Ivonne's mom even raised chickens so they would have fresh eggs. She was there every day when Ivonne came home from school and had a full, home-cooked meal waiting. As a working mother, Ivonne inevitably does less for her children than her mom did for her. A hot home-cooked lunch, if Ivonne can even be there, is grilled cheese. How can she say no to any of her children's requests? How can she deny them any of their precious needs? The answer is, she can only do so with great difficulty. At our home, it usually takes Stevan to remind her that she has to settle for doing less. He usually puts it this way: "Ivonne, you have to take some time for yourself, so that you have something left over to give." Then Stevan makes the sandwiches while Ivonne sits (finally) and gives him detailed instructions on which child likes his or her lettuce which way. We tell the kids that the sandwiches were made under mom's supervision.

Supermoms have a very difficult time admitting that they need to refuel their jets. Ivonne often helps women in therapy with this but is sometimes hard on herself. As she says:

I'll tell you what I tell women in therapy: that they are like a cup of honey. In order to keep giving honey to your family you have to replenish your supply. The way to replenish your supply is to get your needs met. This means different things for different women. For some of you it means time to work out and get exercise. For others it means time alone with a book or maybe even time for a nap. It also means allowing yourself to be nurtured. Be like your partner and children: Ask for nurturance and expect it.

If you drain your cup, you just won't have anything to give. You owe it to yourself and to them to make sure your needs are being met, too. You dip into your own resources to give to others all the time. Allow yourself and assert yourself to be sure that your resources are being refilled.

Men certainly contribute to the burden of housework on women, but the supermom syndrome and the continuing need to be the perfect 1950s mom also play a major role. Supermom cannot allow dad to do a sizable portion of the household chores, because that will mean that she is a mere mortal. She cannot allow her partner to care for the children, because then they will be vulnerable, because they were not touched by her supermom powers.

Meeting Mother's Standards: An Impossible Quest

If you are a dual career family and you do not have full-time household help (Who does?), your house should not look like your mother's (unless she was also employed). Unfortunately, many men and women still aspire to this impossible standard. Women often demand it of themselves, and sometimes men demand it of their wives. It is a major stress producer. Keeping a house spotless demands an ungodly number of resources. If your resources are dedicated to perfect order and cleanliness, other goals will be ignored or neglected.

This is also a way some women sabotage their partner's contribution to housework. Sometimes when men try to take over a share of the housework, they do not get it just right (or even come close). Unless they have had a bit of practice, men who try to make the beds, do the laundry, cook, or clean the kitchen will probably not do the best job. We made a list of all the things you need to do to fully clean the kitchen—it was two pages long, single-spaced. Cleaning the oven and stove top alone took up a full page with all the dos and don'ts. If your standard by which help is judged is how well your mother cleaned, it's hardly worth asking. It won't happen, at least not at first, and maybe not ever.

This is connected to the supermom syndrome. Supermom tries simultaneously to match the standards of the hard-driving executive male and of the ideal homemaker. She feels that her work will only be accepted by the family if she also succeeds in being the perfect housewife and mother. At the same time she feels that her performance at work should in no way suffer from the resources drained by her work as a homemaker. This is an Alice in Wonderland fantasy. Alice, you will recall, wanted a world as she thought it should be, but her fantasy kept going awry. She could not sit for a moment and sip her tea at the tea party. What is most amazing is that the supermom is an ideal for some of the most egalitarian-minded women. They cannot seem to give up the idea that the home should look perfect.

Half-Baked Housework: Men's Attempts to Plead Ignorance and Incompetence

Nor can you men use half-baked housework as a way to get yourself "fired" by supermom. If you have ever assembled a bicycle, you can follow the instructions for any task. Watch how a bed is made properly, how the laundry is done, and how a meal is made. Even if your partner's expectations seem unrealistic and unnecessary to you, try to meet her halfway.

Brad often sabotaged his part of the housework. He would make a mess of the kitchen, leave more to be done than he had accomplished when he gave the kids baths, and on three occasions had ruined loads of laundry.

He and Beth decided that they would switch off planning and preparing dinner. Beth did the first night. Brad totally forgot the second night, so he picked up some fast food. Beth did the third night. Brad forgot to thaw out the chicken for the fourth night, so he took everyone out to dinner. Beth did the fifth night. Brad burned the hamburgers the sixth night.

Beth was so angry at Brad that she really felt ready to walk out. Instead, she went on strike. She stopped cooking, cleaning, and doing the laundry. Brad tried to patch things up, but he had really gone too far this time for a simple "I'm sorry."

Beth put it like this: "For ten years I've done it all, now it's your turn. I'll pick up the kids and do things with them, but that's it. You're in charge."

Brad got scared. He had never seen Beth so angry. He realized that he might actually be wrecking their marriage because of housework,

*and he knew darn well that he was guilty of sabotage when things he
didn't want to do fell on him.*

*He bought a book on stir-fry cooking because he had heard it was
simple and had liked Beth's stir-fried meals. He did the laundry and
cleaned the house (after a fashion). He couldn't believe how much
time it took to clean. He worked an hour on one bathroom. Folding
laundry took forever. He never did get to the beds. He really worked
at the house as best he could.*

*By the end of the week Beth's anger had cooled. She set up a time
to negotiate over the housework and they came up with a comfortable arrangement.*

HOW MUCH SHOULD EACH OF YOU DO?

There are two factors that we believe you should consider in determin-
ing the division of household labor. The first is the number of hours
each of you has available after work and commuting. The second is the
importance of each partner having a diversity of tasks to perform. Let
us consider the second factor first, because we have seldom, if ever,
seen it discussed and we think it is even more important than time
considerations.

Diversity of Tasks

Diversity of tasks refers to the kinds of things that you do. Let's consider child care. There are several important reasons why you should
share individual household labor, but one is specific to child care.
Caring for your children brings you closer to them. We discuss this in
depth in Chapter 9, but for now let us mention a few key issues.
Children are from another nation. They have their own culture and
way of doing things. Child care gives you a passport into their world.
If you involve yourself with them only occasionally, they will treat you
like a stranger, a tourist. You will not be considered dependable and
available to meet their regular needs. Many fathers come home and
feel as if their partner and children are part of a club; although they
are loved, somehow they lack full membership. By involving yourself

with your children, you learn their ways of doing things, share their inside jokes, and become a part of their world. They still think you are weird because you are an adult, but you are one of the good members of that culture.

The second reason that both partners should share jobs is that the same task can be a joy when performed occasionally and a drudgery when done constantly. This is especially true of child-care tasks, but it holds for other kinds of chores as well. Giving the kids a bath is fun, but it can become a tug-of-war between parent and child that frazzles nerves already frayed by the day's labors. Cooking can be fun, but it feels like indentured servitude if you have to get dinner on the table every evening.

The third reason work should be shared applies equally to all kinds of tasks. When major tasks fall on one person's shoulders they become overwhelming. There is no time for a break and no chance to gain some distance and solve problems more creatively.

Two women in one of our workshops complained that their husbands were not planning well enough for their retirement and had made some bad investment decisions. On further inquiry, they admitted that they had never wanted to deal with the subject and felt it was men's work. They knew nothing about investing, never looked at a finance magazine, and avoided listening to financial news. Both said their husbands had tried to talk to them about finances, but they had resisted. Ignorance is bliss.

By placing the burden on their husbands, these two women avoided taking any blame. However, if they had been involved, better decisions might have been made, or they might have understood that it is not always possible to avoid mistakes in the complex world of finance.

We heard a similar story in family therapy:

Chris blamed Estelle for problems they were having with their daughter, Jane, who was introverted and rather depressed at fifteen. Estelle

felt she had done everything she could. She realized that Jane's prob-
lem was in part a product of her own low self-esteem. However, she
also felt that Chris was never around when she or Jane needed him.
He was always busy with work or golf or was away on business trips.

When men blame their wives for problems with the children, it is unjustified if they have opted out of daily child care. Child care, financial decisions, and running the home should be the joint responsibility of two full and equal partners.

We encouraged Chris to participate in child care because Jane needed two parents. A single parent can do very well in a single-parent family, but in a two-parent family an absent parent is seen as a deserter. Chris's daughter needed his love, guidance, and attention as she entered adolescence and young womanhood. A good relationship with her father would provide the basis for good relationships with other men.

Time Considerations

Time considerations, although much more straightforward than diversity considerations, are important, too. If the two of you are spending different amounts of time at work and commuting, it does not make sense for the household labor to be split down the middle. Figure out your respective employment and commuting hours when dividing up the household labor. Then follow the following rules, which mirror the points we made about having a diversity of tasks.

- Don't give the person who works less all the worst tasks. It tends to drain energy and is demeaning.
- Divide child-care tasks as equally as you can. Your children need you, and your partner needs you to share the responsibility.
- Allow time off from the most demanding tasks. Fill in for each other. Tucking the children into bed can be fun, but it can become a burden if you do it every night. Watching a two-year-

old can be a harrowing experience after a while if you don't have the possibility of a break.

- Show your partner you appreciate what he or she is doing. Praise each other to the heavens.

CREATIVE SOLUTIONS

Please do not fool yourselves that one or two little adjustments will reduce the stress caused by the burden of household labor. Your stress level will be reduced to the extent that household labor is fairly shared by both partners and by other family members. We lived for a short time on an Israeli kibbutz (collective farm), where we saw this put into practice. No matter what the job, everyone pitched in and tried to do his or her share. In fact, folks tried to do more than their share. The result was that even when the work was hard, no one felt it was unfair and everyone felt like an important part of the team. We learned that a sense of being treated unfairly is more stressful than hard work itself.

In our combined practices and workshops, we have virtually never seen housework and child care to be a source of problems between partners who pitched in more or less equally. Not that such couples did not sometimes have other problems, but they were not stressed out over the work load at home. Indeed, as we have emphasized, sharing household labor is a key to intimacy.

Even if you still fall into bed exhausted at the end of the day, wouldn't you rather fall into the arms of a partner who was there sharing the work with you than one who was out bowling or at home reading the paper? Imagine yourself scrubbing the kitchen floor; how do you feel if you know your partner is playing cards? Does this feeling change if you know that yesterday she took over the household (kids and all) so that you could go out for the evening with your friends or to play tennis? So don't fool yourself with a few creative solutions to the problem of dividing household labor. Division of labor must be "fair and caring."[9, 10]

Still, we can't resist adding a few tips for more creative housework. Over the years, couples have shared with us their creative solutions to household labor, and we have also invented our own. All of them are guided by COR principles. They either reduce the need to invest precious resources or produce resource gains. Here they are:

Purchase labor from your children. Make the tasks appropriate to their ages. Heck, they'll get the money from you anyway, so you might as well enjoy the fruits of their labor. Some tasks should be your children's family responsibility, but others are worth extra bucks. A couple in one of our workshops made Sunday afternoons a sacred family time, but everyone had chores on Sunday morning. Rather than being divided up, however, the chores were done together, like old-time barn raising. If each of three children does three loads of wash a week and everyone puts away his or her own clothes, most of the laundry will be done.

Men, take a cooking class. Cooking schools are all around. Talk to the organizer about your level (complete ignorance). One fellow we know took one class on stir-frying and another on salads. That is all he knows how to do, but now he plans and prepares three meals a week. There are also easy cookbooks, some even designed for men. Buy one, read it, and take some practice runs. Keep in mind that you are learning another way to show your love, not just how to cook.

Teach your partner to do a chore. Pick one that he or she thinks of as appropriate to the opposite sex. Women's sense of competence is enhanced when they know how to use tools and check the furnace, and men can learn that doing the laundry does not require an advanced degree. We mentioned earlier how many details go into cleaning the kitchen (the wire brush for the burners, certain chemicals that can't be used in the oven or on the enamel, little tricks to clean the faucets). People who don't often clean never consider the dust on top of the cabinets or behind the refrigerator. Take time to write out what needs to be done and go over it with your partner.

Set up a gas grill for year-round barbecuing. For some odd reason, American men are in charge of barbecuing. So be it. Set up the grill in a sheltered spot (not the garage, it's dangerous). You can grill come rain or shine. Meat, chicken, fish, and vegetables can all be grilled. Add a tossed salad and you have an excellent meal. Put some extra chicken on and undercook it by ten minutes; it can be reheated for the next meal in minutes.

Create a low-maintenance environment. Flower beds are high maintenance, ivy is low maintenance. Use containers that food can be served in and stored in. Use fewer dishes and less silverware. Choose rugs and furniture based on easy maintenance and comfort. Colored comforters on beds in place of bedspreads is very European and very in. It's much less work, and a six-year-old can make a bed with a comforter.

Such solutions may sound trivial, but we often see homes that are dual career nightmares by design, with light-colored rugs, copper pans, rugs under the kitchen table, velvet couches, flower beds, and waxed-wood floors. If growing flowers is a way for you to reduce tension, it's a wonderful idea. But choose such activities wisely, because those are precious hours that could be spent with your children or in your partner's arms.

Choose a residence that allows your children independence. We do not expect you to up and move for this alone, but consider it if a move is in the offing. We find it to be a huge timesaver. Our home is within walking distance of the school, library, religious school, drugstore, and playground. This was a top priority in our choice. The end product is that we very seldom have need of a car pool. The dance class and some of the soccer games are too far for the kids to go alone, but we want to accompany them to some activities so we can watch and coo over them. A bad location can easily translate into five to ten hours of car pooling a week. An added benefit is that children gain more self-confidence and a sense of independence by being less dependent on you.

Use fewer rooms. The family room is a wonderful invention. Use it. When the children are spread out in different places while dad is in the den and mom is off somewhere else sewing or designing a spaceship, two undesirable things happen. Most important, the family is apart. You shouldn't be attached to one another at the hip, and people need their private time, but being together generates closeness. Second, a lot of rooms are getting dirty. We eliminated all but one TV, for two reasons. We think TV makes children either passive or aggressive (depending on the child) and we think multiple TVs isolate family members in different corners of the house. Yes, the kids fight over the TV, but they learn to compromise and watch shows together.

FAIRNESS

Karl Marx had at least one thing right: When the burden of work falls on you, you feel overwhelmed, oppressed, and diminished. We were at first surprised to learn that with the end of communism in most of Eastern Europe, many women no longer want to work outside the home; they want to be homemakers. But the reason is obvious. Communism liberated them outside the home but not in the home. Women made up over 50 percent of such professions as medicine and engineering, but when they went home they were still expected to be housewives. The household labor fell on them. They don't believe that their husbands will change with the fall of communism, so the only thing that might improve things for them is quitting their jobs.

Every family requires a tremendous amount of labor. The only question is really who will do it. If you can hire help, you've solved the problem. But unless you hire live-in help, there is probably still an appreciable load left over. In any case, few of us have those kinds of financial resources. So who will do it? If the burden falls on one partner, he or she is likely to feel multiple resource drains. Time and energy are expended, daily life feels increasingly out of control, and he or she feels more and more belittled. Depression and anger often follow in the wake of such resource costs and losses. To the extent that household labor is shared, less energy and time are expended by one person. Even more important, the feeling that one is loved and cared for means increases in key resources.

Here are some TV commercials we would like to see as reflections of the widespread implementation of the changes we have suggested.

Floor cleaner. He is mopping the floor (in jeans and sneakers); she is wearing high heels and has every hair in place. [Hey, it could happen, and it's more realistic than the commercials that show her washing the floor in heels.]

Laundry detergent. Dad struggles over the decision about which detergent to use (mom already knows, for heaven's sake).

New dinner something-or-other. Dad serves dinner and everyone around the table gets excited (they expect it of mom).

Cold medicine. Mom is in bed with a bad cold, but the household still fully functions. Dad enters and tells her, "Here's your medicine, now get some sleep, everything is well taken care of. As soon as the kids finish their baths, I'll send them in to say goodnight. Is there anything else you need?"

Life insurance. A group of women enter a well-kept but not spotless home and one remarks, "Helen, you got that promotion, didn't you? That's fantastic. [And she means it.] Have you considered whether your life insurance policy adequately covers your family, considering all you contribute?"

Beer. Two men (a little pudgy) invite a third (he looks trim and happy) to go down to the bar and have a Shplitzer. He says, "No, I have to make the 5:00 train if I'm to get dinner on the table." The other two smirk, but he quips, "My wife's a lot more interesting than you two guys any day. I'd rather have a Shplitzer with her." (Camera pans to a vibrant woman rushing to meet him at the train. They go home to their family.)

Kitchen cleanser. A couple is heading off to bed with a bottle of champagne. She says, "I can't believe you learned to use Fussy Kitchen Cleanser. You are *so sexy* when you do that. Now could you teach me?"

Well, it's late at our house.
"Ivonne, leave those last dishes and come to bed. I'll get them first thing in the morning."
"But I'm not tired yet, Stevan."
"That's the point, Ivonne."

Chapter 8

*How (and When)
Do I Love Thee?*

Intimacy is the key to sustaining close relationships. We find a partner because we desire intimacy, and we stay with our partner because he or she provides us with intimacy. How in the world do two people who are like ships passing in the night maintain an intimate relationship? This chapter discusses the problem of intimacy for dual career couples and how they can navigate their resources to enrich their relationship.

Dual career partnerships can be an exciting springboard for intimacy. The new equality between the sexes means that you have much more to share than before as partners. On a more equal footing, you can be more straightforward and less manipulative about getting what you want and need. There is increased opportunity for sharing your interests, because both you and your partner are enriched people by having both work-world and home-world characteristics and experiences. This does not mean that dads will be exact copies of moms at home or that women will be exact copies of men at work, but they will share more of the traits and experiences that were traditionally reserved for one gender alone. This mutuality and equality invite a fresh kind of intimacy that will be virgin ground to cover for us as pioneers in our brave new social world that the dual career revolution is shaping.

Unfortunately, dual career marriages can also threaten intimacy. Partners find themselves drawn away from the home. Their attention can become centered around work, in terms of both time and thoughts. When they finally arrive home, partners are drawn to the many tasks demanded of them there. Child care, housework, other family obligations, and personal interests all vie for their time, attention, and energy. Each is a jealous master that could alone fill the days and nights.

It is not unusual for us to come home to a litany of requests and petitions from our children. Jonathan works on us for a half-hour about how he is the only child in the Western Hemisphere without a computer game system. His future popularity and chances of entering law school ride on his receiving one immediately. Sheera needs a clean white T-shirt and sandpaper for a project due the next day (how you use sandpaper on a T-shirt is never clear). The stores that sell these items (only a certain kind will do) close in thirty minutes. Ari has been waiting for a ride (pick up a friend on the way) to a friend's house to rollerblade. He has something important to tell us about school, but wishes to discuss it "later."

The kids have left on the table (in no apparent order) a file drawer full of forms to be completed for the next day of school. Permission for this, teacher feedback on that, demands for medical checkups for sports . . . the list goes on.

WORK WON'T LOVE YOU BACK

So we divide the work and each of us tries to hurdle half the pile of the "to do" list. When do we see each other to be intimate? Maybe we touch base to discuss a question on one of the forms or to coordinate dinner. Then, again, maybe not.

Dual career marriages can also threaten intimacy because both partners are changing and being molded by their careers. Unless you work together, this means you are being drawn in separate directions. If you do not stay in close contact, you are in danger of losing touch, both physically and emotionally.

There is a very funny, painful scene in the movie *Parenthood*. The husband is trying to be amorous in bed with his wife after a hectic family day. As they caress each other, she begins to talk about arrangements for the children and work. Without missing a beat he says, "It's so sexy when you talk like that." Well, it's not very sexy, but when else can these arrangements be made?

How do you switch from dual career hassles and frustrations to romance and lovemaking? How do you find the time for sex, let alone foreplay? Where do you find the time to just sit and talk and catch up on news? So many dual career couples complain that there isn't time for being together, and the days roll into weeks, the weeks into months, the months into years. Like a child who looks for mischief to get parental attention, you may find yourself looking for an argument with your spouse, just to have some kind of contact. What are the odds of succeeding in starting an argument at your house on a typical evening, compared to the odds of having an amorous interlude in the bedroom?

Finally, dual career marriages can threaten intimacy to the extent that intimacy is based on traditional gender roles. If intimacy depends on his "wearing the pants" and her being submissive, a woman who works outside the home can threaten the balance of power. Theoretically, a woman may be masterful at work and submissive at home, but that is probably not very likely. Hence, relationships that are based on traditional male-female gender roles may be challenged by her employment.

In this chapter we begin by defining intimacy and showing you how to determine the level of intimacy in your relationship. Next, we look in depth at the crosscurrents created by the dual career life-style that affect your relationship. As we do throughout the book, we also suggest ways for you to create and sustain intimacy and to offset the resource losses that can undermine intimacy in your relationship. You will learn more about the intimacy between you and your partner and we will explore how best to maintain and enhance an intimate, loving relationship.

WHAT IS INTIMACY?

Why do we use the term intimacy instead of love? We have thought long and hard about this. It is not that we do not think love is critical in relationships. It is. However, we have seen relationships dissolve when two people "only" love one another. Relationships that have both love and intimacy, however, seem better able to stand the test of time. Love is an intense, affectionate feeling for another, which hopefully includes romantic desire when the love is between partners. Love is an attraction to another—a deep, inviting feeling. Intimacy, in contrast, is the closeness two people achieve. We can love someone from afar, but we cannot be intimate from afar. We can love someone to whom we do not disclose our thoughts or wishes, but we must disclose our thoughts and wishes to be intimate. We can be harsh and even destructive with someone we love, but that destroys intimacy. Hence, when we speak of intimacy we are also speaking of love—but of a mature love that invites closeness, caring, respect, and support of the other's self-esteem and well-being.

Intimacy is the product of many aspects of your relationship. It is a critical resource both because it is highly valued in itself and because it is important in stress resistance. Dr. E. M. Waring asked fifty adults what intimacy meant to them. Four themes emerged from their responses:[1,2]

- Intimacy means sharing private thoughts, dreams, and beliefs.
- Intimacy means enjoying a mutual sexuality based on affection and commitment.
- Intimacy requires self-confidence and a sense of identity.
- Intimacy means mutual esteem and prevents anger, resentment, and criticism from undermining a relationship.

It is helpful to break this down further into nine aspects of intimacy—the nine C's. These are derived from the work of some of the foremost researchers on intimacy.[2-4] Think about the extent to which your relationship includes these elements.

1. *Caring*—intimate relationships express caring, affection, and sexuality, which are indivisible from one another.
2. *Cohesion*—intimate relationships include a sense of mutual bonding, trust, and togetherness.
3. *Commitment*—intimate partners are deeply committed to each other.
4. *Confession*—intimate partners are honest and open with each other. They reveal their private thoughts, feelings, and dreams. (This is called self-disclosure in the literature, but we needed another C-word.)
5. *Confidence* in self—intimacy requires that one have confidence in oneself and one's identity.
6. *Confidence* in one's partner—intimacy thrives on accepting one's partner and validating his or her sense of self-worth. (The noted psychotherapist Dr. Carl Rogers called this "unconditional positive regard."[3])
7. *Conflict resolution*—intimate relationships are relatively free of arguments and criticism. Disagreements are worked out without devaluing one another.
8. *Compatibility*—partners find each other's temperament, personality, and interests compatible with their own and of interest to them.
9. *Control containment*—intimacy thrives on interdependence, whereby partners influence each other and encourage each other to grow but do not seek to control each other. Also, intimacy thrives when outside forces, such as parents, are not permitted to control the relationship.

This is not to say that an intimate relationship has all these things going for it all the time. Sometimes a hardship such as a job loss produces more conflict than is usual. You don't have to share your partner's love for model train sets or opera to be compatible. Sex may lose its spark for a period of time. However, when any of the nine C's are lacking for a prolonged period, the integrity of the relationship is challenged. The closeness between you and the feeling that you can depend fully on each other start to fade from your mind and from your daily interactions. Intimacy is multifaceted, but what else can you expect of something as complicated as your closest, most loving relationship?

Zachary and Rebecca had been married three years. Both felt that their intimacy was still growing, but each attributed that intimacy to different aspects of their relationship.

To Rebecca, Zachary's openness about his feelings was strong evidence that he felt close to her. She also felt that she could share her feelings and thoughts with him. He was a good listener and didn't try to judge her. Zachary also supported her by little things, like sitting next to her on the couch reading a book while she watched TV or waiting downtown a half-hour each day for her to finish work so that they could take the train home together. Finally, she felt great intimacy with him because he had held off on a career move when it was not a good time for her.

For Zachary, intimacy with Rebecca was based on the big things she had done for him. When his mother died unexpectedly, Rebecca had been an enormous source of strength and support. She had handled the funeral arrangements and all the guests, allowing him to mourn and reach within himself to make sense of his loss. On another occasion, he was fired from a job for which he had competed with a colleague, and he had been afraid that this would diminish him in Rebecca's eyes. Instead, she helped him understand the event for what it was: The company had been looking for an older person for the position and was just not going to allow a person five years out of school to head a department. She suggested that he go after a position in a smaller, more dynamic firm, and he was doing very well after a year at the new job. She was right. The more dynamic firm fit his pioneering spirit much better. Now Rebecca seemed to be reading his mind when she said he might not really be happy until he started his own company. Such thoughts had been on his mind for a while, but he was afraid that Rebecca, who took less chances in life, would not support such a risky venture. He felt close to her because she had the courage to fight down her own need for stability so that he would be happy.

For Caroline and John, who had been married eighteen years, intimacy was based on similar experiences. However, having been through more years together, their intimacy was more strongly established and had faced greater challenges.

The marriage had a rocky beginning. Financial pressures weighed on them considerably. They had a child early on, and Caroline had a daughter from a previous relationship. Both were very controlling early in the marriage. John wanted Caroline to work, but Caroline wanted to stay home with the children until they reached school age. John also tried to control her by making all the major decisions— where they lived, what car they drove, how much they budgeted for every item, and who they had as friends. Caroline tried to control John, in turn, by trying to make him into something he wasn't. Other men earned more money, were better husbands, helped more around the house, dressed better, and were more dependable. She expressed her dissatisfaction in many little ways, but would deny it if John confronted her about her feelings.

Their intimacy grew as John and Caroline became more confident in themselves. They were excellent workers and were rewarded for their efforts. As financial pressures lightened, that cloud over their marriage dispersed. Over time, they came to a kind of understanding. John would handle large decisions but would always seek input from Caroline. As he became more self-assured, he came to rely on her as an equal partner in decision making. Feeling less controlled, Caroline no longer felt that she had to try to control John. She became more supportive of him as a man, a husband, and a father. She showed her support by telling him of her increased confidence in him and by turning to him more for help.

John did not express his feelings verbally. However, he recognized this and so would often pick up a special greeting card or small present for Caroline. He also expressed his feelings by showing love and affection equally to Caroline's daughter and to their own daughter. He adopted Caroline's daughter and always showed great pride in her accomplishments. He learned to talk more about work and found that Caroline was very insightful about personnel problems he had as a manager with employees.

Intimacy grows along different paths in each relationship, but the nine C's are apparent whatever the path. Rebecca and Zachary were getting off to a good start in marriage, gaining a maturity that does not always develop so early. Caroline and John had to endure a more stressful and conflictual period and develop more self-confidence as individuals before their intimacy could develop. In some measure, just staying together during this rough period confirmed their commitment to each other, making them feel safer about taking the risks that go along with trusting an intimate partner.

EVALUATING YOUR INTIMACY

The nine C's can be used as a tool for evaluating the intimacy in your relationship. We have devised a questionnaire on intimacy for you and your partner to complete. Answer the questions individually and then share your responses. Indicate the degree to which you agree or disagree with each statement by circling one of the numbers from 1 (disagree very much) to 6 (agree very much). Figure your score by adding together your ten responses. Scores can range from a low of 10 to a high of 60.

Warning: If you find aspects of intimacy lacking in your relationship, acknowledging this to yourself or your partner may be painful. If you feel that your relationship lacks facets of intimacy that you consider important and that you think will be hard to acquire without professional help, we recommend marital counseling. Our experience

Partner *1*

The Nine C's—Plus One— of Intimacy

1. My partner and I care for each other and show affection. 1 2 3 4 5 6
2. My partner and I feel close to one another. 1 2 3 4 5 6
3. My partner and I are committed to our relationship and to our being together. 1 2 3 4 5 6
4. My partner and I share our innermost feelings, thoughts, and dreams. 1 2 3 4 5 6
5. My partner and I support and esteem each other through thick and thin. 1 2 3 4 5 6
6. My partner and I are both able to accept each other's esteem and support. 1 2 3 4 5 6
7. We enjoy being with each other and sharing activities together. 1 2 3 4 5 6
8. Even when we disagree on something, there is a feeling that both our opinions and feelings matter. 1 2 3 4 5 6
9. We do not try to control each other or allow others (parents, friends) to control our relationship. 1 2 3 4 5 6
10. We enjoy having sex with each other. 1 2 3 4 5 6

Score: _____

Partner 2

*The Nine C's—Plus One—
of Intimacy*

1. My partner and I care for each other and show affection. 1 2 3 4 5 6

2. My partner and I feel close to one another. 1 2 3 4 5 6

3. My partner and I are committed to our relationship and to our being together. 1 2 3 4 5 6

4. My partner and I share our innermost feelings, thoughts, and dreams. 1 2 3 4 5 6

5. My partner and I support and esteem each other through thick and thin. 1 2 3 4 5 6

6. My partner and I are both able to accept each other's esteem and support. 1 2 3 4 5 6

7. We enjoy being with each other and sharing activities together. 1 2 3 4 5 6

8. Even when we disagree on something, there is a feeling that both our opinions and feelings matter. 1 2 3 4 5 6

9. We do not try to control each other or allow others (parents, friends) to control our relationship. 1 2 3 4 5 6

10. We enjoy having sex with each other. 1 2 3 4 5 6

Score: _____

has taught us that people usually know how intimate they feel with their partners. However, they do not always know how their partners feel. Especially when intimacy is lacking, you may be shocked and hurt to find how much you have drifted apart. We hope this is not the case, but we realize that some will have acquired this book precisely because their dual career relationship is "on the rocks." You may be able to work this out between you. If not, marital therapy can be very productive and can help you through difficult decisions and changes in your relationship.

We also suggest a possible detour route. If, as a couple, you already know that your relationship is lacking in intimacy, skip the questionnaire. Instead, read on in this chapter and work on gaining intimacy in the ways we suggest. Later, when you feel intimacy is on the rise, go back to the questionnaire and share your responses with each other.

Your Intimacy Level

Let's look at your scores. Remember, although this survey is based on a number of research measures, it should be used cautiously. It is only a guideline. No survey is more meaningful than your personal feelings. All that the survey can do is help provide a yardstick with which to measure feelings you already have.

A score between 50 and 60 indicates that you feel you have a very intimate relationship. You are very satisfied with your relationship and what it provides. However, you may still have disagreed with one or more statements concerning an aspect of intimacy that you feel is important. In that a case, there is room for optimism because the other aspects of your relationship are strong enough to help you work on the isolated problem area.

A score in the range from 40 to 50 is positive but suggests there is room for intimacy growth. You may be in a new relationship or you may recently have gone through some difficult times; either may be depressing your responses somewhat. We would like to see you increase your intimacy further, but an important question is whether you feel comfortable with the current level of intimacy. It does not matter if the intimacy you have is enough for us; the point is whether it is enough for you or your partner. Statements you disagreed with are areas to discuss with your partner and in which to invest your resources.

A score between 30 and 40 indicates that you may be unsure about the level of intimacy in your relationship. Were you being cautious because you were unsure of your partner's responses? Do you have difficulty expressing these kinds of feelings? If you do, your scores may underestimate your deeper feelings. If there were statements with which you disagreed, try focusing your attention and your discussions on these areas of your relationship as you read this chapter.

A score below 30 may indicate a lack of intimacy in your relationship, at least in some critical areas. Be cautious, however, in making this interpretation. Are you the pessimistic type, one who paints things blacker than they are? Do you have difficulty expressing or acknowledging love? These traits may be limiting your scores. On the other hand, they actually may be limiting the intimacy in your relationship.

If you feel that this book and the discussions we recommend that you have with your partner are not helping to raise your intimacy score significantly, or if you feel especially troubled by the low level of intimacy in your relationship, we once again urge you to seek professional help. If you are more comfortable speaking to a member of the clergy, by all means do so. The clergy today are increasingly well trained in relationship counseling.

─────

Courtney and Stephanie had significant problems in their relationship. They tried to present themselves as a model couple, but that was far from the case. Stephanie often belittled Courtney, and among friends she would make "innocent" jokes at his expense—how stupid he was, how much he spent, how crazy his family was. Courtney, in turn, was very controlling of Stephanie. Every time she began to advance at work, he would decide that his career demanded they move or that she should stay home with one of their children for awhile. He claimed the relocations were necessary to meet her spending level, and that since he earned more, his career should come first.

Courtney and Stephanie spent little time together. They worked separately, seldom ate together as a family, and did things alone with their two children. Courtney seldom helped around the house, and Stephanie constantly felt exhausted from her "second shift" of work at home following work at work. When they were both home, the house was filled with tension. Stephanie often took Valium to calm her nerves, and Courtney's drinking was at a dangerous level.

Stephanie was afraid of intimacy. Her father had been verbally abusive and distant. She was close to her mother and sister, and had had close but anxious relationships with two men before marrying. She would typically break up with a guy after a few dates. Stephanie used sex as a source of power, giving and withholding it, depending on whether she wanted to reward or punish Courtney. Recently Courtney had begun to do the same, and the result was that they had sex about once a month.

Whenever Courtney and Stephanie argued, they belittled each other. When their arguments became intense, one of them always threatened divorce. After nine years of this (the first three seemed better), they wondered why they were still together. Oddly, both felt that they loved each other and were committed to being together.

Stephanie and Courtney might benefit from marital therapy. The fact that they still love each other is an important basis for rebuilding trust, intimacy, and mutual support. Without professional intervention, however, their personal problems, never-ending power struggle, and dual career pressures are likely to result either in divorce or in a marriage that is painful to them and damaging to their children. A self-help book such as this one might help them begin the process of repairing their relationship, but is not likely to be nearly enough. A book might be a catalyst in getting them into therapy, and could also be used as an adjunct to therapy with an understanding marital counselor, psychologist, or minister.

———

Courtney made the first move by beginning to help more around the house. He committed himself to coming straight home from work and lightening the burden on Stephanie. He also began to share his feelings about being pushed away whenever he felt that he and Stephanie could be closer, and he admitted to feeling threatened by the independence she gained from work. He felt that the women in her family "didn't need men" and feared becoming obsolete.

This might have fallen on deaf ears, but a crisis brought them closer together. Stephanie found a lump in her left breast and the doctor was also concerned about a possible growth in the right one, too. In the days prior to the biopsy, Courtney took off work to go with Stephanie to all the tests and appointments. He was very strong for her and told her that she would be beautiful to him whatever the outcome. They stayed awake together, crying for most of the night before the biopsy.

The biopsy was negative; no cancer was detected and the benign mass was removed. Right at this time, Courtney's firm offered him a major advancement and a move. He told Stephanie about it, adding that it probably was not good timing. They needed to enter counseling and work on their marriage. They used the positive momentum of the previous weeks to overcome the hurdles that had been preventing them from seeking outside help.

Comparing Intimacy Levels

Now it is time to share and discuss your intimacy score with your partner. Even if both your intimacy scores are high, discuss what you thought about when you considered each item. Share the good feelings you had. If you disagree, first try to understand whether one or both of you are biasing your scores. Are you trying to minimize the closeness that you feel because you fear being hurt or because "real men" don't share their feelings? Are you angry over something that recently occurred, and so were harsher in your answers than you might otherwise have been? Are you trying to paint a rosy picture where in fact there are many thorns and thistles?

Before proceeding further, try to determine what your genuine responses are and compare them with those of your partner. If you feel there are ways in which you would like to be more intimate, focus on

WORK WON'T LOVE YOU BACK

these as we discuss intimacy and dual career partners in the remainder of this chapter.

WHY IS INTIMACY SO IMPORTANT?

Resources, you will recall, are those things that we most value or that allow us to obtain these things we value. Intimacy is a key resource in both instances.

Intimacy as a Resource in Its Own Right

People seek intimacy from the earliest stages of life.[5, 6] Infants seek to bond with a nurturing adult, and their development is deeply affected if this attachment process is disturbed or interrupted.[6] The infant seeks to nestle in safe arms, to suckle at a life-giving breast, and to be warmed by another warm body. In the famous studies of Dr. Harry Harlow, infant monkeys that were denied nurturant contact as infants were disturbed throughout life and could never adjust to mature adult relationships.[7]

Human infants who are kept from nurturing have similar problems. Work by Dr. Phillip Shaver and his colleagues suggests that if early attachments are troubled, this may be reflected in adult attachments.[8] Insecure relationships during infancy and childhood may lead to continued anxiety, jealousy, and insecurity in adulthood. Virtually all personality theorists, be it Freud, Erikson, Sullivan, or Maslow, argue that healthy early attachments are critical to the development of a psychologically healthy adult.[9–12]

Children continue to seek their closest attachments within the family, from parents and siblings. During adolescence, they begin to seek them in friends to an increasing degree. Make no mistake, however, close relationships with parents and siblings remain critical at this stage. You may not see your teenage daughter or son much, but their well-being remains dependent on a close relationship with you. Nor does this mean they will not argue or seek to distance themselves from you. This is the time when they are trying to figure out who they are apart from you. Research shows quite clearly that even this process of identity formation depends on a stable, close relationship with parents.[10]

In late adolescence and early adulthood, the primary relationship with a parent should change from an adult-child relationship to more of an adult-adult relationship. Simultaneously, an intimate attachment should begin with one or more romantic partners.[10] We have all gone through this painful stage of testing love, trying to understand our lovers and trying to find the right one. Two things are clear from this process: First, the search for an intimate partner is a strong human motivation. Second, we take a beating, but are not deterred in our quest.

By adulthood, individuals have usually entered into an intimate, romantic relationship (in fact, typically into more than one). And for those of you reading this book, this relationship entails commitment to a life together. Women may be somewhat better at talking about being intimate, but research indicates that both men and women feel strongly about the need for an intimate relationship.[13] There may be conflict over the degree of commitment people are willing to make to achieve intimacy, but its importance and centrality to their lives are unmistakable.[5, 14]

Intimacy as a Barrier Against Stress

Intimacy is not only a resource in its own right. It is also a resource because those who possess an intimate relationship are more resistant to the effects of stress. We have seen this both in our research and in clinical work.

Stevan's work with the Israeli army showed that soldiers who had close ties with their comrades-in-arms were less likely to experience psychiatric breakdown under conditions of intense combat.[15] Returning soldiers who had experienced stressful combat readjusted to civilian life much more quickly if they had intimate ties at home than if they lacked such relationships. Soldiers with loved ones at home were less anxious and successfully resumed their jobs and education, whereas those who lacked intimacy were more anxious and had difficulty readjusting to civilian life.[16]

Intimacy was also found to buffer the effects of health crises on stress. In research on women coping with the stress of miscarriages or unanticipated cesarean sections, an intimate partner was found to be a key ingredient in limiting depression.[17] In still another study, mothers of acutely and chronically ill children were less likely to be depressed and anxious if they had an intimate partner. Women who lacked an intimate partner were at appreciably higher risk for these stress reactions. This does not mean it is not normal to be anxious and depressed when your child is ill, but it is at those very times that you must cope most effectively to support your child and family. Intimacy is an important stress resistance resource, enabling women to do the job that has to be done during difficult times.

Intimacy has also been found to be a critical resource in dealing with everyday stress from work and financial and home pressures. Research by Dr. Beth Vanfossen found that an intimate relationship was an important stress buffer for both men and women.[18] Showing confidence in your partner was most critical. Those who dealt best with stressful circumstances felt that their partners appreciated them, brought out their best qualities, and helped them become the person they wanted to be.

Intimacy acts as a stress resistance resource in a number of ways. Being accepted by an intimate partner conveys to you that you are valued and wanted, despite your faults or difficulties. It says that your partner is committed to being there with you, which means that you will not have to overcome difficulties and bear the pain of setbacks and defeats by yourself. Dr. Seymour Sarason sees this as a key to building what he calls your "psychological sense of community."[19] An intimate partner also instills confidence by letting you know that he or she believes in you and in your ability to master challenges to your resources.[20]

When major losses occur, an intimate loved one is there to mourn with you and nurture you through difficult times. In her book on surviving tragic loss, Dr. Kathryn Cramer shows how your closest ties are a critical resource in working through tragedies, such as the death of a loved one or survival after a personal trauma.[21] Dr. Cramer agrees that intimacy does not work alone, however, but rather is built on the basis of a confident self. Close ties help to instill in you the belief that you can weather even the most terrible storm.

As you can see, intimacy is a critical resource in itself and is also tied to two other key resources that we have considered throughout this book—mastery and self-esteem. As illustrated here, intimacy, mastery, and self-esteem form a triangle of resources. Each promotes the others

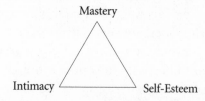

in a gain cycle and diminishes the others in a loss cycle. Thus, being rejected by a partner not only affects the relationship but also our sense of mastery and self-esteem. In contrast, when our self-esteem is heightened, we are more capable of providing intimacy and support to our partner. Because intimacy, mastery, and self-esteem are strong, robust resources (see Chapter 3), they are more resistant to the storm of stress than many others. This creates a kind of breaker wall between our sense of safety and well-being and the raging sea of stress.

Now that we have a better understanding of the nature of intimacy and of the degree of intimacy between you and your partner, let's look at how dual career life challenges intimacy and how we might best withstand that challenge. We will examine how we can preserve the nine C's and build greater intimacy in our lives. Dual career life can be a foundation for greater intimacy, or it can interfere with intimacy at every turn. You must make a commitment to plant the seeds of intimacy and nurture their growth and harvest.

THE FIGHT TO MAINTAIN INTIMACY

There are many aspects of dual career life that may undermine intimacy in your relationship. Let us examine different resource drains that challenge intimacy and try to find ways to counteract them. It is so common to look for the problems in any life-style that you may not realize all the ways in which the dual career life-style can promote intimacy. We need to look for these, too.

Time

When do I love thee? Lack of time seems to be a complaint of all dual career couples. Work pressures, child care, personal interests, and household chores absorb most of your day. Businesses are demanding more of their employees as they strive to become more efficient, and a tough economy means that they can pressure you without too much fear of your leaving the firm. Providing quality and nonquality time to your children takes up another portion of your day. And still the housework isn't done.

Well, you vote with your feet. If intimacy is important, you *must* carve out time to be with each other. Some of this should be family time together with the children. Learn to discuss some topics openly in front of the children—not serious conflicts or last night's bedroom interlude, but your day, your ideas, and, yes, minor conflicts. Children will gain by seeing their parents work through problems in a supportive way and show interest in each other and in them.

However, other time together must be one-on-one. Begin by having at least two dates a week. Make one a going-out date and the other an at-home date when the kids are in bed. One date can include another couple, but not both. We speak to many couples who go out less than once a month, and then usually in company. Make this date time sacred. Show it at least as much respect as you would have for a business date; if you are irresponsible, you risk losing the account!

Do some things together that you might otherwise do separately. We play racquetball together even though we usually play in separate leagues. We take walks together. We clean up the kitchen together. We wrote this book together. Do different things in the same room— she reads, he watches TV. Just being in the same room will produce much more conversation, especially if you make an effort to be in contact. If you are making tea for yourself, make some for him and go and sit down on his lap. You're dangerous with hot tea, so he can't talk back. Make luncheon appointments with her—and keep them!

What we are trying to say is that time is an energy resource that can easily slip through your hands. Or you can take it into your control and use it to your best advantage. Just talking and being together two hours more a week can have an enormously positive effect on your relationship. For many couples we talk to, it more than doubles the quality time they have together.

You think time is a tough issue—well, time is the easy one. Here are some harder ones.

Power and Control

Whenever two people get together in a partnership, the issue of power arises in some form. In a sense, the main purpose of a business contract is to lay out the ground rules for using power and to equalize it. There is no such contract for your relationship with each other—the major partnership of your life.

POTENTIAL POWER CONFLICTS

Dual career relationships affect the balance of power because the woman gains in status by earning income and self-esteem outside the home. But the woman also loses a certain amount of status as the nurturing parent and head of the kitchen. Because men's lives have not been as altered by the dual career family, their status changes less than women's. According to sociologists, the major adjustment for men was the migration from the agricultural economy of rural areas to the industrial economy of cities. In the dual career revolution, the main adjustment men must make is to changes in women's status. In other words, his power in the relationship changes because he and his partner are now on a more equal footing.

Often our partners gain certain powers by mutual consent: You handle the insurance; I'll do the kids' baths and the mutual funds. You do the dishes and decide when we need a car; I'll take care of home repairs. However, using power in a way that is not mutually agreed on undermines intimacy. It's okay for the man to wear the pants in the family, if you both agree to it. Many couples have high levels of intimacy within traditional male-female roles. Likewise, a woman may make the financial decisions, as long as her partner agrees to the arrangement. However, when the use of power is not in keeping with spoken or tacit agreements, intimacy is challenged.

Research on marital relationships suggests that those in which power is equally shared have the least conflict and provide the greatest satisfaction.[22] Both men and women say they want fairly equal power in their marriage. However, men want it a little more in their favor. Even this slightly tipped scale can be the basis for a harmonious relationship, because women tend to be a little less concerned about power than men. However, if the scales are more than a little out of balance, intimacy suffers.

Power issues most often arise when the woman wants a more equitable relationship and the man wants a more traditional relationship. As a group, women are more liberal than men about gender roles, and many couples find themselves in this situation:

Edwin and Abigail were both traditional when they married. However, Abigail became increasingly liberated through both her work and her involvement as a volunteer in a traditional women's church group that supported a rape-crisis shelter. She was very much affected by what she saw in these women's lives.

Edwin was clearly threatened by Abigail's increasing independence. This conflict came to a head when Abigail started to earn more than Edwin and behave in a somewhat distant fashion. He became uncharacteristically controlling, calling her at work over minor household issues, taking less responsibility for child care, and making a number of financial moves without her knowledge. It was as if her larger salary was an assault on his manhood, which he countered by being more traditionally masculine in other areas. On introspection, Abigail came to understand that she was villainizing Edwin and punishing him for rapes committed by other men on other women, which he found as abhorrent as she did. She was doing this precisely at the time when he needed her assurance that her increased independence did not mean she didn't love and need him.

GREATER INTIMACY FROM SHARING POWER

If you can be comfortable sharing power more equally, a dual career relationship has great advantages for intimacy. In traditional relationships, male and female roles are like those of parent and child. When it comes to work, finance, and major decisions, the man is the parent and the woman is the child—father knows best and father decides. If the man is the head of the household, mom's position is down with the children or somewhere between dad and the children. In either case, she is not an adult. When it comes to the household, the tables are turned—dad is the child and mom is the parent. She scolds him for leaving underwear on the floor, for not helping to clean up, and for not getting his Mr. Fix-It jobs done. In the Blondie cartoon, Blondie is constantly after Dagwood to get his jobs from the job jar done. She is in the nagging mom role and he is the delinquent child. The result of this conflict is that the resentment between men and women increases and intimacy is lost. The intimacy between two adults is fuller and more mature than the intimacy between a man and woman alternating in the roles of parent and child.

In every relationship there are some unresolved power issues. Experience tells us that whatever the level of power conflict in your relationship, you have a better chance of gaining intimacy if you put the issues on the table. Discuss your feelings and how the situation is bothering you. Often the need for power arises when one or both partners feel insecure in the relationship. Be sure to express clearly your need for and commitment to your partner. This is especially important when the balance of power in your relationship is changing because of work, children, or your own personal growth.

Self-Disclosure

WHY IS SELF-DISCLOSURE IMPORTANT?

We refer to self-disclosure as "confession" in the nine C's. Close relationships are characterized by a high level of self-disclosure. Dr. Sidney Jourard reached this conclusion in pioneering research on the degree to which people disclose their heartfelt thoughts, feelings, and concerns.[23] Such disclosure engenders intimacy. By sharing their innermost selves, people invite us to be closer to them and tell us that we are trusted not to harm them. We know their areas of weakness and are expected to protect them and never use that knowledge against them, even when we are angry or hurt and certainly never in front of others.

There are some important differences between men and women when it comes to self-disclosure. It is not so much that women disclose more than men as that they disclose different things. Men are more likely to talk about their opinions and thoughts, whereas women are more likely to air their emotions and feelings.[23] Unfortunately, this can make for a kind of apples-and-pears conversation. In the realm of intimacy, it is the sharing of feelings and emotions that encourages intimacy,[13, 23] not the sharing of political viewpoints or even outlooks on life. This gives women a certain advantage because they are more comfortable disclosing such things.

What women may be bad at, however, is expressing their needs. Partly because of the supermom syndrome and partly because of their role as nurturer, many women have difficulty in this area. In the sexual realm, expressing needs has been associated in women with "loose" morals, and this has encouraged women to be more submissive in the bedroom. Likewise, in the family room, women have been taught to attend to others' needs. It is hard for many women to say they need more of this or that from their partner. Women may even devalue support and affection if they are not given spontaneously. Because they have been taught to be so sensitive to everyone else's needs, they expect their partners to be the same way. Many women tell Ivonne in therapy, "If I have to ask for affection or help, it is not 'true' affection. Why should I have to ask for love?"

So both men and women have something to learn: Men need to learn to disclose their feelings and share their fears. Women need to disclose their needs and be more accepting of the support that follows.

HOW DO DUAL CAREERS AFFECT SELF-DISCLOSURE?

The traditional single career life-style limits self-disclosure on a number of different planes. Many men report that they do not want to disturb their wives with work problems. In a way, these men are treating their wives like children. Perhaps there was some validity to their argument when women did not work outside the home and had less experience separating office politics from real job problems. Dr. Robert Weiss interviewed seventy-five men and found that they felt their stay-at-home wives would overreact to their job difficulties or not give helpful advice.[24] For women at home who depend on their husband's income, problems at work may be particularly threatening.

In dual career couples, in contrast, the spouses are resources for one another and can share work concerns and receive helpful feedback. With two incomes, the temporary loss of one income is less threatening, so each partner can share with less fear of upsetting the other.

However, work can limit self-disclosure if you are in a job that discourages the sharing of feelings and emotions. This is particularly likely for men or women who work in jobs traditionally associated with either gender. "Men's occupations," such as engineering and business, discourage sharing on the emotional level and encourage "rational" discussion, void of emotions. "Women's occupations," such as social work and nursing, are nurturing, sharing professions by nature. They are not irrational, but integrate rational thinking with the emotional content of people's lives. These traditional male and female professions may instill in men and women an even stronger division along gender lines in how they disclose their feelings. Engineers and social workers bring home their work personalities, and this may result in a greater communication gap than might otherwise have existed.

When women work in traditional male occupations, they may be asked to sacrifice their feelings and be more like men. When talk at work about family and feelings is given short shrift, women learn to suppress this part of themselves, at least at work. As a result, neither partner may be capable of or comfortable with self-disclosure at home, further limiting intimacy.

Cynthia and Ben, both attorneys, were experiencing significant communication problems. In marital counseling, we could not get over how much they spoke to each other as if they were preparing legal briefs. Neither spoke spontaneously, and each word was carefully chosen for its possible "legal" implications. When either misspoke, his or her words were thrown back like a sprung trap. Like the good attorneys they were, they kept their cards close to the chest. The consequence was that neither knew what the other felt, thought, or wanted. They only knew their "liability," what they owed each other.

Cynthia and Ben's profession was severely hampering their ability to share with each other. Their profession did not create the problem (they probably chose law precisely because they were like this already), but it confirmed that it was unsafe to be open and that you could not trust others.

A dual career life-style can enhance self-disclosure by increasing compatibility. Now that you are both experiencing the work-a-day and home-a-day worlds, you have more in common. It is no longer the case that all she has to talk about is diapers and dust and all he has to talk about is money and management. You share many work experiences, you are out among interesting (and not so interesting) people, and you have the same kinds of good and bad days. Your family concerns are also more similar. How are your children doing in school or with the babysitter? Who can pick up Lauren for her dental appointment on Tuesday? When will the lawn get mowed? Even if everything is not exactly the same at work and exactly equal at home, inevitably there is much more overlap in your responsibilities, concerns, and experiences. This should translate into easier self-disclosure and more mutual interest, which encourages further disclosure.

Work as a Direct Challenge to Intimacy

Work may be a direct challenge to intimacy by absorbing the resources that are necessary for intimacy's growth and sustenance. Our culture values the family on one level, but it also undermines the family in many ways. Successful people in business often tell us that if they showed any sign that their families come before work, their careers would be jeopardized. A good employee is expected to travel at the company's behest, move when the company requires it, work until it is convenient for the company that he or she go home, and take work home to infringe on family time if that is in the company's best interest. Doing otherwise means you are on the "mommy track," whether you are a mom or a dad, a husband or a wife.

By making these demands, work challenges a number of the nine C's necessary for intimacy. Caring is challenged because you must decide whether to stay at work, travel, or move without regard to the needs of your partner or family. Cohesion and commitment are challenged because work demands your allegiance. Confidence in your partner is undermined as well. When you put so many resources into your job, it often prevents you from supporting your partner in his or her job.

Sebastian was a rising star at the university. He also tried to be a devoted husband and father. He considered Joy's career to be important and supported her in it. However, his job made this very difficult. Staying at the university depended on his getting tenure, and his university did not give it easily. At the same time, he was increasingly placed on departmental and university committees.

To write the necessary research papers, prepare his courses properly, and serve on committees, Sebastian had to work many evenings and weekends. He often left early in the morning and came home late. He felt in a bind. He knew that his schedule meant he was supporting Joy less and less and that the burden of child care and housework fell on her. On the other hand, he also knew that if he did not publish more, he would not receive tenure and he would lose his position.

Sebastian's dilemma is a common one for both men and women on the fast track at work today. In many positions, in fact, you will be on the "unemployment track" if you fail to put in extra hours and by so doing ignore the support you owe your partner and family. It is true of academia, health care, law, business, plumbing, and retail—competition is up across all work sectors. Perhaps it is a coincidence, but it seems that just when women are making gains in the workplace, both men and women are being asked to put in more hours and work harder. This call to arms challenges the family and results in both the loss and redirection of resources required for intimacy. Just when women need more support from their partners, their partners are less capable of providing it.

In Sebastian's department, the successful men and women were those who spent most of their days, nights, and weekends working. For many of the women, this meant not having children; for the men, it was more likely to mean ignoring their families. Joy was a psychologist at the university's medical school, and she saw the spouses and children of many of Sebastian's colleagues in therapy.

Sebastian and Joy decided that he should seek employment at a less high-powered university, so that they would be better able to balance their intimacy and family needs with work demands.

Work, Children, and Guilt

When work is over and they are finally home, dual career parents must attend to the needs and demands of their children. Everyone has been made very aware by the media that both fathers and mothers must participate in child care. In Chapter 9 we address how best to allocate your resources to meet your children's needs amidst your other demands, but for now we consider how children can get in the way of intimacy with your partner.

Women, especially, may feel a knot of guilt when they devote precious resources at work instead of on their children's behalf. The more committed they are to work, the greater the conflict. Men, having become more aware of their children's needs for their attention, are now spending more time with them. We do not want only to meet our children's basic needs for food and clean clothes, we want to spend time with them, help them with their homework, cheer them on at Little League, and read to them at bedtime.

As men become more nurturing, their partners' feelings of guilt may increase. If you are a mother, imagine your child falling down and cutting his knee and running past you into his daddy's arms. Do you feel good because dad is such a loving father, or bad because your commitment to work has caused your child to look to dad for comfort? Perhaps you feel both. In blended families, these feelings may be exacerbated if mom sees her biological child being nurtured by his or her stepparent; she may feel threatened by the challenge to her unequivocal role as chief and sole nurturer. We often hear about men feeling threatened if their partners earn more, but women may feel threatened if their partners nurture more.

For all of us, the combination of children and work can drain resources that are essential for intimacy between partners. Children thrive when their parents have an intimate relationship, and although they may jealously compete for both your attention, they will suffer if they completely succeed.

This is a tough balance to achieve, but it is essential to the intimacy between the two of you as partners and lovers and between the two of you and the children. Allocate time and energy to both your partner and your children. Make some times sacred for both, and honor your commitments. Some of this can be accomplished through family time when everyone is together, but your partner needs your undivided attention as well.

_____

June was anxious about balancing work and family. She was anxious at work because she felt she was depriving her daughter Bethany; she was anxious at home because she felt she was not as committed as she should be to preparing her classes. She had a hard time separating from Bethany, and Bethany herself had become an anxious, worried child. She began to be able to sleep only in her parents' bed. At first, Bethany would be returned to her own room when June and Dan came to bed. But then she began waking up and crying. For the past four months, Bethany had been sleeping between her parents most nights. Needless to say, this was hampering Dan and June's sex life and intimacy.

You must set limits on the time you spend at work, with your children, and with your partner. Your partner might come last, because the demands of work and children are more obviously pressing. All the more reason why you must strive to develop intimacy with your partner. You must spend time as a couple, talk openly when you have the chance, provide emotional support, and help with tasks. If the two of you are intimate, you will be better parents. If intimacy is lacking, you risk creating an unsafe emotional environment for your children.

Social Support and Intimacy

Perhaps the most important thing you can do to increase intimacy in your relationship is to provide your partner with social support. The work of Drs. Barbara Sarason and Irwin Sarason has blazed a clear trail of understanding about the interconnectedness of intimacy and social support.[25, 26] Social support is a critical tool in preserving the family during times of stress. It includes both communicating emotional support and providing help with tasks. It's how we show that we care and will be there for each other. We discussed this resource in depth earlier in the book, and now we wish to relate it to intimacy.

Once again, dual career relationships have a decided advantage over single career relationships. Because both of you have work and home responsibilities, you have a better understanding of the support each of you needs. Thus you can anticipate each other's needs and provide the right kind of support. Men are learning to nurture their children and in so doing are taking a crash course in being more nurturing in general. As a result, they can more easily be nurturing of their partners. Women are learning more about office politics, finance, work pressures, and work challenges. This allows them to support their partners more fully. Support often comes out of empathy—the ability to put yourself in the other person's shoes. By sharing so many roles, you both not only know in general what the other needs; you can feel what the other feels when support is needed. You are much less likely to minimize the stress your partner is experiencing, either at work or at home, because you've been there. You yourself have survived a period of conflict with a power-mad boss, and you yourself have survived three hours with a power-mad two-year-old.

PROVIDING SOCIAL SUPPORT

Years of careful research on social support give insights into how best to offer and receive social support. Based on this research[25-27] and our clinical experience, we wish to share with you the secrets of successfully providing and accepting support.

Emotional support and the sharing of tasks are both essential. Emotional support means

- Listening to your partner and being a sounding board, rather than lecturing and being a know-it-all
- Making it clear that you stand behind your partner
- Saying that you believe in your partner and in his or her ability to succeed and master difficulties
- Making it clear that you love your partner and will be with him or her through thick and thin

- Offering a shoulder to cry on and being there during hard times
- Expressing the importance of your partner to you and to the family
- Being available to hear about your partner's dreams, problems, and fears
- Showing interest in who your partner is and what he or she wants to be

Research indicates that without intimacy, help with tasks is not considered important.[28] The message is clear: First you must support your partner's need for self-esteem and mastery, your partner's belief that he or she is valued and has a special relationship to you and your family.

Although not as crucial as emotional support, help with tasks is also important. Task support includes all the help with housework and child care that we discuss in Chapter 7. It also involves other tasks that may arise through work, community activities, or special problems.

LEARNING TO INVITE AND ACCEPT SUPPORT

There is a catch to social support, however: We have to be willing to ask for it and accept it. Sometimes it is offered spontaneously, but that cannot and should not be depended on. Our needs change, and unless our partners are mind readers, then they cannot know just what we want or need and when we want or need it.

Both men and women have problems asking for help, but the problems come from different sources. Many men were taught to be independent and tough. Any request for help that might suggest dependence or weakness will be resisted. Many women, in contrast, tend to figure out when others need their support. Hence, they expect their partners to know when they need support. We have heard so many women say, "If I have to ask him for help, the help is meaningless."

Both men and women have to change their perceptions and understand that the gift is in the willingness to help and be helped. You express intimacy by helping, because you are saying that you love your partner enough to make his or her needs a priority. You also express intimacy by asking for help, because you are saying that you trust your partner to meet your needs and protect you when you are vulnerable. This is the stuff on which intimacy is built. In a sense, it is what this book is all about.

INTIMACY, SEXUALITY, INTIMACY . . .

Sexuality in a long-term relationship depends on intimacy. Intimacy creates the desire to be physically close to your partner. Sharing your sexual self, in turn, develops greater intimacy. The movies have it wrong. Meaningful sex does not begin with a steamy scene; it begins with being intimate. By being open sexually, you are inviting your partner to share your closest feelings and vulnerabilities. You are at your most vulnerable when naked in each other's arms. But if you are loved and cared for, you feel safest at those same moments.

Sexual problems can interfere with intimacy. There are two parts to our nervous system, the sympathetic and parasympathetic systems: One controls "action" and the other controls "play"—rest, relaxation, and sexual response. Work, rushing, and responsibilities activate the action system. On vacation, you not only have more time for sex, you may feel more sensuous because the action system is turned off and the play system is turned on. Clearly, your dual career life-style activates the action system to the detriment of the play system.

We often work so hard at our careers that we go right past the play stage into the exhaustion stage. We are too tired to be sexual. Many couples find themselves at this exhausted stage all the time. If they have sex at all, it's "Let's do it and get it done with." "If it takes more than ten minutes, I may not still be awake. Oh, shoot, I forgot to make the kids' lunches and call the school."

Don't wait until you are so tired that sex is a drudgery, or even worse, there is no time for it. Get to bed a little earlier, sneak away on Saturday afternoon, wake up a half-hour earlier on Sunday morning. Intimacy requires physical closeness—touching during the day, holding during the night, sexual play, involvement, and lovemaking. It begins with sharing a household, moves on to sharing housework, and culminates in sharing your lover's bed. You should be awake for some of the bed part. You need to create and sustain intimacy to sustain love, loving, and lovemaking.

Chapter 9

*Where Do
Children Fit In?*

A *r e* we risking our children's well-being when both parents work outside the home? Evidence from our clinical experience and the research literature is clear: A dual career family can be a superb environment in which to raise healthy, psychologically strong children. There is no evidence that single career families have any long-term advantages in raising children over dual career families. This is not to say that there are not some advantages in both family types when it comes to child rearing, but the advantages and disadvantages of either life-style appear secondary to the other family characteristics that we discuss in this chapter.

We want to devote as many resources as possible to the care and nurturing of our children. In dual career families, there are many obstacles to raising children in a loving, responsible manner. In the single career family, there is one parent whose primary responsibility is to care for the children. Usually this is the mother, but in an increasing number of households men are choosing to stay home, at least during the child's early development.

Most dual career parents, including us, worry about whether day care and babysitters can substitute for a parent. We are concerned about our children being left alone before or after school. We feel guilty about being tired in the evening when we finally return from work. And what about the other household responsibilities? Dinner has to be made, clothes must be washed, and dirt, dust, and disarray can only be ignored for so long.

In this chapter we discuss how you can best apply your resources to promote your children's well-being. We look at how family intimacy and welfare can thrive in a dual career household and what the keys are to success. We also examine some potential child-rearing problems that may threaten your children's well-being and best interests. Rather than merely leave you with more worries, we look at solutions to these problems as well.

RESOURCES THAT CHILDREN NEED

Children require many of the same resources that we reviewed in earlier chapters for adults. Naturally, we need to translate these into children's terms. Where adults need challenging work, children need their school and home lives to be stimulating and challenging. Where we need supportive employers, they need supportive teachers and caretakers. Where adults need control over their lives in a broad sense, infants need to feel that their cries will provoke a response, giving them a feeling of control over their environment. Adults often need peace and stability. Children need these things, too, but they will make do with an environment that is somewhat chaotic, as long as it provides safety, love, and stability. The resources required by children also depend on their developmental stage. Our kids recently made a plea for personal credit cards, but if this appears on the children's resource list in this chapter, then they have been tampering with the computer again. Children *do not* require credit cards!

Let's look at four key resources that children need:

- Protection/safety
- Comfort
- Primary provider(s) of sustenance and nurturing
- Secondary provider(s) of sustenance and nurturing

The need for protection and safety is often associated with infants and young children. We would encourage you to think about the ways in which adolescents need them as well. AIDS, crime, the economy—these problems threaten today's teenagers, in addition to perennial threats like rejection by peers, the challenges of young love, and difficulties in school. Although your role becomes more supervisory and supportive as your children grow, even teenagers who claim to want total independence need your support and protection. They need to know that the family is a place of acceptance and refuge. They need you to set limits and define age-appropriate rules and regulations that you will stand by and expect them to follow.

Children also need a high degree of comfort. This does not mean they need fancy furniture or to be picked up and coddled at every moment. Rather, they need to know that their comfort is being watched out for and that they will receive consistent support from their parents and caretakers. When we were "exchange parents" for a Russian girl, Nika, we learned that many Soviet city dwellers had chosen to have only one child so that they could provide as much comfort as possible despite deprivation. Mom may have stood in line for food and clothing twenty hours a week, but the children had their needs met to the extent possible. Indeed, many of these children did not know about their parents' deprivations, they were so sheltered by the comfort they were provided. Our Russian daughter thought life was good in Moscow, while her mother grimaced both at the thought and at her daughter's naivete. But Nika's mother was doing what working parents try to do everywhere: protect and comfort their children. Parents provide comfort by material means and by their attempt to meet the children's physical and emotional needs whenever possible, often before their own. Comfort is provided by warm, loving arms that encircle the child and offer affection and caring. Comfort comes from working long hours or standing in endless Moscow lines, and making the food on the table seem as if it were easily obtained.

A great deal of research on the importance of "attachment figures" (that is, adults with whom the child has a close relationship) tells us that children need strong attachments to a primary adult.[1, 2] There is every indication that a close-knit group of a few adults may also afford this basic resource for the infant and young child.[3] The attachment figure needs to be available and responsive to the child's needs. Most research on children's primary attachment focuses on mother-child relationships, but there is increasing awareness of the importance of a supportive father. A strong, primary attachment to an adult must be viewed as a critical resource for infants and children.

Secondary providers of sustenance and nurturing, such as child-care workers, teachers, and grandparents, are an additional resource for children. Like the primary attachment figures, these secondary caretakers should provide warmth, comfort, and protection. They should be responsive to the child's needs and provide a stable, predictable environment. For the dual career family, these secondary providers are a critical resource because we depend on them to be there for our children when our careers make demands on our own time.

PARENTAL ROLE SATISFACTION AND MUTUAL SUPPORT AS CHILDREN'S RESOURCES

So far we have focused on your resources, household division of labor, and intimacy between you and your partner, setting aside child care. And we did so with good reason: Research findings are not clear on the effects on children of dual career parents. However, there is agreement on the effects of role satisfaction and work load on your children. Role satisfaction is the degree to which you are satisfied with what you do, whether you work outside the home, as a homemaker, or some combination of the two. This role satisfaction (as a breadwinner and a parent) and the mutual support you have developed with your partner are additional resources for your child. It is also important for you to be comfortable with day-care arrangements for both you and your child to have a successful day-care experience.

Mothers who are satisfied with their role as a dual career parent or homemaker do better as parents.[4, 5] Their children are better socially adjusted and better off psychologically. Indeed, the most at-risk group may be children of mothers who prefer to work but stay home out of a sense of duty.[4] The ability to offer love and nurturing, on the one hand, and to encourage autonomy and independence, on the other, requires high self-esteem and a sense of mastery in the parent. If a woman lacks these qualities, she is likely to be an anxious or distant parent, and this will have negative consequences for the child. There has been no research on how it affects dad to stay at home when he wants to work outside, but we cannot imagine that his experience would be any different from that of women in the same situation.

Laura wanted to work outside the home. However, she also felt that a mother should be at home. When she turned to her own mother for support, her mother suggested that, by taking a few years off, Laura could do her best for the baby and then go back to her career if she still wanted to. Her husband was ambivalent. He felt they needed the extra money, but he also liked the idea of her being home with the baby. Laura stayed home.

Laura worked hard at being a good mother, but she became increasingly depressed. The baby was colicky and often cried. Laura tried to nurse but did not have enough milk, and the baby rejected the breast. When Laura tried to comfort her, the baby would hardly respond, and tended to cry herself to sleep. So did Laura. She felt like a failure as a mother and a wife. She couldn't even handle her child; other mothers seemed to do it, why couldn't she? Laura gained twenty-five pounds over a six-month period, stopped exercising, and constantly felt tired. Her physician told her it was a normal response to the postpregnancy period. When she turned to her husband for support, he said they should take a wait-and-see attitude, and she would probably feel better soon.

Luckily, Laura found support in some friends who had gone through a similar experience. With their encouragement, and before she slipped into a deep depression, she called her old employer and asked if she could return to work. Her boss was overjoyed, as Laura's replacement had not worked out. A week later, she had arranged for child care with a woman who had a three-year-old and loved being home with the children. With Laura working, the baby became more responsive and Laura lost fifteen pounds. She was much happier as a mother and felt she had found the right combination. Her husband was rather passive about the issue, but felt if that was what she needed, he was all for it. Her mother disapproved of her working and let her know it. Interestingly, her mother-in-law was the most supportive member of the family, and she and Laura became closer as a result.

You might think that women who prefer to be caretakers but must work outside the home would have problems with child rearing. Research does not indicate this, however.[4] Research and our clinical experience suggest that such women are highly motivated to spend time with their children when they do come home. They may feel guilty and dissatisfied about having to work, but they make sure they spend time with their children when they can. The amount of time is not as important as its quality, and as homemakers do not necessarily spend more time with their children, employed moms may be able to make up for lost time. Working moms who prefer to be home can still meet most of their goals, but homemakers who want a career are cut off from reaching many of their goals by not being employed.

———

Tammy would have liked to stay home with her children, but finances did not permit it. After being out of work for a year, her husband had finally found a job that paid somewhat less than he had earned before. They were both rather traditional, but Jim was thankful that Tammy had a job and showed his appreciation by helping as much as he could around the house. He said his buddies could just "kiss off" if they had something to say about it. Ideally, he wanted Tammy to stay home but felt that until he earned much more, her working was heaven-sent. Meanwhile, he idolized Tammy for what he felt was her sacrifice.

Tammy switched employers to one with an on-site day-care program. This allowed her to spend lunchtimes with her youngest, Karen. When she arrived home, she made spending time with her five-year-old, Lance, a priority. She would take the two children to the playground, get out a game, or read to them for an hour before preparing dinner. After dinner, she would leave the dishes and laundry for later and spend more time with the kids until they went to bed. Jim was better with Lance than with Karen, and he spent more time playing this or that ball game with him.

After the kids were asleep, Jim and Tammy would clean up together. Often, Jim would make Tammy sit down at the kitchen table while he cleaned up. This was a big turnon for Tammy (the handsome man washing dishes routine), and they had sex on the kitchen table more than once. Jim made her feel very loved and taken care of when he made her stop working at the end of her long day. She was very aroused by his display of love.

Family time was always a high priority on weekends. Jim played in a softball and a bowling league, and spent weekends catching up on the lawn and repairs, but he often took their older child with him. Tammy reserved her time for the kids. She continued to feel guilty about working, and probably should have taken a little more time for herself. But her guilt ensured that the children received maximum attention from her.

Even children who spend much of their day in day care still have a significant primary attachment to their mother.[3, 6] The question is how capable the mother is of providing quality time to foster that attachment. Here household labor becomes an issue. If the "second shift" falls disproportionately on the woman, she is diverted by other tasks, just when she could be spending time with the children.[7] In this situation, both mother and child feel the effects of their forced separation—first by work and day care, then by home labor. This can have serious deleterious effects, on both the child and the mother, as each needs time with the other.

Men's part in this situation is a bit different. Those who work full time tend to work more hours than their partners and farther from home, which increases commuting time.[8] Men who support their partners by providing emotional support for them as wage earners and mothers and by sharing household tasks set the stage for maximizing positive parent-child interaction.[5] We have emphasized that a significant part of the father's role in household labor should be in the realm of child care, which means that a strong father-child attachment should emerge. We might add that although fathers seldom seek to be the primary attachment figure, this is an increasing trend. If the father is the primary attachment figure in your family, then the formula of what we are saying should probably be reversed, giving the father the primary role and the mother the supportive role.

When the mother feels guilty about leaving her children to go to work, the father's role becomes all the more important. A woman will naturally turn to her partner for approval and support of her roles as mother and breadwinner. The benefits of working for women have been found to depend on this support.[9, 10] When a woman does not get the full support of her own or her partner's parents for working outside the home, as is often the case, her partner's support becomes all the more significant. As we point out in Chapter 7, just saying you support her decision and then leaving her with all the housework and child care is tantamount to saying, "You're really alone on this one, baby. You want to work, fine, but I'm not getting bent out of shape to do anything more."

What does a woman need to provide her partner as men's roles also change? In Dr. Lisa Silberstein's recent study,[11] many of the men reported being ribbed about doing "women's work." A man who chooses to be less than fully driven in his career may see other men, not as committed to their families or with wives who stay at home to support the household, rise faster. Men desperately need their partner's support for such a choice. If a man's contribution is never good enough, or quite enough, or quite right, then he will avoid offering support and instead seek the kudos the work world provides. If you would rather see a handsome man do dishes than dance naked, you'd better make clear your love and lust for the guy at the sink.

THE CHILDREN'S RESOURCE LIST

Having considered the special resources needed by children, and their being somewhat different from the resources needed by adults (see Chapter 3), we can present the children's resource list. As in the adult version, some of the resources on the resource list for children are less primary than others. In particular, love, security, and affection can make up for extra clothes and toys. We also distinguish in this version between internal and external resources. Internal resources are those held within the child's self, such as self-esteem and a sense of mastery. External resources are those that exist in the child's environment, such as family stability, shelter, and love.

Take the time here to complete the questionnaire on children's resources: Do Our Kids Have It All? (Again, each partner should make an assessment and then compare the two.) To what extent does your child have each of the external resources listed? Don't worry too much about whether he has expensive, name-brand tennis shoes (even if he worries about it). Concentrate instead on nurturing, comfort, stability, and safety. Now look at the internal resources. To what extent is your child developing an age-appropriate armament of these resources? When you think about identity, don't expect your child to know exactly who she is and what she wants to be at the precious age of six. At that age, identity means knowing she is loved, knowing her place in the family, and being happy with being a little girl. Existential introspection and discussions of Nietzsche will come later.

No, we are not going to give you a way to score your child's resources. You should have a good sense by now that all the items listed (excluding extra material resources) are important. You should strive to maximize these resources and look for solutions wherever a resource is lacking.

HOW WE CREATE CHILDREN'S RESOURCES

Children's internal resources, to a large extent, grow out of the external resources that you provide or that are otherwise imparted by their environment. As dual career parents, you probably have questions about how the demands of job and home influence the intimacy, love, stability, and social support of your children's environment. In particular, you are likely to be concerned about the number of hours you are away from home and how your children are affected by your absence and the care arrangements you have made for them. In this section we discuss problems that arise and how you can prevent or combat them. We begin with your children in infancy and progress (well, some would call it progressing) to their teenage years. First, however, you should know some of the most serious danger signals.

A Special Note: Danger Signs

Before we get into the specifics of children's resources, we want to make mention of some important considerations. Be watchful for danger signs in your children. When these signs emerge, it is unlikely that they are caused by your dual career life-style (although this may somehow be interacting with other problems they are having). When any of these signs appear, seek professional advice and help. We recommend consulting with a mental health professional in your community. Alternatively, you may feel more comfortable speaking with a minister or family physician first.

The signs to watch out for are numerous. They include depression or anxiety; hyperactivity; grades well below the child's ability; aggressive or inappropriate behavior at play, in school, or at home; and frequent tantrums or behavior that you feel is out of your control and dangerous or inappropriate. Sleep disorders may also indicate deeper psychological problems. These include difficulty falling asleep, nightmares, inability to sleep alone, and grinding of teeth or bodily tension during sleep. Children also may express fears to you, and these may be quite normal. However, if a child uses these fears to explain an inability to do ordinary things, that is cause for seeking help. Also, if the fears really bother the child, it can be a sign of deeper problems than a self-help book can address. Frequent stomach problems, problems with eating or swallowing, or other physical complaints should be checked with a physician.

In older children and teenagers, social isolation; association with children you consider delinquent; signs of alcohol or drug use; suicidal

WORK WON'T LOVE YOU BACK

Partner *1*

Do Our Kids Have It All?
Children's Primary Resources

Rating

EXTERNAL RESOURCES

Mother who is satisfied with her role . . . . _____

Father who is satisfied with his role . . . . _____

Parents who provide mutual support . . . . _____

Protection/safety . . . . _____

Comfort (that is, someone available to provide comfort) . . . . _____

Primary provider(s) of sustenance and nurturance . . . . _____

Secondary provider(s) of sustenance and nurturance . . . . . . _____

Time for adequate sleep . . . . _____

Family stability . . . . _____

Adequate clothing . . . . _____

Intimacy with parents (affection and communication) . . . . . _____

Time with loved ones . . . . _____

Necessary school supplies . . . . _____

Positively challenging routine . . . . _____

Adequate food . . . . _____

Stable care outside the home . . . . _____

Intimacy with siblings . . . . _____

Acknowledgment of accomplishments . . . . _____

Friends (increasingly important with age) . . . . _____

Understanding and nurturing caretakers and teachers . . . . . . _____

Affection from others . . . . _____

Help with school tasks . . . . _____

INTERNAL RESOURCES

Feeling part of a social group or family . . . . _____

Feeling successful (feeling that he or she has and can succeed) . _____

Positive self-esteem (feeling of self-worth) . . . . _____

Age-appropriate goals . . . . _____

Positive identity (emerges with age) . . . . _____

Independence (age-appropriate and always with backup support) _____

Ability to communicate well . . . . _____

Feeling that life is not overly chaotic . . . . _____

Optimism . . . . _____

Health . . . . _____

Feeling of control . . . . _____

Pride . . . . _____

Hope . . . . _____

Feeling valuable to others . . . . _____

Partner 2

Do Our Kids Have It All?
Children's Primary Resources

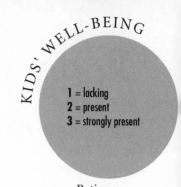

Rating

EXTERNAL RESOURCES

Mother who is satisfied with her role . . . .   _____
Father who is satisfied with his role . . . .   _____
Parents who provide mutual support . . . .   _____
Protection/safety . . . .   _____
Comfort (that is, someone available to provide comfort) . . .   _____
Primary provider(s) of sustenance and nurturance . . . .   _____
Secondary provider(s) of sustenance and nurturance . . . . . .   _____
Time for adequate sleep . . . .   _____
Family stability . . . .   _____
Adequate clothing . . . .   _____
Intimacy with parents (affection and communication) . . . . .   _____
Time with loved ones . . . .   _____
Necessary school supplies . . . .   _____
Positively challenging routine . . . .   _____
Adequate food . . . .   _____
Stable care outside the home . . . .   _____
Intimacy with siblings . . . .   _____
Acknowledgment of accomplishments . . . .   _____
Friends (increasingly important with age) . . . .   _____
Understanding and nurturing caretakers and teachers . . . . .   _____
Affection from others . . . .   _____
Help with school tasks . . . .   _____

INTERNAL RESOURCES

Feeling part of a social group or family . . . .   _____
Feeling successful (feeling that he or she has and can succeed) .   _____
Positive self-esteem (feeling of self-worth) . . . .   _____
Age-appropriate goals . . . .   _____
Positive identity (emerges with age) . . . .   _____
Independence (age-appropriate and always with backup support)   _____
Ability to communicate well . . . .   _____
Feeling that life is not overly chaotic . . . .   _____
Optimism . . . .   _____
Health . . . .   _____
Feeling of control . . . .   _____
Pride . . . .   _____
Hope . . . .   _____
Feeling valuable to others . . . .   _____

thoughts, plans, or actions; and their own acknowledgment of problems should be taken seriously. We are amazed at how many parents fail to take action when their children show warning signs quite clearly. If in doubt, ask a professional's opinion.

Now let's get back to building children's resources.

Maternity Leave and Paternity Leave

There are many excellent reasons for maternity leave, for both the infant and the mother. We have heard stories about superwomen who returned to work two or three days, or even the day after, delivery. At a recent workshop for academic women who had young children or were hoping to soon, such stories were greeted with anger. They were angry that women should be expected to return to work when they still lack strength after the difficulty of labor and delivery. They were angry that women should feel pressured to leave their infants so soon and return to tough, full-time jobs. They were even angry that these women told them their "war stories," as it implied that they should follow suit. They appreciated the pressures on the "pioneer generation" of executive women but did not want these same pressures placed on them.

Maternity leave allows for a resource rejuvenation period. Physical and emotional resources are drained after giving birth. Vaginal deliveries are exhausting, and women are typically already overtired before they begin. Cesarean sections are carried out in a quarter to a third of all births in North America. They are major surgeries and require considerable recovery time. We seldom think about it this way, but the newborn baby has also been through a heck of a battle. He or she was either squashed down a narrow canal or, in the case of cesarean sections, heavily anesthetized (via the mother). Although most births are called "healthy," some medical complication is involved in more than half of pregnancies and deliveries.[12] Modern medicine minimizes the negative consequences of these complications, but they still take a toll on the resources of mother and child.

Both mother and infant need time for recovery and bonding after the birth.

Ivonne gave birth to our youngest child, Jonathan, by cesarean section. After the delivery, Jonathan stopped breathing—a common effect of anesthesia on the newborn. His head was shaved on one side and an I.V. tube was inserted into a vein close to the surface of the skull. He was placed in intensive care overnight for observation.

In the morning when they brought him to Ivonne, he did not look great. With his half-shaven head, he looked like a punk rocker or a miniature Mr. Magoo. After two previous newborn beauties, Ivonne doubted he was hers. Luckily, he received the "most-improved" award, but we also think he received a lot of extra cuddling to make up for his and Ivonne's initial shock.

It is usually suggested that a parent—probably the mother because of her own physical needs (recovery, nursing)—be maximally available to the infant during the first three months. Developmental psychologists and physicians believe that this initial bonding period is critical to the child's future adjustment. Children who develop secure attachments are better adjusted socially, less anxious, higher achievers at school, and subject to fewer disciplinary problems.[13–15]

Paternity leave is an increasingly popular option, although still not common. Our best information about paternity leave comes from the Scandinavian countries, where state law has provided this option for some years. Paternity leave is usually used, it turns out, to support maternity leave and the woman's return to work.[16] It is typical for the two parents to split parental leave, allowing the mother to take the first half. The father then steps in to care for the somewhat older infant, and the mother returns to work.

We need to learn much more about paternity leave, but we believe that paternity leave may offer an excellent backup to maternity leave. However, we think that a mother has special biological needs, especially if she is breast-feeding, having to do with her own recovery from pregnancy that are not addressed by paternity leave. The way that the Scandinavians have responded to the option of equal parental leave seems to support our contention about the mother's needs following childbirth. Again, however, discussion between you and your partner will help you decide what is best in your own case.

Jack's firm allowed paternity leave, but Marion's company only allowed her to take a few weeks' sick leave. They decided that when Marion's leave ended, Jack would step in for three months. When Todd was four months old, they would hire a babysitter.

Jack settled very well into the primary caretaker role. He was comfortable with Todd and not as tired as Marion, because he wasn't getting up nights to breast-feed. Marion pumped breast milk for Todd, and they supplemented this with infant formula. Because Marion missed Todd and her breasts felt painful by noon, Jack would bundle him up and take him to see her at lunch. This had the added benefit of making Marion feel more a part of Todd's day. It also got Jack out of the house. By noon, he desperately felt he needed the change of scenery; he was surprised at how confining the house felt sometimes.

Jack received no support outside the family for his decision. At work he was seen as an oddity, and his parents were strangely quiet about the arrangement. He and Marion realized that they had to support each other throughout this period. Jack felt that he would quickly regain his status at work once he returned.

Child-Care Decisions

Our preference, based on developmental research,[5,17] that women take parental leave does not mean the child will have problems if the mother must or chooses to return to her job shortly after giving birth. However, long hours away from an infant might have negative effects. If you can possibly limit your work hours during this period, or find a way to be available to the infant during the day, or take the baby with you to work, that would be desirable.

There is also evidence that warm, nurturing, well-trained care providers (fathers included) can be a special resource during this early period. Generations of children in the Israeli kibbutzim (collective settlements) have been raised in this fashion. In addition to the mother and father, a small group of child-care specialists on the kibbutz (called "metapelets" in Hebrew) nurture and raise the child.

Mothers go to work but visit their infants frequently during the day. Stability and love are guaranteed by the presence of both the mother and father and the trained caretakers. These children grow up to be strong, secure adults, and they are usually sought after in Israeli society for positions of authority and responsibility.

Sometimes parents who take a break from their job to be with their infant return to work after six months. In many cases, this arrangement suits the parents and child well. Some developmental psychologists, however, think six months is a critical time in an infant's development and argue against returning to full-time work at this particular stage.[5] Between about six months and a year, infants develop a fear of strangers, a normal developmental response. These psychologists believe that abruptly beginning day care during this period may produce a more anxious, poorly attached infant. This is especially likely if the primary caretaker (be it mom or dad) returns to work full time.

There are a number of solutions to this possible problem. One is to expose the infant to an enriching day-care environment before the age of six months. The caretaker, and not a stranger, then becomes a nurturing secondary provider. Beginning with a few hours in day care and gradually increasing the time over a few weeks is also helpful.

It is important that you be comfortable with the day-care arrangements and setting. Ivonne's doctoral dissertation explored the effects of parental satisfaction with day care on the child's social adjustment. She watched how children separated from and reunited with their mothers at the beginning and end of day care each day. Mothers who were more satisfied with the arrangements were less anxious while leaving and picking up their children. Mothers who were unsettled about having children in day care would prolong the separation until the children became anxious and afraid. Likewise, when they came to collect their children, they would be anxious and distressed, communicating once again that the environment was dangerous. There are two aspects to satisfaction with day care: finding quality care and feeling comfortable about you and your child being apart. The two factors are related, but if you cannot overcome your own feelings of apprehension and guilt about leaving your child, you will be uncomfortable with even the most ideal situation.

There are many books that consider day care in detail, but let's look at it from the resource perspective. We want a nurturing, stable, secure, and comforting environment for our children. It is also important that there be nurturing secondary caretakers (that is, secondary to you as parents) and that they have plenty of time to spend with your infant. Look for situations where there are few infants or children per caretaker and where each caretaker is assigned to particular children. We prefer one caretaker having responsibility for four to five children, rather than four caretakers having responsibility for sixteen to twenty. The caretaker-to-child ratio is the same in both cases, but the dynamics of the more familial situation allow for better caretaker-child bonding. For stability, look for low turnover of workers and children; high turnover of either is a bad sign.

The majority of Americans choose to leave infants with women in family settings. Although there is a problem with nonlicensing and lack of supervision in such settings, there is reason to believe that these are the best arrangements for infants, if well chosen. You should be cautious, however. Seek recommendations, take the time to observe at the person's home, and ask if it's okay to drop by unexpectedly (and do). You should become the supervisor and establish a trusting bond with the person caring for your child.

——— ▬

When our oldest, Ari, was born, in Alaska, we had a choice between some excellent licensed day-care centers and some private homes. Had we found a day-care center with few children and the familial arrangement we discussed earlier, we might have chosen it, but private care was more to our liking. We found a woman who loved being a homemaker as much as we loved being dual career parents. She had two young children and four school-aged children. We stayed with Ari during the first few visits, allowing him to get used to the family and the surroundings. June, the caretaker, would hold him and feed him, and we allowed him to do some exploring.

June's children were clearly well loved and well behaved. June spent her time with the children, not on housework. If she baked, the kids were involved, with dough in their hands. We often dropped by at odd times to pick up Ari, as we had variable schedules. Not once did he appear unhappy, and usually he was in someone's arms or playing with an older child.

When our second child, Sheera, was born, we did not find such ideal circumstances outside the home. We chose a very nurturing woman to come to our home and care for her while Ivonne worked in an office attached to the house; with Sheera cared for at home, Ivonne could maximize contact with her daughter. Although having someone in the home was a bit more expensive, we saved money because she also cared for our oldest child when he came home from his half-day preschool.

We think that we found pretty good arrangements for our children. However, we considered between ten and twenty-five women and settings for each of our children, and we did have some setbacks. Some are scary to think about.

———

Before we found the family arrangement for him that we described earlier, Ari had a short, chaotic history of care. When only a few months old he had a wonderful, warm caretaker. She was very devoted to him and had no other young children at home. However, her sister died suddenly and she became too distraught to provide care. The stability we had hoped for was quickly shattered and Ari had to switch caretakers. He spent the next three days (that was enough!) with a woman who was recommended but not at all nurturing. The children were supervised but not loved. She did not believe in cuddling a child not in need of food or a diaper change. Luckily, we eventually found a loving day-care arrangement for Ari.

The caretaker of our youngest child, Jonathan, was initially warm and loving, but after about a year she became bored and irresponsible. One day we found the floor covered with nutshells and half-eaten fruit; he had obviously had some time to shell and

eat the nuts (nuts are very dangerous to a two-year-old). Our neigh-
bors thought a boyfriend had been visiting. The caretaker was let go.
We were both angry and felt guilty that we had not seen the problem
developing. Imagine, two psychologists—we should know better.
Lord have mercy on the poor candidates for caretaker we interviewed
after that!

At times we felt like we were walking along a cliff. We both strongly wanted to work and advance our careers, but at times we felt that one false step would cause doom to rain down on our children as a consequence of bad day care. Even in Israel, where day care is superb for the young child, it was hard to find continuing quality care.

The Exhausted Child/Exhausted Parent Syndrome

For children between two and six, more day-care options become available, although they are very far from ideal and are often expensive. Again, look for a nurturing, stable, comforting environment, where chaos is kept within reasonable limits. Children at this age do not necessarily require the small familial group setting we discussed in terms of infants, but we feel that a low caretaker-to-child ratio remains important. We also continue to prefer one day-care worker having responsibility for a small group of children, rather than a few workers sharing responsibility for a large group. An academically challenging environment is a secondary concern. Children's play, if well supervised, is naturally stimulating, and you can spend evenings and weekends teaching your three-year-old Latin and Chinese algebra if you so desire. If you still want a more academic environment, just be sure it is also a nurturing one in which the instructor provides close contact.

At this age (and to some extent children at all ages), the child who is in care for long periods can become overtired. Up to six hours is ideal but may not fit your schedule. Eight to nine hours, in our view, should be the maximum. If you can arrange your schedules to accommodate late drop-off by one parent and early pickup by the other, we recommend it. We would emphasize that children who remain in day care for longer periods will not necessarily suffer, but in our experience, the risk is higher.

Our recommendation to limit day care to eight or nine hours, which we know will be a challenge to many dual career families, is based on the observation that longer periods can be exhausting for the child and often for you as well. Tired children, and parents, have difficulty enjoying quality time with one another. Children may become irritable or withdrawn and can be unresponsive just when you are finally able to provide care. We have known many parents who try to increase their time with their children by keeping them up late. This only adds to the child's exhaustion and the chances of family conflict. Furthermore, children who are in day care for more than nine hours often experience shift changes among the staff, which increases the complexity of the environment and can make the child's day more chaotic.

Some of you have no alternative but to keep your child in day care for as long as eleven hours. There are still steps you can take to strengthen your attachment to your child and provide the external resources needed to foster the growth of strong internal resources. For one, get up early with the child and have some quality early-morning time. When you pick up the child, make it a time when you give him or her your full attention. Then get the child to bed at a reasonable hour, ensuring a good night's sleep. Make weekends a sacred time with the children. If your weekends are hectic, you risk compounding the problems caused by your long absences during the week. By making weekends a time for quality interaction, you can renew the attachment with your child that was strained during the week.

These recommendations hold for school-aged children as well. Children often spend extended periods in after-school-care programs. Just because the child is older and appears well adjusted does not mean you can relax the emphasis on quality time. Mornings, evenings, and weekends should be treasured for the opportunity they afford you and your children.

In fact, children thrive on one-to-one interaction and family time in the morning and evening and over the weekend. Resist the temptation to make up for lost time during the week by overscheduling weekday and weekend organized activities. Trying to enrich your child's environment is a natural and well-intentioned goal, but it is too easily overdone, further exhausting you and the child. You cannot make up for lost weekday interaction by scheduling baseball, soccer, dance (tap, jazz, and ballet, of course), chess, violin, space scouts, and zither. It is you that your child needs.

Ten-year-old Janice and her parents came to therapy because of Janice's temper tantrums and declining school performance. During the initial interview, her mother and father (Sarah and Joe) said that Janice was enrolled in piano, dance, soccer, religious school, gymnastics, and Girl Scouts. Each of these activities made multiple demands during the week, from piano and dance practice to religion homework. By the time Janice was finished with her activities for the afternoon, it was late evening. Then the family rushed through a microwave or fast-food meal. By then, Janice was too exhausted to do her homework, and it was too late just to relax, read together, or play a game. No time for quiet cuddling and reconnecting.

Now the tantrums began, but they weren't really just Janice's. Because Sarah and Joe were exhausted, too, their tempers were short and they frequently yelled and made impossible demands. They would tell her to do her homework and take a bath in a half-hour, so Janice would take her homework into the bath! Sarah and Joe couldn't understand why Janice wasn't happier with her "enriched environment."

In therapy, Joe and Sarah very quickly disclosed their feelings of guilt about not having enough time for Janice because of their work schedules. They felt this resulted in her being "deprived." For each measure of guilt they felt, they had added another activity, until Janice's schedule was as full as a dentist's.

A plan was devised for them to reduce Janice's organized activities to two per week. Joe and Sarah decided that one of them would be home by 4:00 one day per week so that Janice could have a friend over, something that Janice herself felt was lacking. The rest of the unscheduled time was devoted to one-on-one interaction between Joe or Sarah and Janice or to family time. Janice was even allowed some alone time to read, do her homework, or watch a favorite TV pro-

gram. The family began to eat dinner together, and Janice received the help she needed to do her homework.

Ivonne thought deeper issues had led to Janice's tantrums that she would have to deal with, but these virtually vanished with the changed circumstances. Within a matter of only weeks her grades began to improve and she was making friends. Ten weeks into the new regime, Janice's allergist even reduced her medication (that's right, allergies are often exacerbated by stress and lack of social support).

Loving interaction is the best way to counter the hustle and bustle in your children's lives. However, for loving interaction to work, both you and your children must not be so exhausted that its positive effects are short-circuited before they have a chance to develop. Keeping your child's and your own schedules within the bounds of everyone's stamina is critical for the effects of close interaction to take hold and work their magic.

Dual Careers and Children's Aggression

There is some evidence that children of dual career parents are more aggressive than other children.[17] Three explanations have been proposed. First, children in day care have to compete with other children for the good toys (a good toy is one that another child got to first). Even with quality supervision, children battle over toys, swings, and lunch. It is probably adaptive for such children to become somewhat more aggressive.

The second explanation is that children with two employed parents may spend more time watching television when they are home. Parents often use the television as a babysitter, because even with day care over, they may have to play catch-up with chores and errands. Either before the parent returns, or after parents return home, the television is used to pacify children. Research by Dr. Leonard Eron provides convincing evidence that television violence encourages violence in children.[18] As a result, researchers are seeing increased aggression in such children.

The third explanation is a lack of supervision of older children. With women going to work, this task, which traditionally fell on them, is sometimes neglected. This is especially true for working-class children, but it occurs with middle-class children, too.[19] Some dual career parents are so involved in their work that they abdicate responsibility for child care to the children themselves. We often see these children in therapy. Generally they are either angry and aggressive or angry and withdrawn. In either case, their parents often marvel at their independence, but their independence is a survival technique built on insecurity.

Mark and Cheryl, brother and sister, were fifteen and fourteen years old, respectively. Their parents were successful and very involved with work. In fact, it was not unusual for both of them to be out of town, the kids left to their own devices. Mark was extremely angry and withdrawn. He tried desperately to get his parents' attention through good grades, but they were still inaccessible. Cheryl was a bit stronger but was involved in more dangerous activities. She had recently acquired a seventeen-year-old boyfriend who was into drugs, drinking, and criminal behavior. She was determined to get somebody's attention. The parents did not get involved until the police arrested their daughter for having a drinking party at their home. The parents only avoided their own arrest because of their small-town relationship with the police.

Mark was considered a model child, but in therapy his depression and anger scared his parents. They had seen problems developing with Cheryl but had tried to minimize them, hoping she would "straighten out with age." After making some initial progress in therapy, the family left counseling and returned to business as usual. The parents returned to their absorbing careers.

We expected further problems to arise and they have, the family coming back each time for just enough therapy to allow them to continue their destructive routine.

Dual careers certainly draw you away from your children for a great part of the day. Again, how you handle your resources will determine the consequences of this. You can limit TV time and select programs with your child. Be firm and offer alternatives. Given the aggression that might result from the competitiveness of preschool, your child needs your attention and support at home. You can teach your children how to solve conflicts with their siblings and make them feel that their important needs are being met. Assertiveness may help your child achieve more in life, but it must be appropriate to the situation. Aggression, which is an overreaction inappropriate to the situation, can spell trouble socially and at school.

Chaos and Stability

When we think of healthy dual career families, we think of safe, fast sailing ships. They depend on a lot of factors to move quickly in the water, but, oh, when they do . . .

Like a sailing ship, the dual career family always seems to be threatened by chaos. Virtually all our dual career friends, the families with whom we have worked, and those in our workshops report that some degree of chaos is always present. When both parents work full time or near full time, there is going to be some rushing around to get meals on the table, kids in the dishwasher (oops!), homework done, and children chauffeured to their various and sundry activities.

Maybe the difference is between controlled and uncontrolled chaos. Does your family have a sit-down meal together at least three times per week? Do you have weekly time together free from outside distractions? Do you have time to interact one-on-one with the children? Do your children find that you are available to them? We see many parents who constantly tell their children, catch me later. But later doesn't come and the children become discouraged and stop asking. Chaotic families begin to lose their children through the cracks. The children adapt in a way, but their internal resources are weakened as a result. How important can a child feel if he or she cannot get dad's full attention or mom's interest in a project? The answer is not very important, not very valued.

You must be sure to establish some pillars of stability within your hectic family life. Children need clear rules and supervision. At all ages, they need you to set appropriate limits and stand by them. They need to know the consequences of good and inappropriate behavior. Your family also needs traditions that are anticipated and enjoyed. Not just Thanksgiving, Christmas, and Passover, but Sunday afternoon and Friday night traditions, too. And don't forget bedtime rituals. Babysitters and older siblings can only fill in to a degree; it is up to the parents to secure the sails and navigate the family's course. At no time in your children's lives is it okay for you to abdicate your position as heads of the family.

Stability also comes from being available during a crisis. Parents must be supportive figures in their children's lives. Major stressful events often have serious negative effects on children's well-being, whether you are a dual or single career family.[20] Many crises can be averted when both parents are actively involved in the family's day-to-day activities. A teenage pregnancy might well be prevented by sharing feelings about sexuality and popularity. Alcohol-related car crashes often occur because parents permit teenage drinking or fail to supervise, and household accidents increase when children are left unsupervised. Loneliness, depression, and poor self-confidence can all lead to problems that are preventable if children are offered a stable, reasonably disciplined, nurturing environment.

When stressful events do occur, supportive parents provide the stability and nurturing that help young people weather the crisis. Like the keel of a good ship, parents are a stabilizing force in times of trouble. As dual career parents, you are fully capable of providing all the necessary support and love, but it will probably take some extra vigilance and extra efforts at mutual support.

Ernest and Darlene were shaken when their son, Edward, was badly hurt in a car crash. Edward would lose three months of school and would not be able to participate in sports for over a year. Another youth had been killed in the crash, and Edward felt responsible, even though it was the other boy who had run a red light.

Ernest and Darlene decided that Ernest would take the three months off from work to be with Edward. It would be hard to make it without his salary, but at least his company's leave policy ensured that he would not lose his job. Ernest spent the days tutoring Edward, propping up his sagging morale, and helping him be as active as possible during his recuperation. He and Edward talked a lot during this period and achieved a closeness that would last a lifetime.

Because of Ernest's willingness to take on the nurturing role and to dedicate many of his own resources to supporting Edward, the family was able to weather the stormy seas created by the accident. Ernest also began to feel fuller as a man, not just like a worker bee. He felt he was contributing more to the whole family and that staying home was one of the most important decisions he had ever made. He felt like a hero, and we think he was.

Some Advantages of Day Care

Children who experience day care have many advantages over children who do not. Those who spend an appreciable amount of time in quality programs are better socially adapted than children who are cared for at home.[5] If the setting is well supervised, they learn interactive skills and become better social problem solvers. Social skills help them when they enter school and may lead to greater popularity and leadership roles. Your child does not need to be the most popular child in the class. However, social isolation threatens children's self-esteem and sense of safety in groups. Day care can enhance your children's social resources, which, in turn, can lead to further resource acquisition (see Chapters 2 and 3).

Boys and girls whose parents work outside the home tend to develop less traditional attitudes toward gender roles than children who are cared for at home.[21, 22] Perhaps because they see their mothers working, they learn that women can succeed in many roles and that not only men can be confident and competent. Fathers who spend time taking care of their children teach them to see men and women as more equal.[23] When children see both parents succeed in multiple roles, they learn that neither gender has exclusive rights to or competence in any of them. This is probably particularly important for girls, who otherwise begin to feel lacking in competence and self-esteem, especially as they enter adolescence.[24, 25]

In one workshop, Jim, a police officer, wanted to know if his son would become a "sissy" because his wife worked. He was happy that his daughter might be stronger, but did not want his wife's working to be at the expense of his son.

Research suggests that boys from working-class families do suffer more than girls when their mothers work outside the home.[26, 27] They are shier and more nervous, dislike school more, and get lower grades. However, these effects are reversed by the *father's* investment of resources. The sons of fathers who are actively involved with their children and who support their wives as mothers and co-breadwinners had few, if any, of these problems. Another important predictor of boys' well-being is mom's satisfaction with her role, whether or not she works outside the home. As we have said, mom's satisfaction is in large measure dependent on dad's support.[9, 10] As to becoming effeminate, this, too, depends not on mom, but on dad. Men who are involved with their sons in a caring, nurturing manner produce men who are more secure in their gender identity than the sons of distant, aloof, macho fathers.[28]

So the only thing that Jim really should be worried about is how he dedicates his resources to his children and partner. He holds the key to his wife's role satisfaction and to his children's well-being.

A dual career family may have a particularly positive influence on girls. Girls who see their mothers successfully managing both career and home see themselves in a more positive light. They see more of the world open to them and generally feel more capable of succeeding. To the extent that the traditional homemaker is a less powerful role than is the breadwinner role, girls in traditional families tend to see themselves as less potentially powerful. A mother who works outside the home serves as a valuable role model for girls.

Our daughter, Sheera, is twelve. She says she might be an artist or a physician—she sees advantages in both. She is fond of saying that "all men are created equal . . . women are created superior."

Even with their enhanced self-esteem, Sheera and girls like her experience conflicts because they are still getting mixed messages about women. Women on television and in film are clearly chosen for their beauty. Our kids have remarked that the weatherwoman is about ten times better looking than the weatherman, who strangely resembles a possum. Women are often portrayed in movies and television as helpless victims of violence. Children's books and TV commercials still present traditional mom-at-home families.

These mixed messages notwithstanding, Sheera sees that women have choices about what to do with their lives and that women's words and actions count. She will have to reject the message that the teacher communicates when she asks, "Whose mom can bake cookies for the Friday party?" or "Whose dad can coach soccer?" She will have to allow her dad to bake cookies for Friday (announced on Thursday), with chocolate swirls and colored sprinkles, and mom will have to step up and coach a little soccer.

ENRICHING YOUR CHILDREN'S RESOURCE GARDEN

Now that you have considered your children's external and internal resources and have read and thought about the factors that influence these resources, it is time to tend to the garden. Think about and discuss with your partner what resources your child lacks. If you see weaknesses in external resources, devise a plan for enriching your child's resource environment. Enhancing your children's external resources often means that you intervene on the level of their environment. This may mean changing your working hours, making adjustments in how you spend your leisure time, finding new ways of spending time at home with the children, and changing your child-care arrangements.

Both Dave and Betty felt that four-year-old Jenny was spending too many hours in day care. Although Betty's job allowed her the flexibility to pick Jenny up at 4:00, she was dropped off there at 7:30. Betty had a master's degree in business, but was working as a

glorified secretary and was dissatisfied. She felt she would be a bet-
ter mother if she were happier with her career.

Dave and Betty agreed that Dave would catch a later train in the
morning and work an hour later. Betty would look for a better job
that started early in the morning. This would allow Jenny to spend
fewer hours in day care. They also decided to wait until Jenny started
school in September to make these changes, thus allowing for a more
natural transition.

Now examine your children's internal resources. Oddly enough, when children are lacking in internal resources, usually the first place to make changes is, once again, in their external resources, which are the fountainhead of their internal resources. Identify internal resources that are lacking or not as strong as you wish them to be. Remember, a child in the gifted program at school does not necessarily have self-confidence, and a child not in the gifted program does not necessarily lack internal resources. Self-esteem, a feeling of control over one's environment, and a sense of accomplishment all are fostered by a nurturing, stable, intimate, supportive atmosphere at home and in other settings.

———

Alice and George's ten-year-old son Gordon was shy and with-
drawn. He lacked self-esteem and often spoke negatively about
himself: "Oh, I can't draw" or "No, I wouldn't be any good at Little
League." This surprised George and Alice because they were the
epitome of self-confidence. They were successful and were seen by
others as leaders.

After looking at Gordon's external resources, they had to admit
that they actually spent little time with him. He was often juggled
among babysitters. George accused Alice of being overly critical of
Gordon and paying attention to him only when he did well in school.
Alice blew up, saying that at least she spent time with him.

When the dust settled, they realized that their careers and high
expectations for themselves had caused Gordon to feel that he had to

meet impossible standards for two people who weren't even there to reward him when he did. Alice and George were going to have to increase their time at home and be more supportive of their son. Further discussion revealed that they had lost much of the intimacy of their early marriage, and so they began to discuss how they could better support each other as well.

Being supportive of each other as partners also means getting a handle on guilt and helping each other keep things in perspective.

We are very proud of our children and feel that we provide them with many resources. Nevertheless, both of us have at times focused on some lapse in self-confidence or achievement on their part. Maybe a teacher wrote that one was not performing up to snuff in class, or we saw another back off in a soccer game while a teammate strove forcefully forward. As a result, one of us becomes filled with self-reproach about not being the best father or mother, being too hard or too soft, too unavailable or too pushy.

Stevan has very high expectations for the children and sometimes can be overpowering. He chastises himself for this, and Ivonne steps in and puts things into perspective: "You give them self-confidence and goals to strive for. You have to expect that if they are truly strong, they will assert themselves right back at you when they disagree. That is not a sign of weakness, it's a sign of strength. So listen to them and back off when they tell you."

Ivonne sometimes feels that she gives in too easily and spoils the children. When they fail to go after some goal, she blames herself for making it too easy for them. Stevan steps in and reminds her that she is usually very strong and that it's a parent's prerogative occasionally to spoil the children. Why else would mothers receive such great Mother's Day presents?

When one of you begins to exaggerate the negative (probably because of the very high standards you set for your children), that is the time for the other parent to plant two feet on terra firma and assert a little common sense. Children are not perfect, and neither are we. We do what we can; we even try to do a little more than we can. We offer love and attention. Sometimes we lose our tempers when we should keep our cool; sometimes we are a bit lazy and lie on the couch instead of getting out there in the yard with the kids and a ball. Each parent must always encourage the other to be a better parent, but you must also reward each other for what you have done and validate the positive influence each of you has had. Remember, too, that criticism should be rendered privately and supportively when you are alone. Compliments should be paid publicly.

You (and we) must learn to accept our children as individuals who, like us, have positive and negative traits, who sometimes accomplish and sometimes fail to meet our most lofty goals. Are things going reasonably well? How can we make them better? These are different questions from why aren't our children perfect.

MAKING CHILDREN YOUR DUAL PRIORITY

Thinking about the effects of dual career family life on children has convinced us that some shifts in how we view this challenge are in order. We cannot think about child rearing in the same ways our parents did and still expect positive results. The world has changed.

First, you should not see child rearing as a woman's task, any more than you should see working outside the home as a man's task. Parenting is a partnership, and if there is one thing the research is clear about, it is that a fully involved father is critical to raising psychologically healthy, successful children. Children do best when their fathers share the household labor, because that lowers the stress on their mothers and allows both to be more effective parents. Children thrive when their fathers participate fully in child care, because dads are cool, too. In most (but not all!) cases they can throw the kids higher in the air, they (still) know more about fastballs, and they look pretty impressive to someone under forty-eight inches high. Dads provide an extra set of arms to hold them and protect them, and an extra pair of ears to hear their stories and plead their case. In fact, we have had some striking counseling successes simply by getting dad involved in bedtime rituals—bathing, storytelling, and tucking in—leading to a closer family all-around.

Second, the search for success and the pursuit of material resources and personal accomplishments should not be allowed to cloud our judgment. Few of you think your work is more important than your children. Fewer still will look back when your children leave home, or when you are old, and say, "Gee, I wish I had spent more time at the office." Many of you, however, spend more hours at work than you need to, considering the commitment you have made to having and raising children. There are millions of American children whose parents' careers are succeeding at their expense. When you are offered that next raise or the opportunity to move to a new job, consider what the costs will be for your children. How will the kids cope with the loss of resources—friends, stability, status (oh, yes, kids are very involved with status, especially from middle school on), and community? Don't dare minimize the effects of your absence, if that will be a part of the "better deal"; you are very important to your children.

Third, many women must come to terms with the fact that they are strongly pulled in two directions. You want to have a career and you want to provide your children with all the time and attention you received from your mother, or wish you had. You must learn to accept and live with certain compromises without feeling bad about yourself. As we discuss in Chapter 3, we all tend to focus more on what we lack and have lost than on what we have and have gained. You must learn to be more gain-oriented and self-appreciative. Spending time on a craft project, your hands touching her little hands, may mean you won't have a spotless counter top, but so be it. Focus on what you and your child have gained.

We have tried not to minimize the costs to your children of your life-style (reading that everything is not roses may have been hard), but you must not falsely glorify the alternative either. Keep in mind that your resources and those of your children are intertwined. As you enrich the garden of your own resources, you will also contribute to your children's well-being. When you remember that they need your time, nurturing, and attention, they will share in your successes.

Chapter 10

Molding a Family-Sensitive Workplace

*I*n this final chapter we examine the future for dual career families. How are families and the workplace changing, and how will these changes benefit the resources of dual career families? We are in an exciting transition period that almost inevitably will enhance both the way employers make resources available to families and the way the workplace allows you to use your resources. For the present, it is up to you to make the most of your current employer's policies, to explore and propose new options, or, if necessary, to search for a new employer more sensitive to the dual career family and its needs. Many employers lack family-friendly policies. However, we are excited that many employers of all sizes are responding to family needs and dual career pressures. There is a movement afoot to see employees as critical resources, and companies are looking for ways to take advantage of you as such. Because so many of today's most valued workers come from dual career families, the means of doing business is open to change.

Many workplaces have already implemented these exciting changes, but you may have to do some searching to find them. If a job hunt is in the cards for you in the near future, we recommend your keeping resource-enriching aspects of a new job in mind. Money is a resource, but there are other facets of employment that dual career partners should make equal priorities. Personnel departments have been renamed human resources departments, but if a company does not offer many of the family-friendly programs that we discuss in this chapter, it has not taken the spirit of the new name to heart. If human beings are resources, employers must cater to their needs in order to enhance their ability to perform well on the job and stay with it. Those of you who are self-employed may even have to learn to be your own more caring boss.

AN OFTEN ADVERSARIAL RELATIONSHIP

The American workplace has long resembled the military in many of its attitudes; we'll use the British Army as an example. Soldiers were sent to India as an opportunity for military advancement and as a matter of service. Wives and families went along faithfully. No matter that they were far from home and England; they also served country by supporting their husbands and fathers. If orders came up for a move to Burma or some other reaches of the British Empire, then so be it. The soldier and his family responded, whether they traveled together or separated. Soldiers were treated well (for soldiers, anyway) and could look forward to an exciting career. If children could not be educated in that country or region, well, there were always good schools back in England. If wives could not follow, then back to England they went. Clearly, no one ever thought to base soldiers' assignments on how they influenced families, wives, or children. It was good for the military, it was good for country, and it was a man's world.

Many of us are familiar with this separation between work and family. The U.S. Chamber of Commerce opposed the Family Leave Bill and opposes family legislation in general, contending that business should remain out of family life and family life should remain out of business.[1] In fact, changes in one realm tend to affect the other. Historically, the family has always been asked to sacrifice for the workplace, whereas the workplace has rarely responded to the family. When work is dangerous, the family is asked to expose family members to the risk of death or disability. When companies needed women and children, women and children went to work. When companies needed long hours, family members worked long hours. When employers ask folks to move, they move. When American retailers see they can make money by keeping stores open twenty-four hours a day, families disrupt their lives to adapt to twenty-four-hour work schedules—holidays included.

Let us at least be realistic. Employment has been intertwined with families since there has been work. The two are indivisible. And work has often placed a heavy burden on families. Indeed, the relationship has often been adversarial. Child labor laws, maximum work hour laws, safety regulations, social security, and now family legislation have been imposed on businesses by the government. When government did not step in, unions often did, fighting for reasonable conditions for workers and their families. Those aspects of the workplace that remain outside of governmental or union regulation are the most family-unfriendly. Part-time work, for example, does not pay medical benefits. Workers who are employed illegally (usually immigrants and the poor) have no benefits whatsoever, and can be asked to work whatever hours and under whatever conditions the employer wants. Indeed, many American companies with good workplace records in the United States open plants elsewhere so that they can avoid humane policies, let alone family-friendly policies, if that is what it takes to be more profitable.

Employers have not placed these burdens on families because they are the Evil Empire. In fact, business is made up primarily of people who love their families and feel that the institution of the family should be supported. However, they are also realistic, in that they must make money to survive. They must make money to pay workers so their families can live, and they must pay owners or shareholders profits or risk losing their investment. What this means is that it is very dangerous for businesses to make any move that places them at a disadvantage with their competition. If one employer has people toiling for slave wages, receiving no benefits, and working under dangerous conditions, a competitor usually cannot pay the price of righting all these wrongs and remain competitive.

A business will seldom, if ever, make a decision to become less competitive, even if it would like to provide better conditions to workers and their families. All the businesses in a given field have to make the plunge together. For an entire business sector to change simultaneously usually requires that government step in and legislate change. Business may fight it, and almost always does. However, in the long run, business survives because change is demanded across the board and levels the playing field. If all companies in an industry have to change, none receives an unfair advantage.

There are also conditions under which it is more competitive to become worker- and family-friendly. This occurs when there are fewer qualified workers than positions. Hence, if Company A treats workers worse, it loses its competitive advantage because qualified workers go to Company B, which offers better conditions. This is increasingly common as jobs become more technical and require better educated and more skillful workers.

THE TIMES THEY ARE A-CHANGING

For perhaps the first time in history, many companies are well ahead of government legislation or union demands to protect family interests. Have they gone mad? Have they been invaded by wild-eyed liberals or subversives? Hardly. What is occurring is that business is beginning to see that family interests are its interests—that business and families share a common resource garden. As a dual career pioneer, you can be very proud of this turn of events, because you have brought it about. You have changed the nature of the options available at the workplace, because in order to keep you, the highly valued employee, companies must help make your dual career life manageable. They are interested in surviving in this new world order, so they are having to make family-friendly adjustments. You will see more and more businesses developing family-friendly policies and practices.

WORK WON'T LOVE YOU BACK

Most likely, in twenty years people will take these benefits as much for granted as we do social security, retirement benefits, and plant safety regulations.

Employees who come from dual career families are in demand today and will continue to be in demand for two reasons. First, there are so many of us. When some 70 percent of two-adult households are dual career households, business has few other options than to invest in dual career families.[2] With women increasingly well trained and well educated, it is becoming impossible for businesses to rely on an all-male or mostly male work force. With members of dual career families among the best educated and best trained available, business would be limited to a less qualified pool of potential employees if they overlooked dual career family members.

What companies are leading the way in pro-family policy? Which ones are courting dual career families? You might imagine, perhaps, that they are small firms, or firms that are not competitive, or perhaps government- or union-controlled companies. The fact is that among the leaders in pro-family policy are many of the giants of corporate America. Their names read like a list of Fortune 500 companies: IBM, Johnson & Johnson, DuPont, Citibank, Dow Chemical, Hewlett-Packard, HBO, The Prudential, and Westinghouse. They span the marketplace from banking, to computers, to chemicals, to defense, to insurance.[3] They are the companies that have read the writing on the wall. These companies are aggressively leading the way in pro-family policy because they want to beat the competition.

"BREAD AND ROSES"

The changes in family policy that are occurring in the workplace are largely a product of the women's movement. We are not talking just about the most recent version that began in the 1960s but also of the long-term accomplishments of the movement that began over a century ago.

In the early days of the union movement, women had a somewhat different agenda than men, which they called "bread and roses." While union men were focusing on "bread and butter," pay-related issues, women saw these as only part of the story. They felt that employers also needed to be aware of the "roses," or quality of life, issues.[4,5] Not just pay but vacation time, time for individual enrichment, and medical benefits. In today's terms, not just pay but family benefits.

Since the 1960s, women have been forcing further changes in workplace policy by entering a broad spectrum of professions in record numbers.[6, 7] Traditional male occupations such as law, medicine, and business have opened their doors to an increasing number of women, such that the male-to-female ratio is becoming fairly equal in many professions.[8] This will inevitably translate into more adjustments in the workplace during the next three decades, at least. As most of these women expect to have families, the cadre of dual career families can only increase.[2]

Stevan met recently with the chief officer of a large corporation who was teaching real-world business ideas and strategies at a major college campus for a year. What this CEO found there was the future, although he was not completely comfortable with it.

He told Stevan that his female students were brighter and more verbal than their male counterparts. He found their work to be more thorough and their writing skills better developed. They were better prepared for class and asked more questions. What he said next, however, was the big surprise. He said he would hire the male students over the female students because "business needs men" and "it's a man's culture."

Personally, we doubt that there are quite so many differences between male and female students. In fact, at Stevan's university we checked entry scores on standardized examinations and found no remarkable male-female differences. This senior executive had probably never been exposed at his level of business to many women. He was familiar with the lofty levels of business that are still a "man's world" because fewer than 3 percent of senior American executives are female. To a sixty-year-old male executive who had always been surrounded by assertive men and supportive women, it was surprising to find so many accomplished women. The reason he thought they were less suited for business was merely that they were not a part of the male club—so we're back to the British Army in India.

We went a step further and looked at the policies regarding women and families of this executive's company. They were actually quite good, and the company was a local leader in employing junior women executives. True, there were few senior executive women, but they were clearly rising in rank, considering the late date at which they had entered the firm compared to men. We guess the CEO had long seen the writing on the wall. He was just having a hard time living with it. He was still more comfortable with men, but he had not allowed that to interfere with realistic business decisions—women were an excellent option within the competitive labor pool. He might still resist making women senior vice presidents, but he would soon retire and the younger men who took his place, having risen along with a cadre of women, would be used to seeing them as peers.

Women bring both direct and indirect pressure on business to change. The direct pressure springs from women's responsibility for child care, the home, and the elderly. As they enter the workplace in greater numbers, employers must respond to their needs or face disgruntled employees, the loss of employees to other firms, or their exit from the labor market and return to the home. And increasingly, women are rising to positions that allow them to make policy decisions.

Indirectly, women cause change because they influence their partners. Men must take more responsibility for the home and child care when their partners work, and so they, too, place pressure on the workplace to change. When men live with partners who are employed, they are inevitably influenced by their partners' needs. As managers, we wouldn't want to return home to a woman who works outside the home and tell her that we just decided against a family-friendly policy. The first generation of managers confronted with increased female participation in the labor force were men whose wives did not work. More and more, however, those in management will be either women or men whose partners are also employed. Inevitably, they will see the world differently, and we believe that their perspective will favor dual career families.

No pressure is likely to be as direct as that exerted when women enter the most senior echelons of management and government in great numbers. When Stevan was planning workshops on how business needs to respond to women in the workplace, he sent out two hundred brochures on the program. Fifteen companies responded, which in marketing terms is not a bad hit rate. However, what was most intriguing was that all fifteen of the interested personnel directors or vice presidents were women. Not one single male personnel director responded! The women, however, saw that problems existed and wanted change. As women fill decision-making roles in appreciable numbers, pro-family decisions will be made.

FITTING YOURSELF AND YOUR WORK TO YOUR LIFE-STYLE

When talking with dual career families and even with personnel directors, we have been surprised at their lack of familiarity with some of the more successful pro-family initiatives that are already working for many companies. A good job will both add to your resources and allow you to use the resources you have to your best advantage. A smart employer will target resources that also work to its benefit. If an employer is investing in you, it should want to keep you around.

Choosing the Right Employer

We all know that men's salaries and opportunities for advancement are better than women's. (We discuss some of these trends in Chapter 1.) But don't base your job decision on statistics. You do not need the "average" salary for people like you, and you are not looking for a job "typical" of married women or men with college degrees. You are looking for one particular position. Neither are you a social experiment. You are a person with certain specific needs, desires, and goals. Some employers will advance your financial resources, sense of accomplishment, and career more than others, and sometimes there are even important differences among divisions within the same company.

Some of you may see women's salaries and opportunities for advancement as only a "women's issue." Maybe you think women's issues are important, maybe you don't. Maybe you think they are important, but for another book. However, there is one women's issue that has a big impact on you as a dual career family: The more money a woman makes, the more money goes in the family pot. The more career satisfaction the woman achieves, the happier she will be and the more she will be able to give to her partner and children. In contrast, the more discrimination a woman meets, even if she overcomes it and advances at work, the more exhausted she will be and the fewer resources she will have to share with her family. It's a family affair.

There are a number of indications of an employer's policies. Usually it is women who need to be cautious, but in some special instances, men can get the short end of the stick as well. This may occur, for example, when only women are considered for promotion or new hires to correct historical gender discrimination. In any case, both women and men can get a clearer picture of an employer's practices regarding women by evaluating the following factors:

- Number of women officers
- Number of women in senior management
- Women's salaries in different jobs
- Assignments given to women versus men
- History of advancement of women (recent and long term)
- Position of women in the specific division or job category being considered
- Attitudes and practices toward women by their immediate superiors
- Recent hiring practices

Such facts can be attained by talking to current employees, examining public records if the company is public or governmental, or asking for recent personnel reports to employees on the topic. These factors will tell the story better than a prospective employer's stated policy. Changes that have occurred over the last five years are the most critical, because management and policy before then may not reflect the current environment. Women may not have been available in great numbers to fill your job, or the firm may have been less receptive to women than it is today. A green light for women may also mean a red light for men. However, because few employers have achieved parity, men still tend to have the advantage.

In employment counseling, Christina asked for a female adviser because she felt only another professional woman could identify with her concerns. She and her husband, Nathan, were college graduates. He was having a difficult time finding work as a designer at his level of training and experience. She, on the other hand, had a steady salaried position as a midlevel manager.

Christina was the only female manager in her division, among twenty-five males. She felt that the other managers shut her out of the group decision-making process. They talked behind closed doors and came to meetings with decisions already made. In her own department, however, she was clearly the boss and received support from her superiors for her decisions. Although most colleagues treated her respectfully, there was the occasional "Hey, babe," or stare at her legs. Despite this, she was being promoted ahead of her peers and receiving excellent reviews. Her boss had made it clear that she was in line for another promotion.

Christina felt dizzy from the mixed messages. In one way she was the token female, and in another way she was a trusted manager with increasing responsibility. To some male colleagues she was a novelty, at best, whereas others treated her as an equal. At home she also had to tread lightly, because her success made her husband feel even worse about his career difficulties.

Christina's situation is typical of a field in transition. She is enmeshed in a web of inconsistencies, and how she should behave in response is unclear. Should she challenge the company to get the men in line, or take legal action? Should she confront or ignore men who treat her other than as a respected colleague? Should she find a firm with more women, or enjoy her current success? Who can she confide in at work about her concerns? The issues she is dealing with are issues that many women and men are facing, each from his or her own vantage point. Her employer is not consistent about providing equal opportunity regardless of gender, but is making progress. Christina has the unenviable task of being in the vanguard. Junior women in her firm are already finding life easier in her wake.

Working with the employment counselor, Christina found a sound-
ing board for solving her problems. She was encouraged to discuss
her concerns privately with her boss, who had always been sup-
portive. She found that he was in fact well aware of the difficulties
she was experiencing. He pointed out that most of the men who were
a problem were not advancing in the firm and that she would have
to get used to their jealousy, which always went along with success.
He promised to be more sensitive when he could intervene. He also
encouraged her to confront anyone who treated her disrespectfully
and assured her of his full backing. He could not, however, change
the fact that there were no other women at her level. The company
had a policy of promoting from within, and women were rising, he
felt, at a good pace. Christina felt more in control now that she better
understood her boss's thinking and the company's policy. As she
worked out her problems, her husband worked out his, and they
found they could further benefit by being supportive of each other.

Leadership versus Maintenance Tasks

One factor that we think is most important—and little talked about—
is assignments given to women. Even for people with the same job
title, work assignments can be one of two types: leadership or maintenance. Leadership tasks are those that advance or change the way
things are done to meet goals. Maintenance tasks involve doing things
in ways that preserve the status quo. Women are more often given
maintenance tasks and men are more often given leadership tasks.[9]
Leadership tasks are higher risk, but they are the ones that offer recog-
nition and the opportunity for advancement. Employees identified
for fast-track promotions are tested in leadership positions.

Rhonda was a midlevel insurance executive who had been forced into
a career move when her husband was transferred. She was glad to
make the move because she had progressed as far as she could in her

old job and their new location offered greater opportunities. She examined two prospective employers.

At Company A there were more women in middle management than at Company B, but they were not entering senior management. Company B had fewer women overall, but women there were advancing and there were two female vice presidents. At Company B, more women were in leadership positions, whereas at Company A, women were largely in service positions such as personnel.

At Company A Rhonda would be entering exactly at the level of the glass ceiling. This is the level at which women are stuck by the invisible ceiling that prevents their further advancement. Company B was less proactive about hiring women, but once hired they were treated well. Had she been considering an entry-level position, Company A might have been the better choice, but now Company B was clearly preferable. In her third year there, Rhonda was made an assistant to the executive vice president, one of the most visible positions for future advancement in the company.

Her new employer appreciated the fact that Rhonda said that she and her family were unlikely to move for the next five to eight years, with the children in school. A number of people had been promoted recently, only to leave for other firms. The company wanted a surer bet.

This also provides a tip about how you can bring about change in your current position. Go for leadership tasks; volunteer, take the initiative. If you perform well, you will often be rewarded.

Maternity Leave and Paternity Leave

Maternity and paternity leave can provide an important period in which to bond with your children, as we discuss in Chapter 9. Women we speak to usually want at least three months to recuperate and develop their attachment to the new baby, and fathers, too, often find it a valuable period for forging bonds with the baby.

Maternity leave is not sick leave, although many companies categorize it as such. Because many more women take maternity leave than men take paternity leave, women are at an unfair disadvantage if their time away is considered sick leave. Having used up their sick leave, women are more vulnerable to job loss or sanctions if they actually become ill. Also, many firms allow unused sick days to be aggregated for retirement, which also places women at a disadvantage if they use their sick days for the healthy time of bonding with their child.

Paternity leave is an added benefit. As we said earlier, in Scandinavia, where it has been policy long enough to be examined, paternity leave is typically used to supplement maternity leave. When the mother needs to go back to work, the father takes over in order to extend time for his bonding with the child and to postpone the need for out-of-home care.

Few jobs offer more than three months' paid leave, but many offer other options. These include up to a year's unpaid leave, a period of part-time work followed by a resumption of full-time employment, or a period in which the parent can perform his or her job at home. There is little regulation of these policies and, even where they are available, they often must be negotiated.

Look for clear and supportive maternity and paternity policies. They tell you that a dual career employee's contributions are valued and that your special needs are being considered.

Flextime

One of the most well-publicized family-friendly policies is flextime. Flextime programs are often misunderstood, however, because people are unfamiliar with their core elements. Typically, workers are allowed to arrive and leave up to two hours earlier or later. They must, however, be at work during the core hours of the workday to be available for meetings and communication. Most flextime programs also demand that workers commit themselves to a schedule for no less than a month at a time to facilitate planning and scheduling.

Flextime is one of the few programs that has been studied in a controlled fashion. Dr. Richard Winett and his colleagues studied the effects of flextime on families with children in an urban setting.[10]

Workers were employed in two federal agencies and were allowed to flex their schedules by about one hour. The researchers found that most workers chose to begin work earlier. Workers reported that with flextime schedules they could spend more time with their families, had more time for educational advancement, and found it easier to complete shopping and other chores. They also reported more relaxing evenings, which included time for family dinners. Commuting time was reduced by enabling employees to avoid traffic. This not only represents a time savings for the worker; it also means that he or she is less frazzled at the beginning of the workday (to the company's benefit) and at the end of the day (to the family's benefit). As you will note, these are some of the key areas for resource enhancement that we have discussed throughout this book. In addition to the reported worker satisfaction, few, if any, managerial problems were found. Flextime is clearly a winner for dual career families.

Flexplace

Flexplace programs give employees control over where they perform their work. As in flextime, a core period is required at the central workplace for meetings and communication. For example, the hours between 10:00 and 2:00 or Tuesdays and Thursdays might be the times when all employees must be at the office.

Clearly, flexplace is only practical for certain jobs. Many sales jobs have traditionally been flexplace, because the salesperson is on the road meeting with clients for appreciable periods during the week. Sophisticated computer networks will open up more jobs to this possibility. Conference calls and emerging visual screen technology will further facilitate the utility of flexplace.

We have heard of the informal use of flexplace by women and men in the months following maternity or paternity leave. One university's psychology department assigned committee work that could be done at home for a semester to a woman who wanted to spend more time at home. An attorney we spoke to negotiated a new contract with her law firm that allowed her to work at home three days a week and at the office twice a week. A social worker took his paperwork home and saw clients at the office. A senior executive arranged for a second office to be rented near his home so that he could avoid interruptions and cut travel time. He goes in early and leaves for his second office each day by 2:00. His computer is part of a network, so he is able to communicate with secretarial staff and colleagues at the central office.

We know of no studies to confirm this, but the instances of flexplace we know of have occurred with employees who are proven commodities. They either are self-employed or have convinced their employer that they can be trusted to work at home. Those who own their own business, of course, can do as they please, constrained only by the demands of the business. Many lawyers, accountants, store owners, independent contractors, and violin teachers can work wherever the tools of their trade are available and arrange their schedules accordingly.

Flexplace does not work well if you have young children who need supervision. However, it can be a workable solution when children are older. We often worked on this book at home. This made us available to answer important questions like "Can I go to my friend's house to play?" ("Yes, be back by 6:00.") and "Can I punch out my younger brother for going in my room?" ("No, you may not. I'll talk to him about that later."). Still, we could usually get fifty good minutes out of every hour, and we actually had fewer interruptions than at our offices.

We have spoken to many women who tried working at home with infants, only to become doubly frustrated at being both a bad parent and a bad worker.

Ellen ran a learning center that provided tutoring for children. She wanted to be home more with her six-month-old, Daniele, and was able to make her own schedule. Although she could not tutor at home, she tried to take her paperwork home. She had records to keep, accounting documents to prepare, and proposals to write for contracts with local schools.

Nothing was ever accomplished. When she could get Daniele interested in a toy, it was only minutes before she needed a diaper change. When she went down for a nap, the phone would ring and wake her. With mom home, Daniele always wanted to be picked up or played with. Ellen would become short-tempered, even though she knew Daniele was just being a normal baby.

Flexplace worked better for Mark, who enlisted other resources while working at home.

Mark wanted to spend more time with his two preschool children. By working at home Tuesdays and Thursdays instead of at the office, he would save two hours of commuting time twice a week. He wanted to spend those four extra hours with his children, but had no illusions about being able to care for them while working. He and his wife, Chris, kept the babysitter but gave her time off when Mark was free to take over. There were fewer interruptions, and Mark found that he actually worked more efficiently at home. Some days he would play with the kids and some days he would take them with him shopping. He was very satisfied with the arrangement, and Chris was happy that he was spending more time with the children and sharing house- hold responsibilities.

We predict that you will see flexplace more in the future. Although it can be an obstacle to planning and communication, it can be a workable solution for many businesses and individuals. Flexplace can cut office costs, if it is well organized, by reducing required office space and attendant energy costs. It can also provide energy savings to society at large by reducing rush-hour traffic and commuting.

On-Site and Near-Site Child Care

Many businesses are offering on-site or near-site child care. This ar- rangement allows at least one parent to spend more time with his or her child and feel more assured of quality care because the facility is nearby. It can save commuting time because extra trips are not needed to drop off and pick up the child. There are sometimes financial savings when the program is part of an employment package and is thus tax-deductible.

Think about how your own needs fit with a company's day-care arrangements before you decide this is a resource for you. Is it convenient for your child to be so far from the home? Are your hours so long that your child will be in care for a longer period of time? How long is too long? Does the program decrease access by your partner because it is at your place of employment? Would you feel comfortable complaining to your employer about the day-care program if problems were to emerge? On-site care may be good for you, but you should approach it cautiously. We know of a program at one large firm that was so unpopular because of the children's long commute with their parents that it was dropped after three years. Because only large employers can offer such programs, we think they will be common in the future but limited to a certain segment of the job market.

Leaves of Absence

There are many reasons why dual career partners may need leaves of absence from work: a sick child, an ailing parent, burnout, an extended vacation. In the past, asking for a leave of absence was difficult because of the fear that the employer might reject the request or even dismiss the employee who made it. Recent family legislation mandates that employers hold open for a set period the jobs of employees who need to care for a family member.

Clearly, such leaves place a burden on businesses. It may be impossible to find a temporary worker to replace a key player during his or her absence. Some jobs require months of training, and the permanent worker might return by the time the temporary employee is ready. Despite these costs, some major employers like IBM decided, even before family leave legislation was passed, that it is worth the expense to offer leave programs, some of which even go beyond the minimum requirements of the current law. The reasoning behind such initiatives is that a valuable employee will be available for rehire at some time in the future, instead of being lost to the competition. Many employers even allow employees to co-pay for benefits during extended periods of leave. Sometimes companies require a given number of years of employment after the leave, so that their investment cannot immediately be lost.

We believe that leave programs will increase. In many sectors they will offer more than legislation requires, and they will be most flexible where employees are highly trained and valuable to the employer. Going without pay for a period is a difficult decision for most families, but at least you know that your job is waiting for you and that your leave will not be followed by an additional period of unemployment. When they offer some continuity of benefits, leave programs will be increasingly attractive. Family stability is often a product of responding well to a crisis. The inability to cope with a crisis results not only in resource loss but in loss spirals that, once initiated, are difficult to halt. When the best way to deal with a crisis is to take an extended leave, the availability of this option will be key to offsetting devastating loss cycles and ensuring long-term resource gains.

———

Salvador took advantage of his company's leave policy in order to care for his wife, Carmelle's, dying father at home. Salvador's own father had left when he was quite young, and Carmelle's dad had been the father he had never known. Given their traditional family values, both Salvador and Carmelle would have been racked by guilt (and also saddled with extreme financial problems) had they placed their father in a nursing home. This, in turn, might have led to family conflict, extra work to pay bills, and even a questioning of their underlying family values. Such difficulties could easily snowball into problems with their marriage and children.

We cannot be sure about what would have happened otherwise, but we do know that Carmelle's father's last few months of life were peaceful and as he would have wished. The family shared his pain but also his joy, because this was how he wanted his family to be. He could see the legacy of his own lifetime labors of love for his family (although he did think it odd that Salvador and not Carmelle was allowed to take off from work!).

Maggie was less happy about her part-time job, into which she felt she had been forced. Both she and Carl wanted someone to be home more with the children, and it was obvious that that someone was to be Maggie. Carl did not earn more than Maggie and was not better educated, but he felt that he could not work part time because work was too important to him. Maggie was pulled between her desire for a career and her desire to spend more time with the children. She and Carl had always talked about the importance of their careers and their families, but when push came to shove, it was Maggie who got shoved.

Maggie's unhappiness about working part time would interfere with their intimacy for years to come and contribute to her long-term dissatisfaction with her life. She always felt that if they had tossed a coin and she had lost, she would have been content. But being forced into part-time work failed to meet a major requirement for intimacy—fairness.

Maggie feels as many women do, even when more family-friendly options are available. As long as taking these options is equivalent to being placed on the slow track at work, and as long as women are pressured to be the ones to ride the slow train, there will be continued reason for resentment. Certainly it's better than having no options at all, but it still unfairly places women in a second-class position.

Sick Leave

Typically, companies allow sick days for being sick. Makes sense. What do they have to say, however, if you take sick days for a sick child? Does this place you on the mommy or daddy track? Does it say to your employer that you are not serious about work? Does your company allow personal days with no questions asked?

In a sense, sick leave policy and practice are the best indicators of an employer's attitude toward employees for whom both work and family are important. If your employer has an either-or attitude about work versus family, it will be reflected in its sick leave policy and practice of this issue, because sick leave for child care places only a minor added burden on business. Indeed, for the many businesses that pay for sick leave not taken, it has no real cost whatsoever. Hence, an employer's position on this issue is likely to be just a reflection of whether it believes that employees can be dedicated to their work and still occasionally need to take a day off to be with a sick child.

Medical Benefits

Not all medical benefit policies are created equal. Some will be a major resource and some may increase your stress and strain considerably.

A good family medical policy obviously covers all the members of your family with a minimal or no co-payment. Most people stop thinking about medical insurance at this point, but there is more to consider. Does the policy cover orthodontal and dental care? What is the coverage for mental health, in case you or your children require counseling or psychotherapy? Many plans force people to choose psychiatric hospitalization by not providing cheaper outpatient coverage and paying only for inpatient psychiatric care. This can turn a problem that could be handled in an outpatient setting into a larger problem.

Many medical policies today control which doctors you can see. Insurance companies often contract with physicians and other providers on the basis of price rather than location. This means that your child's dermatologist may be an hour from your job or from home. In fact, a means of cost cutting for insurers is to discourage visits to specialists by limiting their availability. Check the list of accepted or preferred providers for location as well as hospital affiliation.

Relocation Policy

The transfer of employees to different locations is seldom, if ever, considered part of company policy. How your employer approaches this issue, however, may be the most serious potential threat to your resources. Many firms are downright callous about moving employees to different locations. It's back to the British Army; generals make decisions and officers and soldiers are expected to follow. Even stellar executives can risk losing their positions or being denied future promotions by refusing a "suggested" move. Companies may not consider whether you are in the midst of grieving for a loved one or whether your spouse just became president of his or her firm.

We discussed earlier how moves may result in the loss of many dual career family resources; we should also say that they can enrich your resources if they are well timed. Still, moving is a risky business. How will a move affect your partner's career and salary? The vast majority of career moves still involve men, with wives following. How would this one-sided attitude influence the intimacy in your family? What about your children? Moves can enhance children's self-esteem and sense of mastery if they are handled successfully and occur at the right time. Frequent and ill-timed moves may have the opposite effect.

So what is your potential employer's policy and practice regarding career moves? Are employees consulted well in advance? Is the feasibility of a move for both you and your family something the firm takes into consideration? What happened to others at your level who turned down moves in the past? Are they in the closet somewhere or perhaps no longer around? Can you talk to them? How are moves likely to occur? We live in a community where the average family of young to middle-aged executives remains for less than eighteen months. That is the average, so some families are moved within a year of arrival.

A pro-family company will ask its employees to move infrequently. Moves should be optional, and career advancement at the same location should be possible. When moves are necessary, the company should allow time for long-term planning. This should include job-search assistance for your partner, as well. Some firms hire spouses with useful skills for an interim period while the spouses search for a permanent job at the new location. Companies often have good connections in the new community, and the question then is whether they are willing to put those connections to work for you.

Couples and a Single Employer

Another policy of importance to some dual career couples concerns whether a company permits both partners to be employed at the same firm. Some companies wish to avoid even the appearance of nepotism or fear that spouses cannot be impartial toward one another when it comes to work decisions. When fewer women were in the work force, this was less of a problem for employers, but now it has become a major concern. It has always been a problem, however, for dual career couples, especially when both partners are in the same profession and there are few potential employers.

Companies should carefully reconsider such policies. Many dual career couples have a great deal to offer, and it does not make sense to exclude a competent employee just because his or her spouse is already an employee. However, because partners cannot be expected to be impartial about one another, they should not be placed in supervisory positions without appropriate safeguards. At one organization, the department manager's boss makes decisions for a man whose wife is department head. Another firm transferred a woman to a new, higher position after she married someone in her department. This employer was also smart enough to realize that by furthering the careers of both partners, it was increasing the chance that both would stay. It is often difficult for partners to find two good jobs in the same area, and it is therefore a hard situation to replace.

Vacations

It is wise to explore vacation policies with a potential employer. As we have discussed repeatedly, one of the main resources you need is flexibility. When both of you work, you may never have a family vacation if your employer demands that you take time off at its convenience. Many dual career parents also need to use vacation days to cover periods when young children are not in school. Schools do not consider parents' schedules, and the result can be a nightmare search for appropriate child care.

Employers also differ in how much vacation time they allow. If at least one partner can obtain a generous vacation package, the family's flexibility will be greatly increased. This is mainly a "roses" issues, but even in terms of "bread," extra day care may cost you more than the additional income earned at a company that offers two instead of four weeks' vacation with a little higher pay.

THE BEST OF THE BEST

We have put together a checklist of pro-family policies that you should look for when considering a job. Try to examine the fit between what

WORK WON'T LOVE YOU BACK

Partner *1*

*A Checklist for a
Company's Pro-Family
Policy and Practices*

	Importance	Availability
Salary and position		
Equivalent salaries for men/women		
Good ratio of male/female officers		
Good ratio of male/female managers, vice presidents		
Opportunity for advancement		
Good history of advancement for men/women		
Recent advancement for men/women		
Child care		
On-site		
Near-site		
Pretax set-aside		
Medical benefits		
Conveniently located providers		
Diverse services covered		
Elder care		
Maternity and paternity leave		
Referral service for child care/elder care		
Part-time/job-sharing programs		
Flextime		
Flexplace		
Leaves of absence		
Good sick leave policy/practice		
Good relocation policy/practice		
Open phone policy		
Employment of both partners		
Good vacation policy		

Partner 2

*A Checklist for a
Company's Pro-Family
Policy and Practices*

BREAD AND ROSES

1 = not important
2 = somewhat important
3 = very important

	Importance	Availability
Salary and position		
Equivalent salaries for men/women		
Good ratio of male/female officers		
Good ratio of male/female managers, vice presidents		
Opportunity for advancement		
Good history of advancement for men/women		
Recent advancement for men/women		
Child care		
On-site		
Near-site		
Pretax set-aside		
Medical benefits		
Conveniently located providers		
Diverse services covered		
Elder care		
Maternity and paternity leave		
Referral service for child care/elder care		
Part-time/job-sharing programs		
Flextime		
Flexplace		
Leaves of absence		
Good sick leave policy/practice		
Good relocation policy/practice		
Open phone policy		
Employment of both partners		
Good vacation policy		

the employer offers and what you need. The company may have the best maternity policy imaginable, but you may be done having babies. Go for what meets your family's needs. Complete the checklist alone or with your partner, indicating whether each issue is 1, "not important"; 2, "somewhat important"; or 3, "very important." Then check whether or not each is available at the company being considered. By this point, you should have developed the communication skills necessary to share your thoughts and feelings about the importance of each issue with your partner. Clearly, you want to look for employers whose policy offerings match what your family finds important.

Below we discuss some programs offered by a few of the leading pro-family companies.[3] Even if their policies change over time, these companies should be acknowledged as industry leaders in this area. Their policies can also serve as good models by which to judge those of potential employers.

DuPont is the largest U.S. chemical company. Recent reports indicate it supports five near-site day-care centers and an on-site summer camp. It operates a referral service for child care and elder care. Employees can make pretax set-asides for child care and take up to six months' leave for childbirth. Flextime, part-time, and flexplace programs are available where the job permits. It also offers up to one year of unpaid personal leave with benefits to pursue personal development opportunities.

Patagonia makes a fine line of outdoor wear. It operates two on-site child-care centers and after-school and holiday programs. Women can take up to four months' leave for child care, two of which are paid, and men can opt for two months' paternity leave. Flextime, part-time, job-sharing, and flexplace programs are available for certain jobs. Elder care and child care advice and referral services are also offered. Unlike some companies that offer family-friendly benefits to attract women but do not advance them, Patagonia does both. The majority of their senior managers are women.

IBM's trailblazing in this area is perhaps most impressive, since we remember friends returning from interviews twenty years ago in which they were told which of three suits they could wear to work (all dark blue or gray). The world's largest computer manufacturer funds on-site or near-site day-care centers, awards grants to improve the quality of local care centers that serve employees' children, and offers up to three years' leave for child care, with an option for part-time phase-in. If you choose to adopt a child, it offers financial aid to ease the cost burden. Flextime, part-time, and flexplace programs are also available where the job permits.

With such major players offering programs such as these, the future looks bright for family resource-enriching options at work. Although the availability of such programs is still limited, employers will probably have no choice but to offer them if they wish to stay in line with the law and attract the best employees.

NEGOTIATING A BETTER PACKAGE

Consider negotiating a personalized package of benefits before you accept your next job. Another good time for negotiation is at a transition in your career, such as a promotion, relocation, or move to a new job or schedule. One of the best times to negotiate is when you receive a job offer from another company and your firm wants to keep you. Some firms leave no room for negotiation, but we know people who have negotiated special arrangements with employers as bureaucratic as the U.S. Army. Some agreements are formalized in writing, some are communicated in private memos, and some are unwritten "understandings."

Consider these tips for negotiating. First, develop a clear idea of what job characteristics would enhance your resources. Consider what you might be willing to trade for some of these. You might not need medical coverage if your spouse has a policy that adequately covers you, but perhaps you could use an extra week's paid vacation. Know the costs of what you are asking for and know how they might interfere with your job. Have solutions ready to minimize or avert the cost of your proposal to the employer. Don't present your ideas as ultimatums but as suggestions that you wish to be considered. Make your priorities and bottom line clear, but be open to counterproposals. Always remember that you are negotiating for your whole family. Seek advice from your partner.

Here are some successful negotiations with which we are familiar.

- Wanda was offered a secretarial job at a real estate agency that was close to her home. She knew she would be trading salary for the convenience of the job location. She wanted four weeks' paid vacation, and the agency was offering two. She agreed to work Saturday mornings (which was important to the employer) in exchange for Friday afternoons off and settled for three weeks' paid and one week's unpaid vacation.

- Rick wanted it understood from the beginning that he was not going to miss all his children's plays. He had lost a child and regretted with a wrenching heart every performance he had worked through. He offered to make up during evenings or weekends any work that he missed.

- Chris was a teacher. He negotiated with the school principal to teach half time one out of every five years. This would allow him to catch up with his family. In exchange, he was willing to be a department head, which offered little extra pay but increased his responsibilities.

- Alison was a sought-after architect. She had moved to a new city for a new job at an architectural firm. Luckily, her husband was offered a good job downtown, but in order for him to accept the position, Alison needed to be home mornings to get the kids out. She wanted to work at her home studio once or twice a week, and she wanted to begin at 10:00 the other days. She was a "hot performer," so the firm was willing to accept her unprecedented requests. In return for flexplace and flextime, Alison guaranteed her employer productivity in the top 20 percent of the firm. She promised to return to a regular schedule at the end of the year if she failed to meet the agreed-upon objectives.

- After working as an accountant for five years, Victoria felt that her children needed more time with her. After-school care arrangements were not working out well. She knew that part-time work was not available at her firm and was planning to look for part-time work elsewhere. Her boss almost collapsed when she heard that Victoria might leave. She proposed that Victoria come in one hour earlier, take a half-hour lunch, and leave at 3:30. This schedule worked out to only thirty-eight hours, but her boss was willing to call it forty if Victoria agreed. She did. Victoria's boss negotiated the agreement with senior management.

Oh, yes, whenever you turn down a job that offers few family-friendly benefits, be sure to say that this was a deciding factor (even if it wasn't the only factor). Employers need to hear that people are considering family policy in their decisions. When you make a choice in favor of family-friendly policies, tell your family, and tell them you did it because you love them!

A WORD TO THE SELF-EMPLOYED

The same general principles of negotiation apply to negotiating with yourself as the owner-operator of a small business. In our workshops and clinical practices, we often encounter people with small businesses, "mom and pop" stores, and small professional practices (doctors, lawyers, and such). Sometimes the owner is the only employee or has only a small support staff.

One physician felt that she had to accept every referral or she would lose the referral source, not just that one patient. She gave herself little vacation time, was on call most holidays, worked weekends, and came in early and left late. Her income was enormous, but she was alienated from her family and was nearing an emotional and physical breakdown. We helped her negotiate a more reasonable work schedule with herself, and she contracted with her family to honor the schedule. A store owner learned that his assistant manager could easily handle being in charge two evenings and three mornings per week, and that all did not dissolve into dust when he took a two-week vacation.

We can be our own worst employer if we do not demand a reasonable benefits package from ourselves! Small businesses are not necessarily limited in flexibility, but flexibility can be limited by the management style of the owner. "We have met the enemy and he is us."

THE CAVALRY IS JUST AROUND THE BEND

Dual career couples are besieged by the stress of fitting work and family life together. As you are forging new paths, you will inevitably encounter resistance to your career pattern at work. However, we believe that help is on the way; we can hear the hoofbeats of the cavalry nearby.

There is a clear trend for more family-friendly policies among employers. Family leave is now law, and many companies offer paid personal days, parental leave, and flextime. With more dual career earners in management, they are naturally increasing their understanding of the need to balance family and work demands. The generation of men who have able-bodied assistants at home managing housework and children is nearing retirement. Coming in their wake are men and women whose experience has taught them different lessons for both the workplace and the home. It is inevitable that the demands of dual career employees will be better received by dual career managers.

Yet there is also likely to be a backlash against dual career families and family-friendly policy. Partly, this may come from senior management as a last-ditch resistance before the rules of their game are altered once and for all. Partly, there will be a male backlash against increasing numbers of women entering the corridors of power. However, in the end, demographics will win out, and the demographics clearly favor dual career earners. Women will not return home as they did after World War II, because they are deeply invested in their careers and because their own personal goals have changed. Clean floors and five-course meals have given way to being better teachers, lawyers, postal workers, and psychologists. Both men and women will sort through this transition period and find reward for their roles at work and home, and they will not relinquish these treasures once they are discovered. Nor can society afford the loss of productivity and buying power that dual career families contribute to the economy.

Nevertheless, be prepared to champion your cause at work. Stand ready to plead your case, to navigate through a maze of sometimes contradictory regulations, and even to switch to a more family-friendly employer. Support each other in the special way that partners who share both family and work stress can. Love, affection, and understanding are powerful stress-resistant resources.

Future Use of
Your Dual Career
Flight Manual

We have covered a lot of territory. We have introduced you to a new way of conceptualizing stress and resources. You have learned about conservation of resources theory and how to apply it to dual career life. We hope that you completed the questionnaires and that you have a better idea about your resources, how dual career life can affect you, and what you can do to prevent resource loss and enhance resource gain.

If we have done our job well, this book should be of continued value to you. Your life is a dynamic process. Crises, planned changes, and maturation of yourself, your relationship, and your children all

267

influence your resources. You must constantly reassess your options and your family needs. Look back at relevant chapters and reread points that have special meaning for new periods in your life. Complete the questionnaires again; they will have different outcomes and meanings at different times. As your children grow, the chapter on child care will help you find answers to new problems and concerns. As your relationship changes, the chapter on intimacy will shed a new light on answers you may be seeking in your relationship.

The two of us feel that we have come to know you, as you have come to know us, through the pages of this book. Of course, you have learned more about us personally, but we have worked hard at imagining the different lives and life-styles of potential readers. When we felt we were lacking in information and insight, we talked extensively to people and have tried to imagine ourselves in many different people's shoes. Ivonne came to understand more about what men are going through, and Stevan gained insight about the challenges that women are confronting. We have also grown closer ourselves. We have spoken about issues that we had only spoken around before. We have looked at our children in different ways and learned how to help them become stronger and more resourceful. We have learned more about what each of us has become in our own dual career odyssey. It is not how we started out, it is not even exactly how we expected life to develop, but we are very pleased with what we have achieved and where we seem to be headed. We wish you no less than what we have found.

As we look at our relationship, we can see how much our dual career status has influenced our lives. It affected the timing and care of our children. It determined where we live and how much money we have to live on. When we first married and moved to Alaska, Stevan had to find a very different career while Ivonne finished her Air Force commitment. When we moved to Israel and Stevan found employment first, Ivonne worked in the schools to improve her Hebrew before embarking on her private practice. Moving back to the United States meant that both of us had to create something anew. We had to learn how the schools, child care, and life in general worked in the United States. Although we had grown up here, we had never been dual career parents here, and there was much to learn. During some periods, Ivonne has prepared more of the dinners, done more of the wash, and been the mainstay for child care. At other times, these roles have been reversed or more equally shared. Always, always, it required communication, loving, understanding, and a willingness to give. Always, it required expressing our love and caring in the mundane terms of household chores and the key matters of child care. When one of us stumbled, the other was there to prevent a fall. When both of us stumbled or fell together, we bound each other's wounds, boosted each other up, and held on tight for the next round.

With your partner's help, may you also find your resource gardens rich and overflowing. May you know the difference between which resources are truly important and which are not. May this guide help you to find your way and achieve all the true resource riches you set out to find.

Notes

CHAPTER 1:
Must Two Careers Create Twice the Stress?

1. L. Y. Weiner, *From Working Girl to Working Mother. The Female Labor Force in the United States, 1820–1980* (Chapel Hill: University of North Carolina Press, 1985).

2. M. F. Fox and S. Hesse-Biber, *Women at Work* (Palo Alto, Calif.: Mayfield, 1984).

3. G. N. Powell, *Women and Men in Management* (Newbury Park, Calif.: Sage, 1988).

4. R. Smith, ed., *The Subtle Revolution: Women at Work* (Washington, D.C.: Urban Institute, 1979).

5. R. C. Barnett, N. L. Marshall, W. Raudenbush, and R. Brennan, "Gender and the relationship between job experiences and psychological distress: A study of dual-earner couples," *Journal of Personality and Social Psychology*, 64 (1993): 794–806.

6. N. Bolger, A. DeLongis, R. C. Kessler, and E. Wethington, "The contagion of stress across multiple roles," *Journal of Marriage and the Family*, 51 (1989): 175–183.

7. H. K. Cleminshaw, J. J. Zarski, J. Heckroth, and I. Newman, "Educated women in multiple roles: Well-being, satisfaction, and social supports," paper presented at the National Council on Family Relations, Philadelphia, November 1988.

8. J. H. Pleck, "Are 'family-supportive' employer policies relevant to men?" in *Work, Family, and Masculinities*, ed. J. C. Hood (Newbury Park, Calif.: Sage, in press).

9. J. Pleck, *Working Wives/Working Husbands* (Beverly Hills, Calif.: Sage, 1985).

CHAPTER 2: *A Proven Strategy for Coping*

1. S. E. Hobfoll, ed., *Stress, Social Support, and Women* (Washington, D.C.: Hemisphere, 1986).

2. S. E. Hobfoll, *The Ecology of Stress* (Washington, D.C.: Hemisphere, 1988).

3. S. E. Hobfoll and R. S. Lilly, "Resource conservation as a strategy for community psychology," *Journal of Community Psychology*, 21 (1993): 128–148.

4. S. E. Hobfoll, S. B. Shoham, and C. Ritter, "Women's satisfaction with social support and their receipt of aid," *Journal of Personality and Social Psychology*, 61 (1991): 332–341.

5. S. E. Hobfoll and C. D. Spielberger, "Family stress: Integrating theory and measurement," *Journal of Family Psychology*, 6 (1992): 99–112.

6. S. E. Hobfoll and A. Vaux, "Social support: Resources and context," in *Handbook of Stress: Theoretical and Clinical Aspects*, eds. L. Goldberger and S. Breznitz (New York: Free Press, 1993).

7. C. Lane and S. E. Hobfoll, "How loss affects anger and alienates potential supporters," *Journal of Consulting and Clinical Psychology*, 60 (1992): 935–942.

CHAPTER 3: *Cultivating Your Personal and Marital Resources*

1. S. H. Schwartz and W. Bilsky, "Toward a theory of the universal content and structure of values: Extensions and cross-cultural replications," *Journal of Personality and Social Psychology*, 58 (1990): 878–891.

2. S. E. Hobfoll, R. S. Lilly, and A. P. Jackson, "Conservation of social resources and the self," in *The Meaning and Measurement of Social Support*, eds. H. O. F. Veiel and U. Baumann (Washington, D.C.: Hemisphere, 1992), pp. 125–142.

3. J. R. Freedy, D. L. Shaw, M. P. Jarrell, and C. R. Masters, "Towards an understanding of the psychological impact of natural disasters: An application of the conservation resources stress model," *Journal of Traumatic Stress*, 5 (1992): 441–454.

4. M. Westman, personal communication, June 1, 1993.

5. H. T. Reis and P. Shaver, "Intimacy as an interpersonal process," in *Handbook of Personal Relationships*, eds. S. Duck, D. F. Hay, S. E. Hobfoll, W. Ickes, and B. M. Montgomery (New York: Wiley, 1988), pp. 367–387.

6. M. Clark, "Reactions to aid in communal and exchange relationships," in *New Directions in Helping. Vol. 1. Recipient Reactions to Aid*, eds. J. D. Fisher, A. Nadler, and B. M. DePaulo (New York: Academic Press, 1983), pp. 281–304.

CHAPTER 4: *Her Career Investment and His Reactions*

1. J. Mirowsky and C. E. Ross, *Social Causes of Psychological Distress* (New York: Aldine de Gruyter, 1989).

2. G. W. Brown and T. Harris, *The Social Origins of Depression: The Study of Psychiatric Disorder in Women* (New York: Free Press, 1985).

3. E. McGrath, G. P. Keita, B. R. Strickland, and F. N. Russo, eds., *Women and Depression: Risk Factors and Treatment Issues* (Washington, D.C.: American Psychological Association, 1990).

4. C. S. Aneshensel, "Marital and employment role-strain, social support, and depression among adult women," in *Stress, Social Support, and Women*, ed. S. E. Hobfoll (Washington, D.C.: Hemisphere, 1986), pp. 99–114.

5. I. Waldron, S. Zyanski, R. B. Shekelle, C. D. Jenkins, and S. I. Tannenbaum, "The coronary-prone behavior pattern in employed men and women," *Journal of Human Stress*, 3 (1977): 2–18.

6. S. E. Hobfoll and P. London, "The relationship of self concept and social support to emotional distress among women during war," *Journal of Social and Clinical Psychology*, 12 (1986): 87–100.

7. R. C. Barnett, N. L. Marshall, S. W. Raudenbush, and R. T. Brennan, "Gender and the relationship between job experiences and psychological distress: A study of dual-earner couples," *Journal of Personality and Social Psychology*, 64 (1993): 794–806.

8. P. D. Cleary and D. Mechanic, "Sex differences in psychological distress among married people," *Journal of Health and Social Behavior*, 24 (1983): 111–121.

9. J. H. Pleck, *Working Wives/Working Husbands* (Beverly Hills, Calif.: Sage, 1985).

10. J. Hearn, D. L. Sheppard, P. Tancred-Sheriff, and G. Burrell, *The Sexuality of Organization* (London: Sage, 1989).

11. R. S. Weiss, "Bringing work stress home," in *Stress Between Work and Family*, eds. J. Eckenrode and S. Gore (New York: Plenum, 1990), pp. 17–37.

12. R. C. Barnett, "Multiple roles, gender, and psychological distress," in *Handbook of Stress: Theoretical and Clinical Aspects*, eds. L. Goldberg and S. Breznitz (New York: Free Press, 1993), pp. 427–442.

13. L. Coser (with R. Coser), *Greedy Institutions* (New York: Free Press, 1974).

14. H. K. Cleminshaw, J. J. Zarski, J. Heckroth, and I. Newman, "Educated women in multiple roles: Well-being, satisfaction, and social support," paper presented at the National Council on Family Relations, Philadelphia, November 1988.

CHAPTER 5: *Avoiding the Pitfalls of a Dual Career Life-Style*

1. A. Bandura, "Self-efficacy: Toward a unifying theory of behavior change," *Psychological Review*, 84 (1977): 191–215.

2. S. O. Kobasa, "Stressful life events, personality, and health: An inquiry into hardiness," *Journal of Personality and Social Psychology*, 37 (1979): 1–11.

3. R. Gallagher and S. E. Hobfoll, "The effects of marital status and intimacy on depression among pregnant women," in preparation.

4. H. T. Reis and P. Shaver, "Intimacy as an interpersonal process," in *Handbook of Personal Relationships*, eds. S. Duck, D. F. Hay, S. E. Hobfoll, W. Ickes, and B. M. Montgomery (New York: Wiley, 1988).

5. S. E. Hobfoll, P. London, and E. Orr, "Mastery, intimacy, and stress resistance during war," *Journal of Community Psychology*, 16 (1988): 317–311.

CHAPTER 7: *Household Labor, Or, I'd Rather See a Handsome Man Wash Dishes Than Dance Naked*

1. A. Hochschild (with A. Machung), *The Second Shift: Working Parents and the Revolution at Home* (New York: Viking, 1989).

2. C. Emmons, M. Biernat, B. Tiedje, E. L. Lang, and C. B. Wortman, "Stress, support, and coping among women professionals with preschool children," in *Stress Between Work and Family*, eds. J. Eckenrode and S. Gore (New York: Plenum, 1990), pp. 61–93.

3. H. J. Pleck, *Working Wives/Working Husbands* (Beverly Hills, Calif.: Sage, 1985).

4. L. R. Silberstein, *Dual-Career Marriage: A System in Transition* (New York: Lawrence Erlbaum, 1992).

5. H. Y. Grossman and N. L. Chester, eds., *The Experience and Meaning of Work in Women's Lives* (New York: Lawrence Erlbaum, 1992).

6. M. F. Fox and S. Hesse-Biber, eds., *Women at Work* (Mountain View, Calif.: Mayfield, 1984).

7. R. E. Smith, ed., *The Subtle Revolution: Women at Work* (Washington, D.C.: Urban Institute, 1979).

8. D. Vannoy-Hiller and W. W. Philliber, *Equal Partners: Successful Women in Marriage* (Beverly Hills, Calif.: Sage, 1989).

9. J. Mirowsky and C. E. Ross, *Social Causes of Psychological Distress* (New York: Aldine de Gruyter, 1989).

10. L. A. Gilbert, *Two Careers/One Family* (Beverly Hills, Calif.: Sage, 1993).

CHAPTER 8: *How (and When) Do I Love Thee?*

1. E. M. Waring, "The measurement of marital intimacy," *Journal of Marital and Family Therapy*, 10 (1980): 185–192.

2. E. M. Waring, M. P. Tillman, L. Frelick, L. Russell, and G. Weisz, "Concepts of intimacy in the general population," *Journal of Nervous and Mental Disease*, 168 (1980): 471–474.

3. C. R. Rogers, *Becoming Partners: Marriage and Its Alternatives* (New York: Delacorte, 1972).

4. E. Berscheid and E. H. Walster, *Interpersonal Attraction*, 2nd ed. (Reading, Mass.: Addison-Wesley, 1974).

5. J. Bowlby, *Attachment and Loss*. Vol. 1. *Attachment* (London: Hogarth, 1969).

6. M. Ainsworth, M. Blehar, E. Waters, and S. Wall, *Patterns of Attachment* (Hillsdale, N.J.: Lawrence Erlbaum, 1978).

7. H. F. Harlow and M. K. Harlow, "Learning to love," *American Scientist*, 54 (1966): 244–272.

8. C. Hazan and P. Shaver, "Romantic love conceptualized as an attachment process," *Journal of Personality and Social Psychology*, 52 (1987): 511–524.

9. S. Freud, *An Outline of Psycho-analysis* (New York: Norton, 1949).

10. E. Erikson, *Identity, Youth, and Crisis* (New York: Norton, 1968).